This introduction to the history, house and gardens of Caerhays has only been possible through the work of Charles Williams, his co-authors and others who have provided information, pictures and text. Parts of the sections on the garden and garden tour have previously been published by the Caerhays Estate. Thanks are due to many for their assistance, advice and the use of their material. Wherever possible we have tried to credit contributions to this book.

First published 2011  Text & Artwork copyright 2011 SCSTyrrell
Set in Century Schoolbook 11 on 12.5
Published by Pasticcio Ltd.  Registered in England No 5125728
01326 340153     www.pasticcio.co.uk

ISBN 978-0-9555511-5-4

*Pasticcio*

Ali
Please come again & well slit

# Caerhays Castle

An introduction to its history, owners and gardens

*Charles Williams*

## Charles Williams

Peter Herring, Jaimie Parsons,
Courtenay Smale and Stephen Tyrrell

Edited by Stephen Tyrrell

# The Authors

The writing of this book has been a co-operative effort. Although all chapters incorporate work from other contributors, the first drafts were prepared as follows:

## Charles Williams          Chapters 12, 13, 15, 18, 19, appendices 1-8
Charles Williams grew up at Caerhays Castle and has been engaged with the work, development and protection of the estate since he left University. He left banking positions with Lazards in London to take over management of the estate and its business interests. An acknowledged expert on plants, trees and shrubs, he also runs Burncoose Nurseries, located on the Caerhays estate.

## Peter Herring          Chapters 1, 3, 4, 5, appendices 9, 10
Peter Herring works as an Inspector for English Heritage and had previously spent over twenty years in Cornwall's archaeological and historic environment services. A landscape historian and archaeologist, he has published and lectured on many aspects of Cornwall's landscape. He is married with two children and lives on the Roseland Peninsula not far from Caerhays.

## Jaimie Parsons          Chapter 20
Jaimie Parsons has been the Head Gardener at Caerhays since 1996, having previously worked with his predecessor, Philip Tregunna. Jaimie Parsons is only the 4th man to hold this position in the last 120 years. He was also recently made Estate Manager.

## Courtenay Smale          Chapter 16
Courteney Smale is a mining engineer and graduate of the Camborne School of Mines. He is a former president of the Royal Geological Society of Cornwall, the Royal Institution of Cornwall and the Cornish Institute of Engineers. He has lectured in Cornish Mineralogy and Mining History for over 40 years. In 1983, he was elected a Bard of the Cornish Gorsedd in recognition of his contribution to mineralogical research in Cornwall.

## Stephen Tyrrell          Chapters 2, 5, 6, 7, 8, 9, 10, 11, 12, 13, 14, 15, 17
Stephen Tyrrell is an architectural historian whose working life has been spent principally in the renovation and historic assessment of old houses. The author of several books on architectural history, he lectures in this subject and continues to work with owners of interesting properties. He and his family live near Falmouth.

# Contents

Preface:      Professor Charles Thomas          7
Foreword:    Jim Gardiner                              9
Introduction: Charles Williams                      13

The Landscape and Setting for Caerhays
1   The Settlements around Caerhays          17
2   The Origin of the name Caerhays          27
3   Deer Parks and Parkland                       31
4   The Coast at Caerhays                         37
5   The Church                                        45

The History of the Building at Caerhays Castle
6   The Story of the Building                     55
7   A Castle Tour                                     71
8   John Nash, The Architect of Caerhays   81
9   The Curious Case of the Paper Roof      89

The Families who have owned Caerhays
10   The Trevanion family                         97
11   Trevanion Disaster and Sale             109
12   The Williams Family                          117
13   John Charles Williams 1861-1939       127
14   Plant hunters in China                      137
15   Charles Williams and his successors   147
16   The Williams Mineral Collection          151
17   Recipes from Caerhays                      159
18   Caerhays Today                               165

The Gardens of Caerhays
19   The Gardens                                   177
20   Garden Walks                                 193

Appendices
21   Appendices                                   211
        1-8    Plant Schedules:                  213
        9,10  Historic Schedules:               243
        11     Sources and references          251
        12     Activities and Contacts at Caerhays   255

Caerhays Castle in spring

# Preface
# Professor Charles Thomas

Caerhays, always a delight to visit, has long been the home of my friend and contemporary Julian Williams, whom we admire not only for his chairing of Cornwall County Council but also for his years as presidential chairman of the Royal Institution of Cornwall (a body always in his debt).

This book, as well as giving us a detailed and delightfully illustrated account of the flowers and shrubs for which Caerhays is rightly famous, provides a wealth of information on little-known aspects of Cornish history in this area, and on the early land-use and building history of the place itself. I am indeed glad to see that, unlike many books on country houses, it sets out in detail the early history of Caerhays and the land around it. No country house exists in isolation! And, after a life time devoted to Cornwall's archaeology and early history, it is so pleasant to find that fresh discoveries – who knows what lies behind the beach at Caerhays? – can help to illuminate, not only trading contacts by sea but also the manner in which our forbears managed to live in this part of Cornwall.

Above all, as one of thousands who marvel annually at the height, the colour and the beauty of all the camellias, rhododendrons and other special plants and trees at Caerhays, I find it wonderful that so much expert attention has been given to proper descriptions. Caerhays, viewed from any angle, is an astonishing place. I believe that further discoveries, in both the history of the site and the botanical richness of the gardens, are bound to be made. Welcome to a proper history! And one hopes that other, perhaps comparable, places in Cornwall will take this as a model.

Charles Thomas

Professor Charles Thomas
*Photo: Carl Thorpe*

Caerhays in summer

The view from the 'Four in Hand' across the lake.

# Foreword
# Jim Gardiner
### Director of Horticulture. The Royal Horticultural Society

It is indeed a great honour for me to be writing this foreword on Caerhays, regarded as one of the great woodland gardens of the world.

The site is ideally suited for a garden through having a unique microclimate bathed in moisture and humidity, with 55"-60" of rain each year, an acidic free draining soil, a climate that is generally frost free and grounds protected from the south westerly winds.

The garden, which extends to over 120 acres, was developed by John Charles Williams, known as 'JC'. His interest in plants and their hybridisation was stimulated by the RHS Daffodil Conference of 1884. On moving to Caerhays he first laid out lines of daffodils, some varieties of which can still be seen today. However JC was clearly influenced by the great garden owners/nurserymen of the day such as James Harry Veitch, Lionel de Rothschild at Exbury, Reginald Cory at Dyffryn, Col. Stephenson–Clarke at Borde Hill and Isaac Bailey Balfour, the Regius Keeper of the Royal Botanic Garden, Edinburgh to where the plant discoveries of Ernest Wilson and George Forrest were being sent from China. JC was so committed to new Chinese introductions that he contributed to many of Forrest's exhibitions and funded the entire cost of the third expedition himself.

Jim Gardiner

Surveying the collections today, JC's influence and his introductions of Rhododendron, Camellia, Magnolia and their hybrids is everywhere. None are more visible than Magnolia sprengeri 'Diva', the goddess magnolia which was one of Wilson`s introductions (Wilson 688). At the time, this plant was unique because it was the only pink flowered form of this species in cultivation. Although the original is dead, young plants propagated from the original together with about 300 taxa form the basis of the National Collection of magnolias. This is now one of five recognised by Plant Heritage throughout the UK. Often regarded as Wilson's finest woody plant introduction, seedlings from this plant can be found in gardens throughout the world as well as its hybrids 'Caerhays Belle', 'Galaxy' and 'Spectrum'.

Of considerable influence was JC's involvement with Camellia and Rhododendron. One of Forrest`s introductions was C.saluenensis which JC flowered and then crossed with a single red C. japonica. The resultant seedlings became what we know today as C. x williamsii with the first two named after his wife (Mary Christian) and himself. JC was an astute hybridizer of rhododendrons and 24 hybrids were registered. These include `Veryan Bay` which grows under my kitchen window! Wilson named R.williamsianum in JC's honour and described him as the 'first amateur to appreciate the value of rhododendrons of western China'. JC's continuing presence extended to other genera. This included over 80 Champion Trees (defined as being of the largest in height and or girth) which are recorded throughout the Estate. Many of these, including Aesculus wilsonii, had been planted by JC himself.

The estate passed onto JC's eldest son Charles and then in turn to Charles' nephew Julian. Julian, together with his son Charles, and their Head Gardeners, Philip Tregunna and Jaimie Parsons have navigated the garden successfully, despite the ravages of the 1990 hurricane and Sudden Oak Death in 2003.

As well as nurturing and maintaining the historic gardens, they have been building for the future by clearing old shelter belts and replanting. There is also an extensive programme for new introductions not only from familiar genera, species and new cultivars but also from material new to cultivation.

The garden is probably more accessible today with clearly defined routes developed with an eye to display the significance of its ever expanding collections. It continues to be important for its historically important collections, for its plant associations, for its magnificent vistas and for providing that 'buzz' which a vibrant garden exudes .

Yet it is far more than a garden of international significance. Caerhays is an Estate where there is evidence of settlement for more than two thousand years and of landscape and garden schemes from as early as 1700 to the Repton influenced schemes of the architect John Nash. The book provides not only the early story of the land and house but also that of the estate we now see developed under the ownership and leadership of the Williams family.

But for the Estate to flourish, it must not only continue to manage the gardens and garden enterprises as an attraction, but must also embrace and identify opportunities for future success not just from farms, holiday cottages, country sports, or corporate events, but also from the development of other interests.

My congratulations are given to all of those who have been involved with this book. This is more than just a social history; it exudes interest and passion throughout and a fervent commitment to survival and success in the future.

It is a pleasure to see at first hand the expanding collection of plants, many of which are without equal in the UK, and to know that they too are safe for the future.

Jim Gardiner

The lake and the Luney valley from the entrance to Caerhays (top) and in winter (below).

Charles and Lizzie Williams

# Introduction

Caerhays is famous as a romantic castle. It is of equal importance that the architect, John Nash, designed the building to be part of its landscape. The buildings and landscape may make this one of the most attractive of places to visit, but Caerhays is also famous as the home of the Williams family. This book traces the history of the house and its owners, and is a tribute to those who contribute to its buildings, settings and activities.

Such personal stories include the Trevanions, a name now almost unknown, although it was one of Cornwall's great Medieval, Tudor and Stuart dynasties for 450 years, before failing in dramatic circumstances. It is also the story of the Williams family, who achieved wealth in business and mining activities and then spent it on houses, gardens and their tenants. Caerhays has had, in that family, some of the country's greatest gardeners and plant breeders. Specialists for 120 years in the plants of South West China, they have created the glory that draws thousands to the gardens each spring: the finest collection of magnolias in Britain and possibly the world.

Magnolia: Caerhays Belle

Others have surprising links with Caerhays, not just the renowned architect John Nash but also one of Britain's most famous adventurers, eccentrics and poets, Lord Byron.

The book examines the history of the area from early times onward, goes into some quirky by-ways, and includes detailed tours of both house and garden, together with encyclopaedic information on some plant species.

This is not intended to be merely a dreary record, but a book that celebrates the life, times, disaster and amusements of Caerhays. It also includes a fine recipe for cake, thought to date from around 1700.

Caerhays is not just a great house with fine gardens, but has much more to offer, including a coast and countryside of great beauty. There are also some surprising specialities, such as the Williams collection of minerals, which include items of national importance. These give an exciting and different lustre to a visit. They are fascinating, luminous, sparkling and of many different colours.

A brilliant boulder Opal from Queensland, Australia

The point of this book is to persuade the reader that they should make the effort to visit the house and its gardens.

It is also an attempt to explain how a landed estate such as Caerhays can survive and how such a place can be made to tick as a modern, expanding business.

There are few things as unfashionable or misunderstood as a traditional country landed estate. Such estates are, in effect, small conglomerate businesses with many different sources of income and unbelievable overheads. These overheads are unavoidable and derive from the 'privilege' of owning and maintaining a historic house. The old mantra that a landed estate owner could survive, bring up a family and occasionally reroof a wing on the proceeds of farm rents has long been a fiction. Taxation and inheritance taxes have removed any spare cash and left the estate instead with large liabilities in capital and interest. After 20 years of agricultural decline and stagnation, not to mention 10 years of government disinterest and attacks on the countryside, times have not been easy.

Jaimie Parsons, Philip Tregunna, and Roy Lancaster in April 2009

However, early business training has helped to tackle several diverse businesses at Caerhays with lots of different people, sometimes with wholly contradictory agendas. Expanding those businesses and using the remaining resources and developing them for the future remains, as always, the challenge of Caerhays Estate. Caerhays will continue to develop and adapt to change.

Of course, Caerhays is not just a bunch of buildings, or an outstanding garden. It is also a group of people working to make the place a success. With the nursery at Burncoose, the businesses at Caerhays now require the help of a very large number of people. It is those people who have made and continue to make a success of the place; it is they who should perhaps be the focus of this book.

It is of course invidious to take one example from among so many. However, the gardens at Caerhays have had so few Head Gardeners in the last 120 years and their influence and ability is so well respected that it is right to use them as an example of great achievement and success for Caerhays.

The photograph on this page includes two Head Gardeners. Philip Tregunna served for 40 years in that position and Jaimie Parsons, who took over in 1996, will, we hope, be here as long. He is only one of many important and loyal friends who make this place work.

A couple of miles from Caerhays is a wonderful cast iron fluted and scrolled sign post, one of few survivors of such early types. We hope the finger post will remind you not only to enjoy this book, but to come to Caerhays to see the place for yourself.

Charles Williams

# Section One
# The Landscape and Setting
# for Caerhays

1   The Settlements around Caerhays        17
2   The Origin of the name 'Caerhays'      27
3   Deer Parks and Parkland                31
4   The Coast at Caerhays                  37
5   The Church                             45

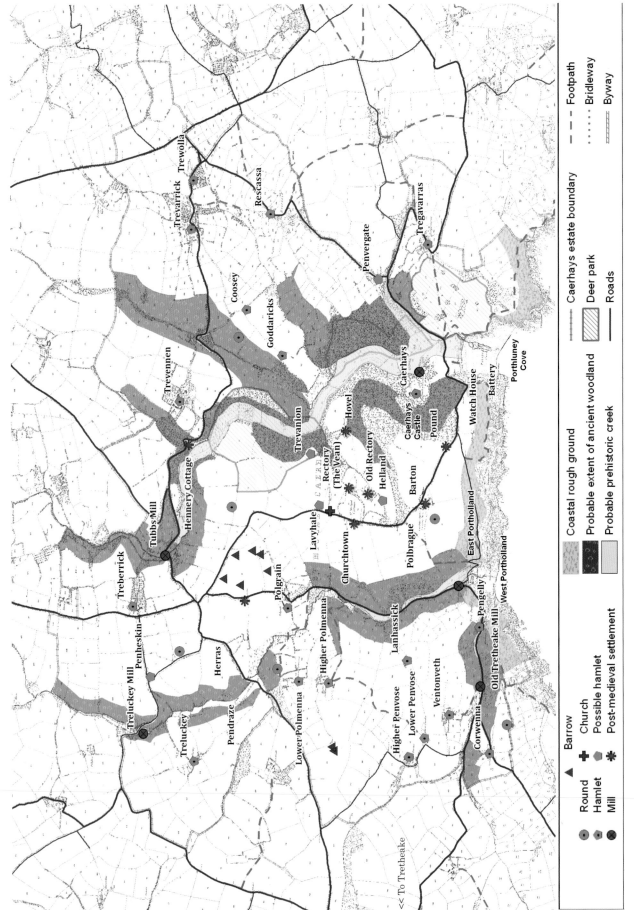

Prehistoric barrows and rounds, early settlements and medieval farm hamlets around Caerhays

# Chapter 1
# The Settlements around Caerhays

Caerhays lies at the centre of a small scale, intimate landscape of great beauty. Although there are some rounded downs, the highest point at Trevarrack barely reaches 330 feet. There is little flat land away from the coast and the landscape is one of twisting valleys with narrow bottoms, each with side valleys and small streams running between hills whose steepest slopes are near the water. Along the south edge of the area the cliffs, broken and precipitous, are around 100-130 feet high. These cliffs give a good display of the area's geology. Devonian sedimentary rocks have pockets of limestone with fossils, volcanic tuffs and lavas, and some minerals. There are hard outcrops and dark angular ridges which run across shingle and sandy beaches. Most of the foreshore is hard to reach save for that around the three main rivers, two of which are at Portholland and one at Porthluney.

The views of the countryside have as their backdrop the Hens-barrow hills and china clay tips to the north and the distant uplands of Bodmin Moor. Caerhays is at the centre of a network of small valleys and steep hillsides which provide drama and a constantly shifting and attractive view of the landscape.

The three main river valleys were once partially tidal, bringing the smell of the sea far inland. The main valley in front of the castle would once have been wide with short navigable side creeks. Tidal waters would have run across the valley and tight to the steep valley sides. This expanse of water probably remained until the early medieval period. A boat riding in on the Iron Age tide would probably have floated as far up as where Tubbs Mill now stands. Short creeks would have cut into Penvergate and also towards the site of Helland, just by The Vean, that stream dividing the site of Trevanion from Caerhays. At Portholland, a boat is likely to have floated up to Polgrain to the east, but only as far as Pengelly on the west. These wide estuaries have now gone, partly because of landscaping at the Porthluney beach, but mainly because of settling silt. The River Luney rises far inland close to a land of tinning and mining, and it is possibly the silts from those mining operations which have helped clog the creeks, turning them into flat marshes.

The valleys give this landscape interest and variety. Their steep sides and ancient woodland, furze and bracken are often too steep for modern farming and therefore give the area a sense of wild country. Many of the early settlements such as Ventonveth, Higher Polmenna,

Treluckey, Treberrick, Trevarrick and Helland, were placed at the highest point where streams provided water, but where some shelter existed. Much of the land retains its early medieval layout and settlement pattern which itself depended on the relationship of steep valleys, rounded hill tops and long stretches of tidal water.

The area around Caerhays remains the most attractive of landscapes and, save for modern buildings on some farms, has been little changed for a thousand years.

## The Early Landscape.

The first inhabitants of the area probably wandered or lived here some 8000 years ago. The varied resources of the land provided the means by which they could thrive.

It is now thought that the woodland that then dominated the environment would have been fairly open. Rather than dense, dark, closed canopy forest, the land would have been kept clear by herds of wild grazing animals. Except where the ground was very steep, the norm may have been a grassland landscape with small clumps and single trees, some growing ancient with vast spreading branches. The woodland would then, as now, have been thickest on steep land and on the sides of the little valleys. The parkland landscape of modern Caerhays may be surprisingly similar in appearance to that which existed five thousand years ago.

From about 8000 to 1500 BC, the local beaches provided the flint used to manufacture arrowheads, knives and scrapers. Stubby scrapers were used for skinning animals or removing bark from wood; knives for cutting flesh; pointed awls for piercing skins and leather.

The most dramatic change to the recent landscape may have been the infilling of the valleys over the last few hundred years. As with much of south Cornwall, the valleys had until then been long tidal creeks which allowed shallow draft boats to trade much further up what were, at high tide, wide areas of water. Both the Luney and Portholland creeks have since become silted up with detritus from later tin workings and agriculture further upstream.

The original estuaries also had marshes spreading round the numerous springs, making most valley bottoms treacherous, although modern drainage has reduced the extent of some marshes.

The other effect of the long stream or river valleys was to reduce travel in an east-west direction. This gave greater emphasis to the trackways along high ground some way to the north and to the trackway that ran behind the coast at Caerhays, dropped to cross the Luney at a ford and then rose up to high ground to the east. In this area, most travel must have been in a north-south direction.

## Early Ceremony.

In the centuries from 2000 BC, the people built barrows on the high, open, gently rounded tops of the numerous down-like hills. These sites tended to be places with extensive views, either to the Hensbarrow granite uplands or to the Dodman headland. They may have been considered places where people felt lifted high above the mundane world up into the wind among the birds and spirits.

Sites of barrows are known at Higher Penvose and Polgrain, though these have now been ploughed down. Although burial or disposal of the dead seems to have been one of the more important activities that took place at some, but not all, Cornish barrow sites, their rounded mounds were built over the remains of a wide range of ceremonial or ritual activity. This probably reinforced the sense of belonging to a community and to a place: memories would have been invoked and associations and meanings reinforced. People would have deepened their identification with the place that was to become Caerhays.

Polmenna and Polgrain.
The round can be seen in the top right quadrant, behind the buildings.

## The First Farming.

Around 1500 BC, people are thought to have built the first permanent settlements in Cornwall. They laid out enclosures and fields around groups of large, well constructed round houses. These first more settled peoples would probably have considered the barrow mounds, still monumental and sharply defined when the first houses were being built, as belonging to important ancestors.

Much of the Roseland Peninsula is an area of anciently enclosed land, with land long since taken in from woodland or waste. Modern Caerhays is part of a landscape that has been worked intensively since the Iron Age (c 800 BC to AD c 50) and in some places for up to a thousand years earlier.

Scattered through the farmland around Caerhays are several 'rounds'. These were farming hamlets enclosed by circular banks and ditches and dating from the centuries before and after the birth of Christ. They can date from the 4th century BC, though many are of the Romano-British period and some were occupied into the 5th and 6th centuries AD. So for many hundreds of years rounds were a common feature of the Cornish countryside. The most clearly defined example is that which survives as a 36m diameter circular terrace on the crest of steep slopes to the north east of Lower Polmenna. The south side has been fossilised by reuse in a field boundary.

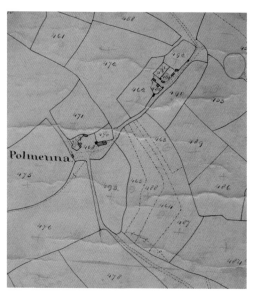

Polmenna as shown in the 1841 tithe map.

A circular enclosure with bank and ditch has been identified north east of the conjectural site of the first Caerhays house. The banked enclosure is at the end of the ridge immediately north of Caerhays Castle. Some of the perimeter has a ditch inside rather than outside the bank. This may be because soil could not be dug on the steeper rock slopes, or that rather than being a 'round', this could be an early farm enclosure dating from between 400 and 1000 AD.

Other rounds of which earthwork remains survive include another circular platform in the valley north-east of Goddaricks in Gorran and part of a tightly curving substantial bank on a ridge to the south of Corwenna in Veryan; the first part of the place-name Corwenna derives from the Cornish *ker*, meaning defended settlement, or round. To the west of Old Park Wood a platform had been suggested as another former round, but this is much more likely to be the former medieval settlement of Trevanion.

Two further rounds have been found at Caerhays, one north of the churchtown and the other south-west of the Barton. In both cases, aerial photography has revealed evidence of enclosures and roughly rectangular fields. However, since these are lost boundaries which do not conform with the later orientation of the medieval fields, they must date from an earlier layout. The round to the south-west of Caerhays Barton is set within a scatter of four or more circular features, probably small round houses; it seems possible that here an open settlement was reorganised into a round, or vice versa, possibly as the status of the inhabitants changed.

It is likely that land use patterns in later prehistoric times were essentially similar to those of the medieval period and, to some degree, to those of today. The distribution of the rounds is similar to that of the medieval farming hamlets. The steep sides of the numerous valleys would have been a powerful geographical determiner of those areas that could be enclosed and farmed.

Iron Age and Roman period farming probably involved a mix of arable and pastoral farming. This is supported by the evidence of prehistoric Cornish artefacts, and from information about prehistoric vegetation or land cover. Although the use of the land may not have been as intensive as it later became, and although valleys may have been more thickly wooded, we imagine that the most exposed hilltops were used for open rough grazing. Even today, bracken and furze survive in many hilltop hedges.

## A Coin Hoard and an Aegean Amphora

Two discoveries are evidence of both settlement and trade.

In November 1869, two ditchers were working on the edge of the valley moor below Old Park Wood. While digging, they found sea sand a metre down. In this sea sand had been placed, between three stones, a jug of 96% pure tin, closed with a wooden bung. The bung had presumably survived by being waterlogged.

The ditchers broke off the jug's neck and handle to discover between 1,392 and 2,500 Roman coins. These coins were mostly of lower denomination brass, some of them washed with silver. Although some of the hoard was lost, most were in good condition and dated from AD 253 to 282. The majority were from the reigns of five Roman emperors, including Galienus, Victorinus, Flavius Claudius, and Tetricus.

Although a large number of coins and the jug are still in Caerhays, coins from the hoard were given to other museums, including the Royal Cornwall Museum, Truro.

Several other Roman coin hoards have been discovered in creek-side locations in Cornwall. It is thought that they were not savings which were hidden to be recovered later, but rather were left as offerings to the spirits of the creeks. The creeks may have been considered special places where tongues of water came and went each day and whose links with the sea facilitated traffic and trade. The location of the Caerhays hoard may show how far up the Luney valley the sea still came in the Roman period.

Another discovery was made by Roger Penhallurick in a molehill on the west side of Porthluney Cove, one of the first safe beaches to the west of the great distinctive headland of the Dodman. Here was found a fragment of imported Bi amphora brought all the way from the Aegean in the fifth or sixth century AD. The amphora, a strong cylindrical vessel used for transporting liquid, may have been part of an exchange where imported wine or olive oil was traded for tin delivered from near the head of the Luney River.

The 3rd Century AD tin jug, discovered in 1865, in which was found a mass of coins.

## Early Farming

From 500-1000 AD, the patterns of settlement that still underpin the shape of the farmland of Caerhays were reinforced. Small hamlets with Cornish names, many with the early medieval *tre* prefix, meaning farming estate, were created or, most often, re-established on or near the sites of prehistoric settlements. Places like Treberrick, Trevarrick, Tregavarras, Trewolla, Treluckey, Trevennen, and Trevanion became the homes of small groups of farming households; they were generally placed on the higher or mid-slope side of a hill. These hamlets were typically less than a mile apart and each was surrounded by fields originally subdivided into strips. The strips were worked cooperatively and communally by the tenant farmers. Beyond the fields, but within the territories, or townlands, of these early hamlets, were valley side woodlands, dominated by oak, valley-bottom meadows and marshes (whose willows provided withies for basketry), and rough grazing land on any surviving patches of downland and on the more manageable of the cliffs.

Trevanion, Caerhays and Trevennen became the centres of important manors in the later medieval period, but at the time of the Norman Conquest these places were subsumed within other estates, as recorded in the 1086 Domesday Book. The details for those Domesday manors recorded in the immediately adjoining parishes are set out in appendix 9.

## Medieval Land Holdings.

At the time of the Domesday book in 1086 and for some hundreds of years previously, the Land of the present Caerhays estate seems to have been part of several different manors. The western section, which was within Veryan parish, probably lay within Tretheake, the north-western section, Treluckey, was within Goviley, and the northern, Treberrick, within Tucoyse. Some of the eastern Gorran land lay within the manors of Treworrick and Trevessan.

However, medieval Cornish estates often held land scattered through a larger area rather than in consolidated blocks, so some parts of Caerhays may have belonged to those distant manors which included the largest in the district. Two of these manors were Elerkey to the west and Bodrugan to the east. However, the most significant manor was that of Brannel to the north. It seems likely that the core of Caerhays was held as part of the manor of Brannel. St Michael Caerhays was also a chapel attached to St Stephens in Brannel, the administrative centre of Brannel to the north. The table in appendix 9 shows that by most Domesday measures Brannel was the largest manor in the district.

The earliest statement of the medieval holdings of Caerhays comes from a survey of 1545, now in the British Museum. In 1545, the Trevanion family held in hand or as demesne the Barton of Caerhays, Trevanion itself (which was still a substantial farm producing £5 per year compared with the Barton's £10), Treberrick (£2 6s 8d) and two now lost farms, Lavyhale and Herras, whose acreages and values were given as 70 and 42 and £2 10s 4d and £2 6s 8d respectively.

Field names indicate that Herras lay to the north-west of Polgrain and the great Cornish historian Charles Henderson suggested that Lavyhale might have stood close to St Michael Caerhays since the name might have developed from *Lan* meaning churchyard and Yvhal

*Please refer to the appendices for further details of early settlements and for the history of the farms around Caerhays.*

standing for Michael.

In 1545 the Trevanions had two corn mills in hand, one at Tolcarne (more recently called Tubbs Mill) and one at Porthe Salen, or Portholland, which was probably on or near the site of the Victorian mill at East Portholland. Free tenants held land at Helland, Polgreen (Polgrain), Trebureck (Treberrick) and Penhesken, while leasehold tenants held land at Ventonveth, at Tregavarras and Rescassa in Gorran parish and at Pengelly (partly owned by Tretheake manor).

Archaeological and historical evidence indicate that by the early part of the Norman period, and probably for some time before the Conquest, the farmland of Cornwall was worked from small hamlets whose households cooperated within communally held strip fields. In these there would have been around ten or a dozen cropping units, each surrounded by a stock-proof boundary and each divided into numerous narrow strips held individually by particular households, but open to each other, divided only by low banks that livestock could step across. Any one household's lands would have been scattered through several cropping units, intermixed with the lands of the other households in the hamlet.

Within what is now the Caerhays estate, there were around twenty such hamlets (see appendix 10). Most survive as today's settlements but a few (Helland, Herras, Lanhassick, Lavyhale, Trevanion and Goddaricks) have been abandoned and effectively lost. We can however identify all these sites, although the precise sites of Trevanion and Herras are still uncertain.

One or two of the surviving farming settlements are still recognisably hamlets – Trevarrick, Rescassa, and Tregavarras – but most shrank long ago to single farmsteads. Some of these are no longer the sites of active farms, being instead the homes of those who either work elsewhere or no longer work.

Traces of the strip fields associated with the various hamlets can still be detected in today's landscape: patterns of enclosed strips at Rescassa; the stony banks of outfield strips on the Corwenna clifftop, to the west of Portholland; and earthworks of others belonging to Tregavarras surviving in the Victorian deer park. Cropmarks visible on aerial photographs reveal more strip boundaries at Rescassa. Within the Trevanions' older deer park, Brownberry Wood, is a well preserved patch of medieval ridge and furrow. The 25 ridges here are narrow, just 2.5m wide (and 0.4m high). These were probably made with spade and shovel as this slope is too steep for a plough. This cultivated patch was isolated by 1517, when the park is first mentioned in surviving records. If our estimate for the park's origin is correct, it is more likely to have been isolated some two hundred years earlier.

## Enclosure and Farming.

Open fields were enclosed earlier in Cornwall than those found up-country. This enclosure took place from as early as the 13thC. This was partly because it was easier in small hamlets for tenants and lords to agree to re-organise holdings. The groups in the villages of middle England, who were larger and bound by tighter rules and customs, found this more difficult.

As communalism broke down so the importance of individual farmers grew. Most of the hamlets at Caerhays had shrunk to single farms by the end of the Victorian period, but in this anciently enclosed land the basic nature of farming regimes (despite increasingly mechanized working) seems to have remained little changed from later medieval times until the middle decades of the 20th century.

The basic land use patterns and regimes therefore stretch back at least to the medieval period and probably to later prehistory. Traditional Cornish farms were almost always mixed, with various forms of permanent pasture and occasional arable fields. Arable fields were mostly under grass, and occasionally broken by plough (or spade). They grew grain for the mill which was then used in the kitchen, sold at market or given as fodder for livestock. A typical farm would support varying numbers of cattle, sheep and goats (all milked and all eaten), horses (used for traction and transport), pigs and poultry.

The best draining land usually became arable land. For several hundred years this was managed through a form of convertible or ley husbandry that appears to have been peculiar to Cornwall, Devon and western parts of Wales. A field (or bundle of strips within the former open fields) would be cultivated for just three or four years. Winter-sown wheat was normally grown in the first year and spring-sown barley and oats in the later years, before the land was put down to pasture and hay grass for around twice as long.

Over six, seven or eight years this grass developed a densely matted turf which, in a process known as beat-burning, was then skimmed off, turned in the sun and wind until dry and then burnt. This process killed most weeds and pestilential insects and transformed the vegetable matter into potash. The potash was then mixed with other dressing material (dung from the farmyard, sea sand and sea weed from the local beaches, ditch cleanings from the fields, etc) and liberally scattered in advance of ploughing.

## Buildings

The farmsteads and farm buildings also reflect the mixed agriculture practised in the fields. Small irregular enclosures were used for a range of purposes, such as mowhays. Mowhays were the stack yards within which ricks of corn stood on wooden grids built on staddle stones, and where hay or fuel (that is gorse or furze) was stored.

In the last decades of the 18thC and in the 19thC, first floor granaries and threshing lofts in two-storeyed barns were constructed for storage of corn. Many were built into slopes so that the first floors could be reached by a short ramp or shallow steps. The ground floors usually housed livestock during the winter. They were also later used for milking, each beast chained to a stiddle in a stall containing a manger and hay rack.

In the 19th century some barns (such as that at Lower Polgrain) had circular or polygonal buildings attached to one side or an end. In these extensions, horses hitched to horizontal bars walked round and round, turning their motion into rotary power transmitted by rods to the threshing barns where leather straps ran threshing and winnowing machines and chaff and root cutters. Although animal powered, the extensions were often called 'engine houses'.

Stables, with their taller doors allowing horses easy entrance, and their mix of stalls and loose boxes, were normally free-standing. They were often close to wagon, cart and implement houses which themselves opened onto the lanes that linked farmstead to fields. Other buildings housed calves and pigs.

Pengelly's main barn is a good example of a local farm building. It has a ground floor cowhouse with a central bay for unloading fodder. On the first floor is a threshing and winnowing barn which has a first floor entrance to the hill behind.

The barns were then extended when small dairies were attached. In these, a portion of twice-daily produced milk was separated and made into butter, cheese, curds and cream. In the early decades of the 20th century some of the functions of these dairies were superseded by transportation of the milk to specialist local dairies, some of which were cooperatives. Churns were carted away for collection by wagon and then lorry from conveniently placed stands. Several churnstands survive, forgotten and overgrown. Trevennen has one cut into the road-bank near the turn towards Trevascus. They remind us that traditional farming has now been replaced by larger operations whose milk is stored in gleaming stainless steel tanks. At first these were squeezed uncomfortably into those old dairies, but most of those have now been replaced by modern sheds from which great milk tankers suck the milk and rush it off to yet larger commercial dairies.

A typical farm barn from the mid 19thC; this one is at Treluckey.

Now national and international economies and the pricing policies of bulk buyers have made it difficult to transform the excellent Cornish grass, nurtured by warm winters and damp summers, into a product that can viably support Cornish families. As a result few dairy farms survive in the Caerhays area.

Caerhays is now the area's principal estate, but as late as the early 19th century there were other important houses and manors nearby at Tretheake, Trevennen and Trevithick. Indeed the western and eastern parts of the current core estate of Caerhays were acquired from Tretheake and Trevennen.

A Barn at Godarricks, in Gorran Parish

## Tretheake

Much of the western part of the Caerhays estate was formerly part of the ancient manor of Tretheake. This occupied most of the eastern third of the parish of Veryan. We have seen that it was surveyed as part of the Domesday Book, but by 1322 the manor was owned by the great Bodrugan family from Gorran. In the Wars of the Roses, the Bodrugans were on the losing side, and their lands passed to the Edgcumbes of Cotehele in the far east of Cornwall, a family with whom the Trevanions were closely connected.

A 1644 rent roll in the Edgcumbe archive listing Tretheake's tenements gives us a reasonable idea of the manor's former extent. It ran from Trelagossick and Trempissick (now called Trevallon) in the north-west to Penvose and West Portholland in the east and Treviskey in the west. Most of the farms were still in place in 1775 when the estate was beautifully mapped for the Tretheake Atlas. This provides some of the earliest detailed representations of farming land in the Caerhays estate. Two other tiny parts, Penheskin smallholding and part of Higher Polmenna, both of which were owned by the Robartes, had been surveyed in 1695 as part of the Lanhydrock Atlas.

The 1775 Tretheake Atlas shows that Tretheake manor ran to the sea at West Portholland and Treviskey. The manor probably benefited from its coastal connections, for which it also had some responsibilities. In October 1690 the manor court heard that *'Melchizadeck Jenking tooke up a peice of Wrecke....'*.

The manor house of Tretheake lies beyond the Caerhays estate, and the manor mill below Ventonveth, in what may be called the Tretheake valley, is now a private dwelling, Some land around the mill now forms part of Caerhays.

Tretheake was sold at auction by the Edgcumbe family in 1919.

# Trevennen

In the later medieval period this manor was part of the extensive and scattered lands of Tywardreath Priory. There was a mill, possibly in the vicinity of Tubbs Mill, but on the Gorran side of the river; a new millstone was brought here in 1447. The condition of this mill had become uncertain by 1513 when the two tenants at Trevennen were obliged by the terms of their lease to use the manor mill 'when that mill is in a state of grinding'. One of those two tenants, Thomas Vyvian, lived in the 'principal place', the main house of Trevennen in 1520. This included with it a culver house, that is a dovecote, a good sign of a more substantial house.

Tywardreath Priory was broken up after the dissolution of the monasteries in the time of Henry the Eighth and its lands passed to the Duchy of Cornwall. Perhaps because this was effectively state land, it was routinely surveyed. In 1650 four different households lived at Trevarrick, two others at Trewolla and one at Tolcarne (where the manor mill had probably lain). There were also other tenements beyond the present Caerhays estate.

# The Slade-Gully Family of Trevennen

The 1650 survey showed that when Thomas Vyvian had surrendered the lease of Trevennen and Goddaricks in 1536 the lands were taken by John Slade. This established a link between the Slade family and Trevennen that lasted for almost 400 years until 1919.

At the end of the 18thC the property came through marriage to the Gully family, who then renamed themselves Slade-Gully. A will drawn up in 1800 by William Slade-Gully (who died in 1816) made a number of provisions for Trevennen. First he allowed his wife Jennifer to stay in Trevennen House and Gardens, so long as she maintained them in good order and repair. The Will also established a trust to raise £2000, enough for a considerable house at the time, for building the mansion house at Trevennen. He asked that his heirs use the Slade-Gully surname, use the arms of both families, and profess to the Protestant religion only.

The Gully family seems to have left the mansion house around the middle of the 19thC, the farmers of the land probably living in the farmhouse in the yard to the west.

It is said that the last owner shot himself, and had no heirs. The house and lands were bought by JC Williams around 1928, when it is said the house was still in reasonable condition. However, during the Second World War the lead was stolen from the roof. Then, in order to stop further damage and pilfering, the doors and windows were removed. This accelerated the decay and the collapse of the house into a ruin. Despite the years of decay, there are now plans afoot for the renovation of this house.

Two pictures of Trevennen c.1900

The shrouded remains of the mansion of Trevennen today.

# The Ornamental Landscape at Trevennen

The Gully family designed and laid out a small ornamental landscape, which was designed to appear larger by the clever use of views of the plantations and of the great trees of Caerhays further down the valley.

The principal approach to Trevennen, from the west (from Tregony, Truro, Mevagissey and St Austell), was made ornamental and dramatic through being swung around the entire length of a small coomb – confirming that those who approached a country house did not do so in a rush. This approach is now used as a farm lane, but retains most of its original features, including a broad roughly metalled surface levelled into the slope to provide a gentle climb. As it leaves the public road it passes close to a rocky outcrop that would have been regarded as a romantically wild feature.

Earlier fields are slighted by this approach road. These fields are obscured by a plantation which, although now being filled by sycamore, was of beech and oak, with some evergreen and with laurels planted beneath them. The new road sliced through an earlier lane and past another earlier and broader lane from the fields to a watering place on the stream.

The approach is seen at its finest as it curves around the far end of the coomb, crossing the stream by a fine bridge with arched opening and parapet walls finished with pyramidal copes. Upstream the brook was restrained by a dam over which the eager water overflows and noisily falls, adding to the drama of the experience. As if to confirm that this coomb was meant to be enjoyed, the wall that edges the drive on the eastern side is a pygmy one, intended only to guide the carriage and not impede any views of the valley. Where the drive leaves the magical valley a gateway was built, using lime mortar; to its south the approach widens and begins a broad sweep decorated by more beech, conifer and sweet chestnut trees.

The landscape at Caerhays has both ancient sites and old buildings. Every visitor has the clear impression of a particularly charming and varied landscape, little altered by the changes of the last thousand years. The landscape of hills, wooded valleys, lakes and streams, edged by dramatic coasts, is a landscape where it is easy to feel alone and enjoy the varied and beautiful surroundings, yet still feel the connection to a few thousand years of occupation.

# Chapter 2
# The origin of the name 'Caerhays'

Caerhays is a word whose origin is uncertain, and whose meaning has generated much debate.

The word now spelt Caerhays is misleading since the present form dates only from the 19thC. Shortly after Caerhays was rebuilt in 1808, two changes were made to the name. First, the word 'Castle' was added and, second, an 'e' was added after the first 'a' of Carhays. The first was presumably to meet the picturesque and romantic requirements of the gothic castle, and the second to suggest connection with the popular conception that Caer meant a castle site. Until the beginning of the 19thC, therefore, the name had been written as 'Carhays'.

The earliest explanation of the name comes from Norden, around 1586. The same definition is given in Richard Carew's Survey of Cornwall, published in 1602: '...Caryhayes...*Kery Haz* in Cornish signifieth *to bear his seed,* or as some others define it, *delighting in seed'*.

A different explanation was given by Hals writing around 1730. 'In the domesday tax 1087, this parish was taxed under the name *cari-crougi'*. He then goes on to explain that the place was most commonly known as *'Cary-hayes'*.

Another historian, Tonkin, probably writing around 1740, suggested that *'Carhayes....*The name of this place is derived from *'caer',* a castle, a house or dwelling, and *'hay'* a hazel hedge as the situation does plainly make out; and did much more so before the great alterations which Mr Trevanion hath done here.'

By 1860 Polsue was suggesting that 'The manor of *Caerhays* or *Carhayes, ....* is supposed to have been the *'Cariorgel'* or *'Cariahoil'* of Domesday', but gives no explanation for the origin of these words. More recent authorities suggest (Padel, Henderson)that *Cariohoil* was never Caerhays but rather Crawle, near Breage.

The three early suggestions would normally be given some credence since, in the time of their authors, knowledge of the Cornish Language, as spoken, was still available and therefore, at that time, the Cornish meaning of compound words might be understood. Sadly, it is now suggested that all these early explanations for the name's origin are unlikely.

Some 19thC historians suggested that the word was a combination of *'car',* for dwelling or strong house, and *hay* or *hayes* for an enclosed fence or yard.

Charles Henderson, writing in 1935, suggested that the 'first syllable should be *Cary* or *Kery* as in Carry-bullock near Callington and Cariorhel (now Crawle) near Breage.' He went on to suggest that the connection was not with *car* or *caer* for castle, but rather with 'ca-rou' or 'cerou' meaning deer.

Peter Herring noted that early forms of the name might derive from '*carow*', the word for 'stag', just as might another place, *Carrow*, which is the name of fields west of Rescassa. However, he also suggests that both Caerhays and Carrow might have names that derive either from an unknown word or from the existence of a former round of settlement.

The existence of an early farming settlement would be like the name given for the round or early settlement at *Corwenna* not far from Caerhays. *Corwenna,* is derived from the Cornish *ker*, meaning defended settlement, or round.

In the area round Caerhays, aerial photographs have identified three enclosures which were probably rounds. These sites are just south west of Caerhays Barton farmstead, on the western crest of the ridge to the south-west of Treberrick, and on the northern crest of the ridge to the north of Caerhays Churchtown. All are probably too far from Caerhays to be identified as the reason for the name.

However, Peter Herring has also identified the remains of a banked and ditched ovoid enclosure on the top of the hill immediately north of Caerhays and just beside the possible site of the pre-1547 house. He suggests that this ringed hill top enclosure is a farm enclosure of the early medieval period. This fits well with 6th or 7thC place name origins and supports the suggestion that the origin of the name was as a hill top farm settlement which retained its name as it moved to the present site some 250 yards downhill.

The name used by Carew, '*Car-y-haes*' has that extra second syllable which may be an important element. The earliest documents show that this extra syllable had always formed part of the name and that the last part of the word was similarly divided into two.

Early documentary examples include the following:

*Karyheis 1279; Karihaes 1259, Sanctus Michael of Karihaes 1259; Karieis, 1297; Caryheys 1297; Kariaes 1300; Keriaes 1300; Caryhaies 1301; Karyhayes 1302; Kerihayes 1313; Kariaes 1336; Caryhays 1366, and often thereafter; Caryheyes 1546; Carhayes, 1568; Carihaes 1578; Cariheayes, 1637; Carihaies, 1642; Carhase,1802; Caerhays. 1818; Carhayes; 1839.*

Since there was for much of the period of these records no accepted way of writing any name, we can assume that these spellings would have been an attempt to represent the way the word was said. Phonetic transfer of these early spellings could therefore suggest that the original spoken words were:

*Kar-y-hay-is.*

A present analysis of these syllables is as follows.

*Kar:* Most of the early examples suggest a short hard *Kar* rather than the softer, longer *Caer*. Dr O J Padel suggests that this word *Kar* would imply a settlement from around the 6thC AD. Although an alternative interpretation could add the second '*i*' sound, to provide '*karrek*', meaning 'rock', no great rock has yet been identified near the site. A further doubt on this interpretation is that it seems unlikely that the name would have survived without some evidence of the terminal hard 'k'.

'Settlement' seems the more satisfactory interpretation.

*Y:* The second syllable '*i*' is a puzzle since it could be an independent element or part of one of the adjoining syllables. It also accentuates the stress on those last syllables which, in Cornish, were the most important part of the word. It might therefore be an inserted emphatic or dialect development. It is difficult to provide a satisfactory explanation or translation for this syllable.

*Hay-is:* If the last part of the name was pronounced Hay-Is, as early written evidence suggests, then the first section can be understood as *Hay-* the word for 'enclosure'. This leaves a second part '*ys*', which is a word with two different meanings, 'place of'' or 'below'. Both these would fit use at this site.

Further research will no doubt provide further explanations. However it seems wise to consider the location and its use as the reason for the acquiring of a name. At Caerhays, the name can be read as meaning the 'settlement below the enclosure'. This is an interpretation which not only has some linguistic justification, but also conforms closely with the site. The only difficulty with this explanation is that although it fits particularly well with the geography, it does not give an adequate reason for the second syllable '*i*'.

We can not overlook the possibility that because '*Cari*' may be an unknown word, no satisfactory explanation can ever be found.

The authority on the meaning and origin of Cornish place names is Dr Oliver Padel. He has written that the origin of this name is 'baffling'. He suggests that Caerhays could be considered as having a similar origin to place names in Brittany such as 'Carhaix', although he notes the differences between Brittany and Cornwall in spelling the second vowel syllable. He suggests it is unlikely that Breton names such as Carhaix were based on the word *ker* for 'camp or fort' (which can also mean 'village' in breton). He reports other meanings of the 'car' element as 'near a cross roads', or 'drivable road'. For the '*haix*' syllable, origins have included the word for 'field', and the name '*Ahes*', a princess who had ancient tracks built.

When the authority on Cornish place names suggests that no definition can be considered satisfactory, and that the origin of the name remains a mystery, it is foolish to argue strongly for any particular origin.

We may be sorry that the Caerhays name has little to do with hazel hedges, or with seed, or even with deer, but we should be delighted to read of princess '*Ahes*', the roadmaker, whose name provides a charming and romantic attribution.

For the present, it is probably best to live with the uncertain definition of *Car* and *Hay-is*, as 'settlement' and 'enclosure'.

However, names continue to evolve. In a development which will no doubt puzzle future etymologists, locals now pronounce Caerhays as '*Craze*'.

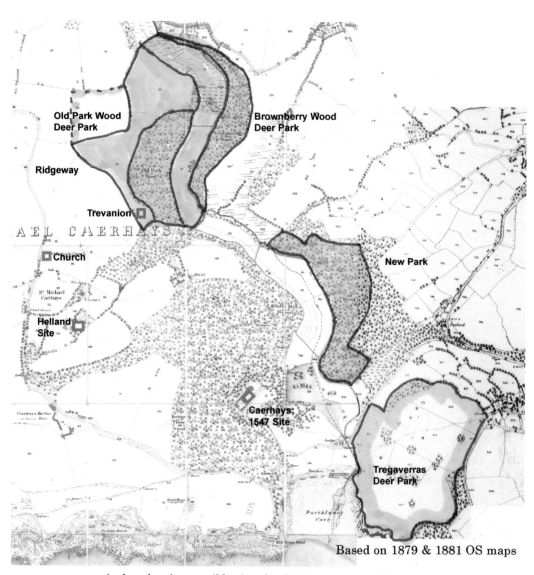

Old Park Wood
Deer Park

Brownberry Wood
Deer Park

Ridgeway

Trevanion

AEL CAERHAYS

Church

St Michael
Caerhays

Helland
Site

New Park

Caerhays
1547 Site

Tregaverras
Deer Park

Based on 1879 & 1881 OS maps

A plan showing possible sites for the deer parks at Caerhays

# Chapter 3
# Deer Parks and Parkland

From the 12thC onwards, Cornish landowners enclosed blocks of their best land to create parks in which to keep fallow deer. Fallow deer had been introduced to Britain by the Normans because of their looks, sportiness and flavourful meat. The enclosed parks were probably intended to keep deer within bounds, to restrict poaching and also to provide sport, energetic leisure, and high status food for higher social circles. Although they may have been primarily for hunting and to supply meat for the table they were normally placed right by the Lord's house as a statement of social position; in later centuries they were viewed as part of the necessary setting for a house.

Over 125 deer parks are known to have been established in Cornwall. Although a number survived as part of ornamental or status landscaping, only one medieval park, that at Boconnoc, continues to hold deer. However there are dozens of other parks, like Caerhays, where substantial remains survive.

## The First Deer Parks.

The earliest deer park was north of Caerhays and was probably established by the Trevanion family while they lived at Trevanion before the 1390s. It was placed either near or, more likely, around the old house of Trevanion. It included an area on the east bank of the estuary, known as 'Brown Berry', for which eastern section rent was paid by the Trevanions to the Prior of Tywardreath. The whole park was still being called Trevanion Park in the early 19thC.

There still remain massive stone-faced 'pales' which show its extent. The most impressive is the curving top hedge of Brownberry Wood, on the Trevennen side of the River Luney. Here the pale has no external height, being cut into a steep slope, but on the downhill side, where the deer would have been, it is 2.0m high and quite vertical, unlike most Cornish hedges which have sloping or battered faces. The walling to much of the pale is of the type known locally as 'Jack upon Jill', courses of stones set at angles to create herringbone patterns. Running beside the pale on its inner side is a broad ditch, up to 3 metres wide. In places, another bank on its downhill side was designed to prevent deer intent on escape from getting a good run at the pale. This inner bank is old, with ancient beeches growing on it; even older oaks (up to 1.2 metres in diameter) grow on the pale itself.

Brownberry Wood has a medieval two metre vertical stone face cut into the steep slope with a ditch and broad low bank beyond it.

The park was long established when the earliest surviving record of the park, the 1517 agreement between Sir William Trevanion and Thomas Colyns, the Prior of Tywardreath, recorded the use of this land as part of Trevanion's deer park. Sir William agreed to take to the Prior a buck (male fallow deer) in winter and a doe (female) in summer.

John Spede's Map of Cornwall: 1610, showing the deer park at Caerhays

The park is also marked on small scale maps of Cornwall made by Saxton in 1576 and Norden in 1597. It was mentioned by Richard Carew in 1602 and its shape was most accurately outlined by Thomas Martyn on his larger scale map of Cornwall in 1748; this contains Old Park Wood and a field on the brow of the western side of the valley that is still called 'The Lawn'.

Charles Henderson noted that the Trevanion park venison had been reputed, with that from Godolphin and Boconnoc, to be the finest tasting in Cornwall.

## A Second Deer Park

The Trevanion family may have created this park as well, some time after their move to Caerhays around 1390. Nowadays, this park is the least well-known, since its best-preserved parts were submerged by the later 19thC development of Forty Acre Wood, which is across the Luney from Caerhays. It then formed part of the landscape park. Still called Deer Park Hills in the mid nineteenth century, this area is bounded by a beautifully built 'pale' with vertical internal face topped with unusual cantilevered projecting coping stones and with a deep internal ditch. It seems likely (as well as logical) that this park originally crossed the Luney to the Caerhays side and may even have been attached to the earlier Trevanion Park, allowing better management of the deer. CS Gilbert, a close observer, noted in 1820 the remains of what might have been park pales on the slopes to the north of the Castle. There are truncated and reduced lengths of what appear to have been substantial boundaries among the plantations above Caerhays. The area on the Gorran side of the river is not really large enough to have worked as an independent deer park although, as part of a larger area, it would have provided beasts with both wooded shelter for fawning and water.

The earliest 6 ft high park walls

By the early eighteenth century this eastern park seems to have been abandoned as Thomas Tonkin makes it clear that there was then only one park at Caerhays. This was the one at Trevanion which was 'well wooded, and having a fine river flowing through it'. It is this park that was carefully delineated by Thomas Martyn in 1748.

The importance of the deer park or parks at Caerhays is suggested by the park being noted on John Spede's 1610 small scale map

'Jack upon Jill' Stone walling

of Cornwall as the only site in Cornwall that is marked with the pale or fence denoting a deer enclosure or park. Whilst this may attest to its importance, it seems more likely that John Spede had inadequate information, or the wrong friends.

Whether or not it was one of the best regarded parks, the Bettesworth family put 70 deer up for sale in April 1789, together with the contents of Caerhays, the lease of the house and the separate lease of the park. This suggests complete dispersal of the park and herd. At normal stocking rates per acre, this may have been most of the deer stock at that time. The first advertisement for sale of Caerhays in 1839 included '45 head of Red Park Deer'. However, earlier sales, the fall of the Bettesworth-Trevanions, poaching and an absence of estate management all ensured that most deer had probably gone by the time of Michael William's purchase in 1853.

Fallow Deer are added to a romantic view of Caerhays from around 1818

## The Last Deer Park.

On the slope below Tregavarras, facing Caerhays, is a very late deer park, created by the Williams family some time after 1858, that must be considered part of the landscape park. The western part of the Tregavarras medieval field system was dismantled. The Cornish hedges levelled at that time can still be picked out as fairly substantial earthworks in the open parts of the park. Some survive intact where they have been enveloped by the several clumps of ornamental trees, which are dominated by evergreen holm oaks. These clumps were designed largely to be seen from the castle as indicators of parkland. Hidden behind a couple of them are the remains of deer shelters. Early maps of the park show that it was compartmentalised by straight fences, of which fragments survive in the clumps, but not in the open spaces. This park was really more important as part of the landscape design than for the deer.

The ancient strip fields on the slopes of Tregavarras were replaced by an ornamental 'new' deer park whose main function was to display parkland from the Castle. The deer sheds were hidden behind clumps of holm oak.

## A Landscape Park

It seems likely that the landscape park laid out to the south and east of the house was begun by John Trevanion in the first decades of the eighteenth century, improved by the Bettesworths, and later much developed by the Williams', in a project that is still ongoing. We know that John Trevanion used a 'great deal of money' to make 'great alterations' to the house and grounds in the early eighteenth century and we also know that a contemporary (Thomas Tonkin) thought that 'there is nothing of regularity observed, it may more properly be called a pleasant romantic seat than a complete habitation.' These slightly sour comments may suggest rather that Tonkin preferred the older more formal fashions in gardening than that Trevanion had failed in his intention to bring Trevanion into the eighteenth century, when landscape was intended to be looked over rather than turned away from.

Cattle grazing in the 'new' deer park

Central to the scheme for a grand castle with inspiring setting and views was the reorganisation of the approaches to Caerhays. The early approach had been either north east along the ridge from the coast road, or along a drive that started at the bottom of the steep hill to the west, a drive that has now vanished in the making of the Williams cut. The ridge road has now long gone and was replaced by the new north drive. The middle drive lingered on until the cut was made

The view from the castle, past the isolated NE tower, to Tregavarras.

and a new road and lodge was made to the south east on a re-sited coast road across the estuary.

The deer park and landscape had formed an important element in the setting and views both of and from the house. The emphasis of the early 19thC landscaping had been on assuring views both from and of the castle. CS Gilbert in 1820 was impressed that the house which preceded the Castle had 'a shew of windows, which seemed to open in every direction', as if intended by Trevanion to allow gaze to be cast over his works on all sides. John Trevanion's Will also made reference to the 'gardens, walks and park at Caerhays' and the last seems to have included a lake. Gilbert described the winding valley below the old house as 'formerly enlivened by a fine sheet of water', 'ruinated' by 1820.

The main landscape park, arranged over the rounded hills south of the house and including the valley-bottom lake, was also conveniently admired from Nash's castle. Its main surviving forms, including the positions of plantations, seem to be of the Bettesworth period. CS Gilbert showed deer grazing this park in his drawing of the castle. However, this may have been artistic licence as there are few signs of deer proof walling or fencing either on the ground or in later nineteenth century representations.

Two pictures of deer from a neighbour's well stocked deerpark show how Trega-varras must once have looked.

## Approaches to Caerhays

Approaches to the new castle were rationalised and carefully controlled so that the family and its visitors enjoyed their arrival at the property, park, gardens and finally the castle. Gradual revelation was a major aspect of the design, as it nearly always was in early landscape parks. Many visitors would have come from the north, from Tregony, Truro and beyond. They entered the park downhill from the churchtown on a terraced drive curving around the hill to the castle's north. For the best part of a kilometre those who had never visited before would have experienced a sense of descending from the open airy world of the churchtown and its surrounding farmland into an increasingly dark and lushly wooded or forested place. This included the ancient oak woods of the old deer park to the north, the new plantations on the hill and across the valley the belts around the upper edges of the middle period deer park, now called Forty Acre Wood. Any visible farmland was notable mostly for its lack of farmsteads. The farm called Goddaricks which would have stood on the hillside ahead appears to have been dismantled at roughly the same time as the development of the Bettesworth expansion of the landscape park.

Coupled with there being no northern lodge until the middle of the nineteenth century, and thus no structure to signal that one was entering a high status designed world, one effect of this descent would have been to put the visitor into a state of uncertainty and heightened excitement. On reaching the ridge end the drive turned south and drew people into a narrow defile, with who knew what lurking in the darkness among either the densely planted trees climbing steeply above or those on the hill falling precipitously to the river below. As you moved through the trees, the world opened up again, the darkness being replaced by drama. Ahead and below was a large lake containing green islands reached by a boat. Further ahead were dunes and beyond them, edged by dark cliffs, lay the sea beyond Porthluney.

But the new visitor, distracted perhaps by these beauties,

would still have been uncertain about where he or she was headed; the lake was within parkland, that was clear – there were the expected scattered trees, clumps of them, and plantations and screens of them, conifers as well as broad leaved trees, but where was the house? Suddenly, set up ahead on a narrow shelf in the steep slope which held the drive, rose a battlemented and turreted curtain wall. Awareness of the size and beauty of Nash's castle was to be further delayed until the carriage rolled through the wall's arched gate and ran along to the covered north door. Even then the design of the house was such that only one half was seen on this approach; the south-western wing was saved for the first walk around the gardens.

Caerhays Park is now mature – the lake is tantalisingly half hidden by conifers and the distant clumps in the new deer park display the extent of the Williams' park.

This northern approach can still be enjoyed in pretty much the same way, although the Victorian lodge now signals that a park is being entered. Ornamental plantings of rhododendron, azaleas and magnolias reinforce this impression.

While this approach works really well, it seems that even greater thought and effort was put into how people entered and enjoyed the park from the south, from the sea. This may even have been the preferred way for showing the place off to most important visitors. Some may have landed on Porthluney beach by boat, but most people would have come from the west, from Tregony for example, or from the east, via Gorran and Mevagissey. In either case, visitors would have met a perimeter wall whether crossing a neat estate bridge over the River Luney, or, from the west, passing beneath a stunning folly arch high above the beach on the west. Both were early signals of estate country. A pair of lodge buildings guarded the opening of the main approach, immediately beside the bridge – these are turreted and crenellated and foretell the castle itself, creating an atmosphere of mock militarism. The castle had already been seen before the bridge had been reached so revelation is not the game here, but instead the piling on of pleasure. It is still a thrill to follow the curving footings of the lodge walls, to slip into the park and begin the slanting climb to the great white castle.

Probably the preferred approach for bringing visitors to Caerhays in the 19thC was that via the impressively turreted south gate near Porthluney.

The Bettesworth Trevanions included the sea and beach in the designed landscape of Caerhays by running an ornamental walk, Watch-House or Battery Walk, along the top of the cliffs on the west side of the beach. This walk, once with a seat at its seaward end, is now largely lost to scrubby growth. In the early nineteenth century a monument was erected to the memory of Captain George Bettesworth, hero of the Napoleonic Wars, on one of Porthluney's Points, probably this western one. No sign of it remains, although it is conceivable that the statue now in the Trevanion aisle of Caerhays Church was originally placed there.

## Views within the park.

Originally a corn mill stood in the middle of the landscape park, which might have appeared mundane in a landscape of contrived beauty, but even here care was taken to make the most of the mill. Its own southern approach was partially sunken so that wagons carrying the corn to and flour from the mill did not spoil views from the castle. This deep lane was crossed by the approach drive on another ornamental bridge, once again turreted to fit with the theme of the castle. The thatched mill was properly looked down upon from here, and its splashing wheel and hard-working miller could thus be admired.

The gothic arch provided a bridge across the original, deeply sunk and steep coast road. The arch, probably designed by Nash, allowed walkers to cross from the house to the coastal path and the Battery viewing point. Re-siting the coast road has made the arch and gateway redundant and forgotten.

This picturesque throwback was replicated to a degree by the red-roofed cottage ornée, the home of farm labourers, provided with a neat cottage garden, that stood on southern slopes near the cliff-top folly. Both mill and cottage were swept away after the Williams family arrived. They changed the emphasis of the parkland's design from one designed to give pleasure in approach, to one giving pleasure in being within it, looking out from the castle and across the garden and park.

Most notably, John Michael Williams enhanced views from the castle; he drew the sea into them by using unemployed fishermen and miners to slice a broad notch through the low rounded hillock backing onto the beach that until then had closed off from the house direct sight of the ocean. This sharp-sided cut's creation entailed the reworking of the south-western road that it sliced through and which it left hanging high and dry, immediately below the folly. The Williams' ran this road further to the south, enabling them to enlarge their ornamental plantations a little. From a new sharp corner they then cut the deep, steep and dark route down through rock to reach the floor of the cut and continue outside the park wall. The cottage was a victim of the great notch made by Mr Williams in the hillside to allow a view of the sea from the house. Both the cottage and the mill were demolished and its lane and leat removed. The mill was resited in East Portholland. The decorative circular shelter, 'Noah's Ark', illustrated in the chapter on J C Williams, was built to house cattle.

The last deer park on the slope below Tregavarras, facing Caerhays, was re-landscaped to form part of the pleasure grounds surrounding the house. The former deer parks in Forty Acre Wood and Trevanion were also brought into the landscaped parkland in the nineteenth century. A spattering of ornamental trees (conifers and exotics) was planted in the southern part of Old Park Wood and an avenue of beech trees, now mature, was planted along the drive at its foot.

Across the valley an arboretum containing numerous massive conifers (plus some palms) was established in that part of Forty Acre Wood closest to the castle. Narrow walks were run among these trees and around natural rock outcrops, providing yet another form of pleasure to the family and its visitors.

Within and between all four parks are multi-purpose plantations, growing timber, acting as visual screens and backdrops, sheltering the gardens from the wildest excesses of the Cornish weather, and harbouring large numbers of game birds. Shooting may be seen as a continuation of the tradition of ornamentalised field sport that had been carried on in the deer parks.

Just as a landscape of farming hamlets can be read as one of co-operation and neighbourliness, so a landscape of parks like that at Caerhays can be read as one linked to wealth and patronage. However, both landscape styles, whether of farming or parkland, are beautiful not just because of simple aesthetics, but because of their association with the history and peoples of past centuries.

Those passing along the coast road have for two centuries enjoyed this view of Caerhays Castle and its parkland.

The castle, viewed through the cut from the sea.

The view of the sea that JM Williams wanted for his drawing room

Birds fly between the lake and Castle

# Chapter 4
# The Coast at Caerhays

Caerhays has one of the quietest stretches of Cornwall's coast. This is partly because the roads between Dodman Point and Portloe cannot be reached by coach because of narrow tracks and weight limits in the stretch between Portloe and Portholland. It is also because the policies for both Caerhays and the Area of Outstanding Natural Beauty are to keep tourism to a level that allows peaceful enjoyment of the coast and keeps the beaches relatively unspoilt.

However, this quiet gives a misleading impression of the historic importance of this coast and of the activities which it once supported. A look at a map shows that Caerhays is fairly centrally placed in the long stretch between the Falmouth Estuary and the port of Fowey.The inlets each side of Caerhays must always have been important. Although it is sometimes difficult to imagine their silted streams as thriving trade centres for a large inland area, this must have been the case. For instance, the inlet at Portholland is probably named after what was once the most important site in the district, 'Helland'. Helland, which has been lost for 1000 years,was just over the hill from the Portholland estuary.

The Caerhays coast, strategically central in the section, remained busy in more recent centuries for fishing, coastal trade, smuggling and wrecking. There are hints of these activities in the remains found along the coast.

Although the most beautiful of landscapes, the coastal fringe is now almost entirely neglected. It is largely overgrown with furze, bracken, thorn and bramble scrub and patches of woodland, which are mainly of sycamores and willows. It is difficult to appreciate that un-

There are few quieter stretches of Cornish coast and few more beautiful.

Portholland

Coastal Grazing

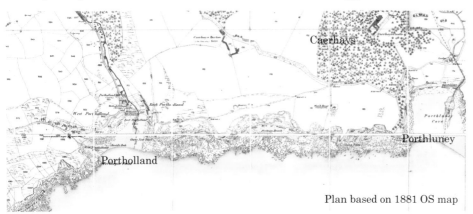

Plan based on 1881 OS map

til the early 20thC this land was part of the resources of the coastal farms. Much of the cliff would have been useful rough grazing, divided into separate holdings by stock-proof boundaries which, though redundant and overgrown, can still be seen. A tiny pound was created just north of the watch house, allegedly extended by Squire Trevanion *'to impound the donkeys which in his time were a great nuisance roaming about the parish'* (Willimott).

Some parts were enclosed as part of a farm's fields and traces of hedges survive, as on the cliff-tops above West Portholland and to the east of Porthluney. Others were orchards, again with hedges, and here a few apple trees survive. For example, on the cliff slopes between East Portholland and the Watch House can be found a Mannington's Permain (eater) and a Primrose (the best Cornish jam apple) and to the west of West Portholland a Sweet Larks (a pickling apple), Adam's Permain (eater) and Costard.

The south facing cliffs on the Caerhays coast were ideal for establishing orchards in the nineteenth century. A few trees survive, yielding this varied crop.

Farming was also linked to the coast through the carting to the land of sea sand and seaweed to sweeten and manure the soil and, of course, through the use of the little ports of Portholland and Porthluney as places from which to send produce around to the larger coastal or estuary towns of Truro, Falmouth and Mevagissey.

Here and there along the cliffs we encounter former quarries, surviving as irregular cuttings, usually hard to penetrate now, being so overgrown. Most would have yielded stone for local building and hedging, but it is possible that some quarries produced limestone used in the kilns at the two Porthollands and at Porthluney. Quarries generally lie beyond the valuable farmland and are on steep slopes where cuttings driven in on the level could most efficiently work into the target rock. It is also possible that coastal quarries were conveniently placed in relation to harbours and hards from which stone could have been exported. Dating of the quarries is uncertain. As they are industrial it is tempting to see them as fairly modern, but some of Cornwall's earliest building stone quarries are along such cliff sides.

A Cliff Quarry on the Caerhays coast

## Cliff Paths and Coastal Walks

Nowadays, the cliffs and coast are seen mainly as places of beauty, of pleasure, and as lengths along which are paths, and look out points. It is certainly true that the paths provide spectacular scenery and on occasion, challenging walks.

However they were not made for the leisure walkers of today, but provided routes for watchers, excise men, smugglers, as well as for law abiding citizens. These walks vary between little zig zag paths, overgrown walks like that to the old battery and more leisurely strolling stretches.

Sand and seaweed from the beach were carted to sweeten the farm soil.

The coast has probably always had lookout places, but it was not until the end of the 18thC that walks and 'prospects' became important. In 1818 J P Neale noted that 'an elevated walk in the grounds towards the sea, to this time retains the name of Watch-House Walk, although very faint indication is left of the former existence of such a building'. Neale must have missed the neat Watch House that now stands roofless on the high ground above the walk. This is almost certainly a lookout from the Napoleonic War. The arched window openings are not just frames for looking along today's coast. Despite the decorative early 19thC gothic form, this building was designed for use at a time when it was sufficiently important to monitor this coast. The

Joe Trudgeon of Caerhays with horse and cart on the coastal path

now roofless Georgian Watch House was linked to other Napoleonic War stations at Nare Head, Dodman Point and Greeb Point, to the east of Porthluney. There must be a possibility that the old Henrician battery was refitted in the Napoleonic War. The Watch House would have provided full time watchers with comfortable if cramped quarters, warmed by a fire.

The coast path

## Raids, Smuggling and Shipwrecks

In the 16th and 17thCs the coast of Cornwall was raided, not just by enemies of the state, but by brigands, thieves and opportunists. There were also raids by people called 'Moors', a word used to describe Arabs as well as the French and Spanish raiders. The Moors came to capture men and women for sale in slave markets. It is sometimes forgotten that most large houses or farmsteads of the time within about four miles of the coast had some protection with a wall or tower to make the quick raid more difficult. Such houses were usually placed away from the sea, not only for protection from the weather, but also from raiders.

On the shoulder of the hill west of Porthluney stands the shell of an early 19thC watch house. This was made more ornamental than many because it stood on the edge of Caerhays Park.

Most raids went unrecorded, but from the south Cornish coast hundreds, even thousands of young men and women were abducted and sold into slavery in Turkey and the Barbary Coast of North Africa.

The St Michael Caerhays parish registers record collections made in the 1630s for 'ye redemption of ye captives in Turkey' and in 1683 for J Hutchings 'a slave in Algier, 6 shillings'.

## Smuggling

Smuggling always gains when government controls and taxes on imports make it profitable, and smugglers had always thrived in Cornwall, which was far from the reaches of the Crown and its officers. Indeed, in the 16thC the gentry practised a mixture of piracy and smuggling, with the Killigrew family being one of the more notorious participants. The growth of tax and central control also encouraged smuggling to avoid the payment of duty, especially in the later 18th and early 19th centuries. The coast became a watch house not only for enemy ships, but also for smugglers, for the landing of trade and for smuggled goods. This meant that, for some, the coast was synonymous with those who would subvert the law and undermine the country's taxed economy: the smugglers.

The Napoleonic watch house was part of a chain that included others at Nare Head, Greeb Point and the Dodman, the last two visible through the left-hand window.

Tradition has it that all elements of local society were involved in the 'trade'. In 1724, Daniel Defoe noticed that *'smuggling and roguing... is the reigning commerce of all this part of the English coast, from the mouth of the Thames to the Land's End in Cornwall'*. The gentry too had their interests and their 'cut' of any profit that might be made. Gates of the Caerhays estate were allegedly left open at appropriate times.

One of the myths common to all parts of the Cornish coast is that associated with the existence of smugglers' tunnels. Stories are told of tunnels cut through miles of granite, when a simple pony trail would have been so much easier. There are many legends of mysterious openings, of hidden caves, or hidden tunnels.

Sadly these are usually a figment of the imagination, or are remnants of medieval mining or cess pits, Victorian drains or limestone fissures. These stories still run and run, and it is always a disappointment to those who believe in them to learn that they may be of dubious veracity.

Caerhays too has a story of such a tunnel, said to run from the Castle down to Porthluney. Why dig when you can go quickly overground, without fear of a tunnel that flooded with the tide?

A drawing on the cartouche of a late 18thC estate map of neighbouring Tretheake manor (which ran to the Veryan coast at West Portholland) actually shows men unloading barrels from a ship into a waiting boat in a bay not unlike those on this coast. Most of the little coves where such boats could be hurried ashore have zigzagging paths protected by banks: covered ways with shallow, widely spaced steps ideal for lugging heavy loads on moonlit nights. Catchole to the west of Portholland and the tiny cove at Black Rock to the east of Porthluney are good examples.

Nowadays, this stretch of the coast is experienced largely by tramping along the South West Coast Path, which was established as a long-distance route used by Excise Men for lookout and to allow quick passage to interrupt smuggling activity.

Such smuggling seems to have been accepted as a normal village activity. A rector of Caerhays remembered that when he arrived in 1852, five old men who had been smugglers and Trevanion's boatmen sat together in the chancel. Smuggling had been a capital offence, but the tolerance of these five by the Trevanions and by the church and the community nicely illustrates what Cornish society thought of their activities.

The Cornish coast path was maintained in the smuggling period to allow Excise Men to rapidly reach points where goods might be brought ashore.

Black Rock path is one of many zig zag paths to a cove which sometimes had covering banks on their seaward sides, ideal for discreet moving of contraband.

## Shipwrecks

Many ships and boats have been wrecked along this stretch of coast. The events of 5th and 6th December 1830 were among the most dramatic. Three foreign ships, from Denmark, Russia and France, were driven by a hurricane onto the shore at East Portholland and the wooden ships were being pulled apart by the force of the sea. The sailors, in mortal danger and stranded hundreds of yards from safety, were rescued by the remarkable bravery of five young fishermen. 'Stripped to their drawers', they grabbed a boat washed off the Russian ship and used it to row out and get a line onto one of the ships. This allowed ten men from the Russian ship and seven from the French to reach solid land. The Danes also managed to get to safety.

As is so often the case, and as happened to a container ship beached further up the coast in 2009, 'country people', sometimes

Smuggling was integrated into local economy and society in the eighteenth century to such an extent that the cartouche of the 1774 atlas of Tretheake Manor in Veryan included this busy scene (Photo courtesy Peter Herring)

known as 'wreckers', heard of the loot. This included wine on the French schooner. The following day they descended on Portholland, no doubt passing the homes of the lads who had risked their lives to save the terrified sailors, and set to their task of stealing whatever they could lay their hands on. They were eventually dispersed when the revenue cruiser the *Adder* was called up and fired shots over them.

Some time after the middle of the 19thC, numbers of wreckers, known as 'the Mevagissey and Gorran Haven men', descended upon Porthluney where a schooner from the Isle of Man had come ashore. Fortunately Lt Walker, late of the Coastguard, Henry Sargent, the gamekeeper, and the Rev Willimott (who recorded the story) got there first and took three very ill men to the Lower Lodge, where they were revived (three of their shipmates had already died). The cargo of marble, bound for Antwerp Cathedral, remained untouched because it did not appeal to the foragers. More recently, in December 1961, the coastal tanker *'Allegrity'* hit the cliffs near Greeb Point and was then driven on to the rocky foreshore below the Watch House where it was scrapped, material being brought ashore by wire rope.

The cove and rocks of East Portholland

## East and West Portholland

Few coastal villages are as unspoilt as the two Porthollands. Arranged at the heads of two sandy coves and at the end of deep twisting valleys, they are separated by a crumbling slatey headland. Since they are mercifully beyond the reach of coaches, and under the conservative management of a thoughtful landowner, they have not developed the standard modern paraphernalia of most Cornish beaches. Two thousand years ago people had to negotiate the tidal creeks running some way inland, but since then both valleys have become silted and sanded up. It is easy to imagine historic communities sheltering here close to the occasionally raging sea.

East Portholland, today

Snuggling close to the sea, the village of East Portholland is now fairly securely protected from storms by curving concrete walls. Although in existence since the medieval period (when known as Porthelland) this is an essentially 19thC hamlet. The terrace was built for estate workers and limekilns; a pub and mill added further activities and colour. The Wesleyan chapel is now a private dwelling.

Pengelly Farm, just yards from West Portholland beach, has been there since at least 1465. The name, from the Cornish *pen* and *kelli*, means head of the wood, suggesting that trees rather than furze and bracken once covered the steep slopes of the valley running inland. With its fine stone barn and its Charolais sheep, Pengelly is now a rare example of the farmsteads that were once common close to Cornish beaches. It contributes to the picturesquely functional character of West Portholland, as do the massive limekiln and adjacent fishing cellars and boathouse.

A low rounded headland separates West Portholland (foreground) from East Portholland, They are linked by a narrow lane and the beach itself.

East Portholland, the larger of the two hamlets, is mainly residential now, but in Victorian times it had a corn mill, two lime kilns and a public house, The Cutter Inn. The exceptionally fine early 19thC terrace housed Caerhays estate farm workers. Each Portholland had a Victorian non-conformist chapel, both now converted to dwellings, but both still dominating their settlements. Each was of a different denomination, serving rival strands of non-conformism: Bible Christian at West Portholland and Wesleyan Methodist at East Portholland.

Both Porthollands are protected from the erosive power of the

Pengelly Farm

sea by strong concrete walls. The defences also extend westwards from East Portholland onto the more exposed headland with its sloping slippery slatestones, along the midslope of which runs the minor road that links the two villages. The boulder and concrete walls here regularly require repair, reminding us that little in this world is permanent.

Steep-sided valleys with fast-running streams such as those running down to the two Porthollands are ideal for establishing corn mills. Disused mills survive in both. Half a mile up the West Portholland valley is Tretheake Mill, to which tenants of Tretheake Manor would have been obliged to take their grain for grinding into flour and meal. The earliest known reference to this mill is as 'Trethake and Behennowes' mills', in 1623. Its dried up mill pond lies immediately upstream of the Penvose turning and the substantial leat that brought water to the mill's overshot wheel can still be seen as a ditch and bank below the Portholland road.

Another mill in East Portholland had a weir in the stream and a leat beside the road. It was recorded as Portsalen Mill in 1545. Portholland Corn Mill is the tall three-storeyed building furthest upstream on the western side of the valley in East Portholland. Its mill race ran along the uphill side of the Polgrain lane and was shown on the O.S. map surveyed in 1879. Little is known about this building, but it may be that its construction followed the removal from within the park of Caerhays Mill; perhaps the grain from the estate was brought down here for milling when the park was improved after 1853.

Although there is limited evidence for recent use of the two Porthollands for commercial fishing, there is no doubt that both would once have served as bases for coastal fishing. These would have been either permanent settlements or places used seasonally, when the great shoals of herring and pilchard arrived off the Cornish coast. Farming communities would then have turned their attention to taking a harvest from the sea. In medieval times smoked pilchards were exported to Spain and Italy and were consumed in their millions during Lent.

By the end of the Tudor period they were apparently no longer being smoked. Pilchards for export were then cured and pressed in hogsheads, such as was practised in the recently restored cellar immediately beside the lime kiln at West Portholland. Its rear stone wall has a line of six sockets. These received beam ends which were weighted at their other ends and pivoted on the lids of loosely coopered barrels or hogsheads into which pilchards had been packed; the pressure of the weighted beam squeezed out 'train' oil from the fish.

The two Portholland coves also served as small harbours for the importing of the limestone that was burnt in stone kilns built in the early nineteenth century in each hamlet. The western of the two kilns in East Portholland has been removed (partly as a result of the encroachment of the sea, but not before it housed a public convenience).

Portholland: Sea walls to protect renovated cottages by JC Williams; 1896

Repairs at West Portholland in 1917

At low tide a great expanse of glistening sand is revealed at Portholland.

The massive limekiln of West Portholland was begun in 1805 with the square left hand block. It had an eye in each side; two further eyes were added in later extensions. The kilns had closed down by 1875.

New Chapels were built at West Portholland and right, East Portholland.

The eastern kiln still survives behind the most seaward cottages. The three-part kiln at West Portholland is now the easiest to appreciate. The earliest kiln, that nearest the road, with an alcove-like 'eye' on each end, was built in 1805 and the two extensions towards the sea, each with a further eye, were not only put up but had also been abandoned by around 1875. The eyes were used for firing and emptying the large round stone or brick-lined 'pots' which widened as they rose to the top of the kilns and in which the lime stone was placed in layers alternated with slow-burning fuel. The lime from the kilns would have been used in the local building trade (in mortar, plaster, etc) and also to sweeten the acid soils of local fields.

At the eastern edge of Porthluney beach are several caves in which can be found tiny 400 million year old fossils.

## Porthluney

Porthluney has the largest expanse of sand between Carne and Vault Beaches and the beach at the mouth of the valley has one of the widest breaks in the cliff line on this stretch of coast.

Exploration of the caves at the eastern end of Porthluney beach reveals the sedimentary rocks in which may be seen tiny fossils of the Lower Devonian Age, around 400 million years ago. The river and the sea eat into a geological framework which is much less timeless or unchanging than it might at first seem.

The geology includes a small patch of limestone east of Porthluney beach that may have been quarried to feed the lime kiln that once stood towards the western end. This kiln existed by 1822, was shown on the parish Tithe Map of 1840 but was demolished by 1879. Fragments were re-discovered during excavations to extend the beach's car park in 1969. Limestone from the rock with sand and seaweed from the beach were so important for improving the quality of farmland that in 1822 they were offered as a benefit for those who took the lease of Caerhays Barton. More recently, the gardens at Heligan have benefited from seaweed collected from Porthluney.

Porthluney is shown on the 1840 Tithe map of the parish. The Luney River had been canalised and ran under an ornamental bridge beside the park's southern lodge; it braided beautifully to water the heart of the beach. At the head of the beach was a limekiln.

Peaceful Porthluney may have seen little military action but, over the last few hundred years, it has often been prepared to receive and repel threats. Dense blackthorn smothers the remains of a small artillery battery on the western point of the cove. On the opposite eastern side bracken and brambles do the same for what appears to be a length of breastwork, a bank on which hand guns could be rested for firing and which also protected a ditch-like covered way along which soldiers could move. It seems most likely that both defences are early and relate to the period in the sixteenth century when, with Catholic Europe a growing threat, Sir Hugh Trevanion of Caerhays was surveying the southern Cornish defences on behalf of Henry VIII.

The western headland is still known locally as Battery Point and the nicely engineered nineteenth century pleasure walk to it was called Battery Walk.

Battery, possibly 16thC, on west point of Porthluney

Early in the Second World War many beaches were considered vulnerable to German landings and considerable efforts were made to defend them. The concrete pill box at the western end of Porthluney beach survives, as does another on the slope above, though that one is largely covered in brambles.

Storms borne on southern winds sometimes rip away enough of the beach's sand to expose the surviving traces of tubular scaffolding poles. These were used to create ranks of beach defences running across Porthluney to prevent landing craft and tanks from making

A Second World War pillbox still guards the western end of Porthluney beach. Another lies covered in brambles a short way up the slope.

easy headway. Mines were also planted in the area now used as a car park. It is said that during the war local children would scramble through the rolls of barbed wire to get down to the beach to play.

Despite the war-time defences, a Frenchman landed from a large rowing boat at Porthluney, escaping the notice of the coastguards. He walked unscathed through the minefields and claimed he had escaped from the Nazi occupation in France. Sadly for romance, he turned out to be a petty criminal who had escaped his captors and was on the run. His boat remained for forty years on the lake at Caerhays, before finally rotting away.

It is difficult now to imagine how different was the scenery of the valley at Porthluney two thousand years ago, since it has changed from a wide tidal estuary which was navigated for almost three miles inland, to become a managed landscape of streams with mills, lime kilns, lakes and deer parks. The stream has been canalised and put under ground and much of the land altered, including the removal of spoil from the 'Williams Cut' to the middle of the estuary; the roads have been radically re-routed and small gothic buildings added, to give drama to the landscape.

It is still, however, the beautiful place shown in the old postcard and in the photographs on this page.

Porthluney is not only a fine beach, but is also the gateway to the castle itself.

Porthluney beach: This postcard from the 1920s shows the now lost boathouse just by the mounds of earth dumped from the 19thC cut made through the hill.

Two views of Porthluney

A last look at the coast of Portholland

# Chapter 5
## The Church of St Michael Caerhays

The church at Caerhays serves a small parish, ranked 202 out of 209 in order of area in Cornwall, and the church is proportionately tiny. The building is largely twelfth century in origin.

It was originally a parochial chapel, '*capella Sancti Michaelis de Karyhays*' when rededicated on the 5th October 1259 by Bishop Bronescombe. Chapel and parish were at that time attached to the larger church of St Stephen in Brannel, six or more miles to the north, a relic of the holding of Caerhays within the manor of Brannel.

The church was built high on the hill, like most churches dedicated to St Michael the Archangel, who is the patron saint, among other things, of windy places. The short tower, a prominent local landmark, was used as a seamark in the early eighteenth century. It was built within what was once a sub-circular or sub-rectangular enclosure. The strong curving bank within the northern churchyard extension reveals the original line there.

Such enclosures were often named *lann* in pre-Norman Cornish Christian settlements. This may also have been a *lann* since there are medieval references to a settlement in the manor of Caerhays called Lavyhale, a word probably derived from *lan-vyhal*, or the lann (churchyard enclosure) of St Michael. This suggests that this is an early pre-Norman site, although its existence is confused by the existence of another, apparently earlier *lann* name in the parish.

The relationship of the present church with the lost site of Helland, some two hundred yards to the south west beyond the site of the old vicarage, may also have played a part in the siting of the church, particularly since the land on which Helland once stood became part of the glebe, or church land, suggesting a distant connection between church and Helland.

This may have been why, in the words of Henderson, 'From the 16thC, the rectors, with complete disregard for the convenience of their parishioners, fixed their residence at Caerhays, so that this [instead of St Stephen in Brannel] became esteemed the mother church'.

As is usual in Cornwall, the church is by far the oldest surviving structure in the parish. Almost all other buildings on the estate are 18thC or later. The main body – nave, chancel and north transept – were already being baked by Cornwall's summer sun and drenched by its winter storms when Richard the Lionheart was on his travels and when his brother King John was receiving the Magna Carta. The local slatestone that makes up its rubble-built walls had been hewn from the hills or cliffs of Caerhays, and the hunks of granite that were worked into the modest dressings and quoins had been hauled from one of the great Cornish uplands, probably from those nearest at Hensbarrow downs, eight or nine miles to the north. Thin grey-blue slate had also been carried here, probably from the Delabole quarries, for the gable-ended roofs. These have since been prettily topped with red crested ridge tiles.

Much of the 12thC cruciform church survives including the nave, chancel and north transept. A blocked 12thC door on the north side of the nave has a tympanum over it containing a damaged relief carving of the agnus dei, the lamb of God.

A 14thC tower was added at its west end. In the 15thC, the southern transept was expanded eastwards into a half length or two-bay south aisle. Although also called the Lady Chapel, this was effectively the private chapel of the Trevanion family.

The simple cusped lancet windows that are such a feature of the church probably date from the 14thC, the time of the Black Death. There is one in each of the north and south walls of the nave, with another in the north wall of the chancel and a pair under a squared hood mould on the transept's east wall.

The Lady chapel was built in the 15thC by the Trevanion family. Most of the window stonework is from the 15thC or 16thC and is in the perpendicular style, perhaps inserted at a time when the Trevanions were benefiting from being on the winning side in The Wars of the Roses. The east window of the chancel is, however, a nineteenth century replacement.

A porch was built in the angle of the nave and south aisle in the late 15th or early 16thC.

The tower has two-light bell openings with slate louvres on the second stage. The original three bells were dated 1540 and there are now six bells in a strengthened belfry. The granite ashlar crenellated parapet was added to the tower in the fifteenth century and presumably replaced pinnacles or even a short spire.

A Blocked 12thC door with tympanum carrying a carved lamb of God.

The church appears, perhaps because of the association with Brannel, to have supported a number of guilds. Such guilds were not necessarily trade guilds but more like charitable gentry associations, with ceremonial and feast day attributes. The word 'guild' was originally a saxon word for subscription. Most guilds did not survive the reformation or survived only as renamed ceremonial days.

At Caerhays, there is reference to three of the local 'stores' in Sir William Trevanion's Will of 1512. These 'stores', are thought to have been guilds for maintenance of the church and for obtaining prayers for the souls of present and former members. Sir William left the sum of 6s 8d (that is half a mark) to each of three 'stores' which is the only known reference to these 'stores' of All Hallows, Our Lady and St Michael.

The south aisle would have been new in 1512, when Sir William Trevanion asked to be buried in *Seint Mighelis Church in Charihays within our Ladies Chapell in the South side thereof where I have appointed my place to lye in and I will [that] there be made a Tombe of Marbull with a picture*

*upon for myself – the pictur to be made armyd with a helde of myne armes thereupon'. His wife – should she die soon after – 'if her mynde be to lye there as I doo and with me – then I woll she have a picture made for her with her armes upon hir mantlett in suche maner'.* He also left money for a priest to sing mass for three years in the Lady Chapel.

A 1680 terrier of the church's property provides some detail on how the church was furnished then: William Sutton the rector mentioned that there were *'three bells, a chest, a pulpit cushion, a font cloth, a surplice, a Bible, 2 Common Prayer Books, etc etc'.*

The screen to the Lady Chapel is perhaps part medieval, part 17thC, rebuilt in the 19thC.

## Nineteenth Century Renovation.

Repairs and alteration started in 1852 when the vicar, the Revd W. Willimott, reported on the difficulties of updating a church that was still behind the times. He installed a small harmonium, improved the floor and seating and changed the singing and service traditions and layout. His changes must have been a considerable shock to the old fashioned and informal congregation. His memoirs were illustrated with his own drawings. This extract gives some idea of the old style of service.

*"The Chancel of Caerhays presented a queer appearance in 1852. Outside the altar were forms on which sat five old men, who had been in their youth Trevanion's boat men and who smuggled not a little. They all chewed tobacco and used the floor as spittoon.*

*William Jolly the clerk also had his square pew up here and having given out the psalm, 'new version', raised the tune. [This was always] one of his own composing, [but one from which he then] frequently drifted into some well known melody. He never rose from his seat until he was fairly off; If he failed, he, scratching his head, would say: "wunna ga Measter" then he would break out into a loud refrain and carry it on triumphantly."*

Another story tells of the arrival of the harmonium, of an over-shy lady player and, when the music began, of the howling from ever present dogs.

The Revd. William Willimott

In the nave is a brass memorial to that Reverend William Willimott, incumbent from 1852 to 1878. He was not only the instigator of the church's first Victorian restoration, but also the craftsman who undertook much of it, creating many of the new stained glass windows and carved woodwork, including the very special oak and mosaic reredos. On the north wall of the chancel hangs a photograph of Willimott. His memory lives on here, in the glass and mosaics, and in the quirky reminiscences written at the end of his life which show a lively and affectionate interest in the lives of his parishioners.

The next renovations were assist-

The five old smugglers and the singing clerk in the chancel of Caerhays Church from a watercolour by Revd.W.Willimott, Vicar.

ed by the Williams family of Caerhays, and it may well be that the Williams family felt greater obligations to the church than had previous landowners. The existence of a chapel at Caerhays, and that chapel's continuing existence in the early 17thC, meant that the connection of Caerhays with the Church was that of influential parishioner, rather than one of patronage and control.

Patronage of the church did not go with Caerhays. Indeed, the new rectory south west of the church, was built on glebe lands by the Revd CT Kempe, (rector, 1806-1852) and owned, it seems, by the church. In fact that rectory, built uphill of the previous site, was empty from World War 1 onwards. In 1948 it was bought in ruinous condition by the Caerhays Estate. It had been empty for some years before being renovated in 2005.

From 1767 absentee Bettesworth owners of Caerhays and the troubled Trevanion years of the 19thC ensured that the earliest effective renovator and supporter of the church after generations of neglect, could only be the Williams family.

Funding for the renovation in 1864 was helped by JM Williams of Caerhays, as noted in the glass of the south aisle's east window. The arrival of the Williams family brought a patronage that envisaged the parish as within an estate which was Williams' responsibility, one where the tenants of the village were his, and the church an important icon in the estate.

Most of the stained glass in the windows dates from the second half of the 19thC and is of unusual quality. The east window to the south aisle depicts the significant episodes in the life of Christ: Nativity, Baptism, Annunciation, Crucifixion, Burial and Resurrection.

The illustrations give an idea of their quality.

Malachite and Gold Mosaic Tablets. The Ten Commandments frame a mosaic reredos behind the altar. Only one of the two sections for the Commandments is illustrated.

Further renovation, designed by Piers St Aubyn, a relative

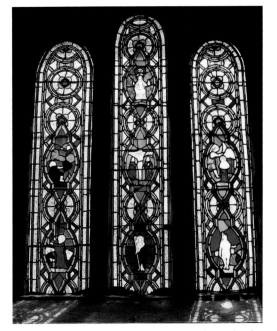

Examples from the ten stained glass windows of the church

of the St Aubyns of St Michael's Mount, was undertaken in the 1880s. Piers St Aubyn was then carrying out alterations at Caerhays Castle, so was able to work on both jobs together, for one client.

Piers St Aubyn was a famous renovator of Cornish Churches and it sometimes seems as though few churches in Cornwall escaped his attention. Much of his work and that of other Victorian renovators in Cornwall, is not well regarded by the conservationists of today.

However the plans that Piers St Aubyn prepared show that the works were relatively straightforward. They included repair of the roof, new ridge tiles, a new floor to the south aisle, an entire new vestry extension complete with organ and fireplace, piped heating, joinery including a new pulpit, lectern and chancel furniture, alterations to the chancel screen, a new slate floor to the porch, and the addition, outside, of his signature boot scraper.

It wasn't too bad, and connection can still be felt with the original small medieval church.

The character of the church's interior was transformed by the nineteenth century restoration; the walls have plain plaster, the floors are tiled, the pulpit, pews and screens are Victorian and the roofs which were replaced with arched-braces have neatly worked wall-plates and collars. The effect on the atmosphere of the place is not as devastating as at many restored churches. The surviving earli-

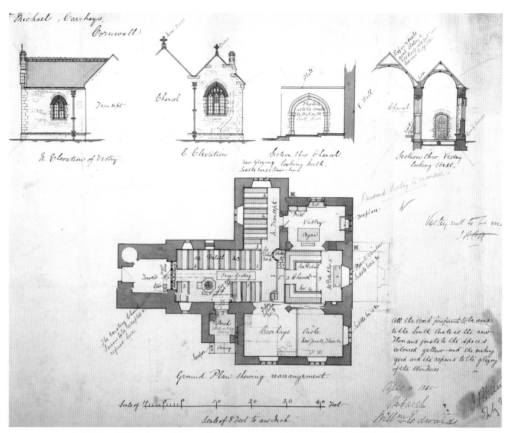

St Michael Caerhays: Plans for alteration and extension by J.P.StAubyn, 1885

Two early photographs of the church

er features are still apparent. These include the strong four centred granite arch to the tower and an arched recess for a tomb (possibly a founder of the new cruciform church) at the north end of the transept. There are blocked doors to what was probably a tightly curving stair to the top of the now lost rood screen.

Three features suggest that while the church may be modest, its patrons, presumably the Arundells and Trevanions, were less so.

Near the south door stands a high quality late Norman font of Pentewan stone. This has leaves carved with great confidence onto the circular bowl, which is perched on a delicate stem.

Another example of medieval carving is on the north wall of the chancel where an angular angel serves as a bracket. Since this bracket was probably intended to support an arch, it is unlikely to be in its original position. On the south wall there is a surprisingly fancy, if crudely worked, 14thC piscena, its ogee head multi-cusped and crocketed.

The south transept and aisle has several Trevanion family monuments. The aisle used to hold the helmet and sword said to have been used by Sir Hugh Trevanion when he was knighted at the battle of Bosworth Field in 1485. Sadly both helmet and sword were stolen in the 1960s. Frightful pikes used also to lean across the aisle, although they have now been more discreetly positioned.

On the south wall is a marble tomb with drapes and urns dedicated to William Trevanion, 'Just, Brave, Sincere, Benevolent and Kind'. He was the last of the Trevanions in the male line and died in 1767.

The grandest monument is the wonderful life-sized statue of George Byron Bettesworth, the heroic younger brother of JTPB Trevanion. He was a naval captain killed fighting the French in 1808, a year after his marriage. The statue appears to be of Coade Stone, an artificial ceramic material, which has been painted shiny black.

The noble George stands with his eyes fixed on the chancel, sword in hand, and cannon, anchor and flag below. This is a statue with that same lavishness of style that his brother was bestowing on the rebuilding of Caerhays.

In the south east corner is a monument both to John Bettesworth Trevanion's first wife, Charlotte who died at the young age of 27 in 1810 and to a child, who died aged two years and eight months.

As John's finances and ambitions began to unravel and the family's honour collapse, one wonders how he felt in the family aisle where his heroic brother stood high, and where, across the aisle, two putti wept over the monument to Charlotte and their only child. Did he wonder what might have been, as he trod down the road to ruin?

The twentieth century saw few major changes, save for those

Illustrations on this page:
1: The angel bracket on the north of the chancel
2: The Piscina
3: A capital to one of the 13thC arches
4: The Font of Pentewan stone

Left:     William Trevanion 1767
Centre: Charlotte Trevanion and child 1810
Right:   George Bettesworth 1808

of church administration. The church is now banded together with other parishes. The most notable addition is an organ which now stands before the tower. This was built by clergyman Canon Miles Brown, who had trained as an engineer. It is modelled on a 17thC pipe organ and arrived at Caerhays in 1990.

The only construction has been a stepped buttress added in 1970 to allow the six bells that hang in the belfry to ring out across the parish once more.

Although there were thefts in the 1960s and 1980s, the church is still regularly open to the public. That apart, there seem to have been few changes over the last hundred years.

## The Church Town

Through the lych gate a small village, Caerhays Churchtown, has developed along the west side of the road, south of the church. The map on the next page shows how few houses existed at the beginning of the 19thC. Churchtown is now characterised by the benign patronage of the Williamses. It is not just that there are estate-built cottages that housed agricultural labourers, carpenters, dressmakers and others over a hundred years ago; there were also Victorian parish amenities such as reading room, school, schoolmasters house and other facilities, including the old poor house. This was in place by 1840, with separate accommodation for men and women. Although now two cottages, it still stands opposite the lane to the *Vean*, the old Rectory.

The church tower, with the buttress added in 1970 to allow the bells to ring once more.

Set back from the road to allow a playing yard to lie in front of it is the old parish school. At the lower end of the village was a small Institute intended to improve the local population and be a place for social gatherings.

However, it was not just the provision of facilities that gave character to Caerhays Churchtown, but also the care taken with stone hedges, architectural design and thoughtful individuality.

The whole place provides a fine setting for the lovely and little known church of St Michael Caerhays.

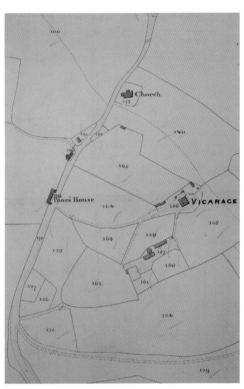

A map of the churchtown from 1840 shows a few buildings scattered along the old ridgeway. The 'Poor's House' was already in place opposite the drive to the newly built rectory. The old rectory site can be seen a few yards to the south west of the new building.

The Lychgate at the entrance to the church.

# Section Two
# The History of the Building
# at Caerhays Castle

6    The Story of the Building              55
7    A Castle Tour                          71
8    John Nash, The Architect of Caerhays   81
9    The Curious Case of the Paper Roof     89

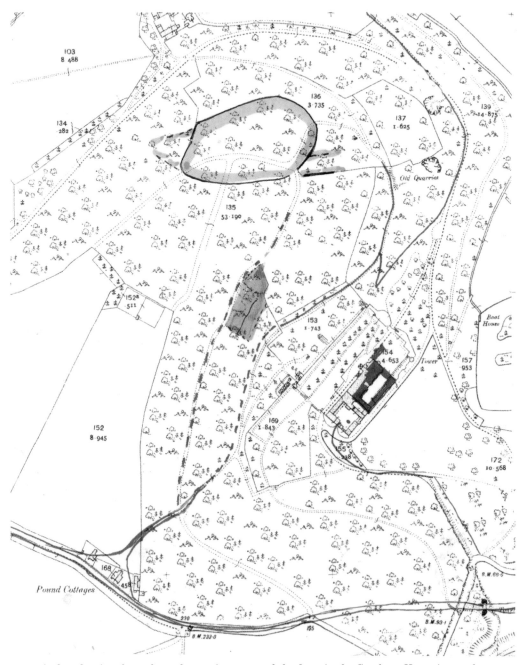

A plan showing the early settlement in green and the first site for Caerhays House in purple.
The early 16thC buildings, as surveyed in 1802 and which are now the site of the modern Castle
are coloured red. Early tracks are marked in red.

# Chapter 6
# The Story of the Building

## The First Settlement

The early farm settlement above Caer-hays is an oval enclosure at the end of a ridge, with a valley to three sides. The bank and ditch run along the top of the slopes on three sides, with a further bank and ditch across the ridge-way. Further banked enclosures run down the slopes to both north and south. These appear to be secondary or entrance enclosures, since one is directly opposite the old site for Helland, and the other runs down a track to the mouth of the small valley and stream to the estuary. In some places, the ditch is cut on the inside, rather than outside the bank, perhaps because the ground there was too steep or difficult for excavation. It is possible that the bank, whose remaining measurements suggest considerable height and size, had on the top a palisade or tight knit hedge. This large banked enclosure is unlikely to have been a ring fort but more likely to have been a secure, scavenger proof early medieval farmstead or settlement from about 700 AD.

An aerial photograph shows the possible sites for Trevanion, (top left), the hilltop enclosure (centre) and the earlier Caerhays house site (lower rectangle).

Maps from the 1802 survey and the 1881 OS maps show a system of tracks which appear to have survived from this early settlement and from the first house. The first habitation, on the top of the hill, but with no easily accessible water supply, had a ridge way running to the coast road. Other tracks ran to the estuary and down the hill towards the site of the present house. Some of those tracks still survive today, together with banks and hedges which may be up to 1500 years old.

## The First House at Caerhays

The site for the first house and its precinct was just down the hill from the first hill top enclosure. The new site may have been chosen to provide some protection from the SW weather and to have been at the centre of tillable fields. Hidden from the sea, it may have given some protection from raiders, but was more likely chosen because it was close to the earliest sites and at the centre of fields and a network of tracks. Tonkin said of this early house that:

*The house anciently stood to the north of the present, towards the brow of the hill, according to my opinion in a far better situation. The place where it was built is still called the haller, that is the hall ; but the odd desire of our ancesters to settle in our vallies, and to get, as they call it, in the luthe, inclined one of the Arundells to remove the house to where it now stands, and that was done so long since that nothing remains but the name to point out this ancient dwelling'.*

It is believed that this early site is about 100 yards west and down hill of the first ring enclosure. Here there is a flatter area, which not only has around its edges some of the earliest banks and hedges on the site, but is also the focus of an early track way system. Further, the building platform has considerable stone scatter indicative of habitation and structures. The 'plat' is long enough to have been suitable for a house of some size with an attached 'townplace' and farmyard. The roads that served this site can still be traced on the 1802 map. A possible site for the house within the townplace is obscured by later stone quarry diggings in the north east corner. This area is also at the centre of former fields which had, in 1802, names like *orchard*, *lower orchard* or *house park*. These names make no sense unless they were derived from this first house site.

## The Move Downhill

Although it is not certain when the move to the present site was made, we assume the new house was built further down the slope as times got safer and shelter and prestige more important. It may also have been encouraged by the wish to provide gardens, water and other amenities within a rectangular precinct. Such a precinct would not have been possible on the slopes of the earlier site.

This sketch shows how the first hall on the site might have looked around 1400, seen from the southwest. The service and well courtyard between hall and onlooker is not shown.

Although the move was said to have been during the time of the Arundells, that is, before around 1400, it is not certain to which house the Trevanions moved early in the 15thC. We assume that Caerhays must have been already a house of some significance, status, and size, because it was this site and building that was preferred by the Trevanion family after they had gained Caerhays by marriage to the Arundell heiress.

It seems likely that the present site had a house of substance from 1400, and that it developed further through the next century. It also seems likely that, as at many other Cornish sites, there would have been a chapel here from around 1420. We know that a private chapel was in use around 1512, probably on the lower site.

It is reasonable to suppose, therefore, that this lower site had a first phase with a hall built, as was common in Cornwall, at right angles to the slope. To this hall were added courtyards and service buildings around the well to the southwest. At a later stage too, the large rectangular precinct around the house was laid out. Such precincts were early examples of garden and curtilege planning and evidence of large and relatively wealthy owners.

We therefore assume that Caerhays was, in the early 15thC, a substantial house, appropriate to a leading land owner, county figure and MP, and that this complex was further aggrandized in 1547.

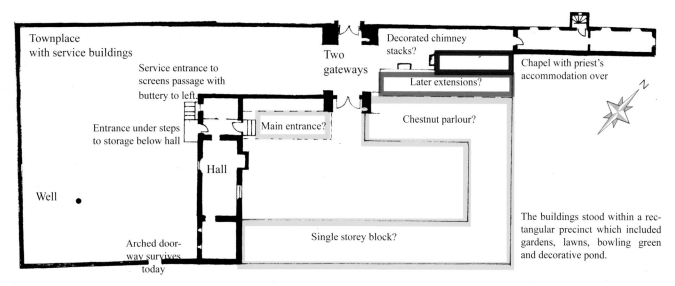

This plan suggests that the site of the early hall house (shown in black) was built at right angles to the slope, within a walled precinct and with well, hall, store and screens passage. The first chapel site may have been to the north west and, if this was always the chapel site, it suggests the courtyard was in place by 1400 or earlier. The courtyard buildings are shown in yellow, and include an extension that covered the main entrance to the hall. The description of the plasterwork and other decoration suggests improvements in at least three phases through the 16thC. This included the remodelling of 1547. The areas in purple and blue show the outline of additional family apartments. The position of the grand parlour, parlour wing and 'chestnut parlour' is not known. The blue and purple blocks with part of the adjacent yellow block were renovated at the end of the 17thC and then refaced and refenestrated around 1710.

*Sketch not to be scaled*

## The Rebuild of 1547

We know a considerable rebuild took place in 1547, since that was the date placed over the entrance arch. It was also a period when funds were available to the Trevanions through inherited wealth, the two marriages to heiresses, the position as Sheriff and the power of the second Sir Hugh Trevanion. It is likely that Caerhays reflected the Trevanions' status as one of the great county families. The house could well have been equal in excellence or magnificence to the grandest of surviving buildings in the southwest, and may also have been influenced by Trevanion friendship with the king, and knowledge of the king's building schemes.

Despite alterations, Caerhays remained a traditional courtyard house and very different, despite a similar date of construction, from that at Mount Edgcumbe, built in 1547 by cousins of the Trevanions. The Edgcumbes, leading lights in Cornwall, lived in Devon just across the Tamar at a great house called Stonehouse. Mount Edgcumbe was unlike the usual run of Tudor buildings since it was probably designed as a villa, deer lodge, banqueting or entertaining hall and general status symbol. Its design as a large hall with four corner turrets is unique in the architecture of the southwest, rare in Britain and has more in common with designs in France than in England. The Trevanion house at Caerhays was probably more old fashioned. It had the older style plan that had been common for a couple of hundred years. It is better compared with the Edgecumbe's other house at Cotehele which, despite later alterations, retained a courtyard layout that had survived from before 1500. This courtyard plan may be similar to an earlier phase at Caerhays with buildings around the well court.

However, 16thC Caerhays was different from Cotehele not only because it was much more splendid in carvings and decorative sculp-

A map of the coastal defences was prepared for King Henry VIII around 1539. It marks parish churches and a few important houses. One house is shown hidden from the sea, east of St Michael Caerhays and north west of the Dodman. The name is obscured, but the last letters might be 'ays', so this could be Caerhays. The map attempted to give an idea of how each house looked, so, if this is Caerhays, it suggests there was a central entrance with accommodation to each side, an image that fits the site.
*British Museum*
*Cotton MS Augustus 1 i, 35-39*

ture, but also because the narrow courtyard design of the north west ranges at Caerhays represented a break with tradition. The 16thC saw a desire for an increase in private accommodation, separate from communal facilities and with more rooms for guests and family units. Because of the narrow width of the standard Cornish range, and the difficulties of roof valleys with double pitches, more extensive accommodation was most easily provided around a narrow long courtyard. Such was the design at Menabilly, built some fifty years later, where the inner yard was reserved for the owners' domestic accommodation and did not reflect the old traditions of spacious service areas and stables. The narrow courtyard design was intended only to provide for domestic accommodation. Services, stables and staff offices were exiled to an outer courtyard. Caerhays seems therefore to have been developed with a narrow domestic yard, built to the north-east of the earlier more traditional outer service yard.

Cotehele is one of few surviving examples in Cornwall of a house with mid 16thC alterations which included a new entrance tower of cut stone, built between 1530 and 1550. It is possible to suppose that a similar tower was added to the outer gate at Caerhays.

We have one description of the house at Caerhays, thought to have been written by Borlase around 1720, but then copied and copied again. This describes a great gatehouse set in the middle of a long range with, to the side, lateral chimney stacks. Off to one side again is the chapel. Going through the 'great gate' brings you through another court to another entrance or 'portal', presumably the entrance to the main Hall. The private rooms include a great parlour where *'In the large chestnut parlour over the chimney are some carvings- a wreath of rose etc: on freestone'*.

The decorative stone and plasterwork and the stained glass in the chapel were seen as important and so the heraldry and figures were described in great detail. The description tells of the Trevanion arms carved over both the first entrance and the adjoining chimney. These arms were repeated over the second inner portal, with heraldic supporters added each side. Over these coats of arms, on the second portal, was also a square block showing Hercules slaying the Hydra and the date 1547, which we assume is the date for either building or renovation. Above this square again was added a pedestal with Queen Elizabeth's Arms. To each side of the blazon were her supporters, a lion and a gryphon, and above was an imperial crown held up by two angels, 'by a good hand'. Alongside the Queen's arms were the arms of Trevanion to one side and of Trewan and Hatch to the other.

This second portal therefore had three tiers of decorative stonework, the reference to Elizabeth presumably having been added rather later. This complexity was common in the internal wood, plasterwork and chimney breast displays of the more extravagant houses of England, although no such extravagance has survived on Cornish exteriors. It suggests that Caerhays was a splendid building.

Charles Henderson paraphrased the old descriptions of Caerhays as '....low and rambling, grouped round a courtyard and entered under a granite archway with a tower or gatehouse over it. On one side was the chapel, its windows full of interesting old glass'.

We therefore know quite a lot about the Caerhays of 1547. Not only do we know of the chapel, great portals, decoration and parlour, but we also know that there was a well, a well court and an outer yard.

This picture of Mount Edgcumbe, Cornwall, drawn around 1717 by Edmund Prideaux, shows that this house of 1547 was not of the same style as most other buildings of the time. Its building may, however, have encouraged the Trevanions to better their old fashioned building to show their status, wealth and court friendships.

The entrance elevation to Cotehele, Cornwall, shows the 'new' tower added c1530-1550 in fresh ashlar stonework. It was placed in the centre of the earlier wall of the main court, and replaced an earlier entrance to the west. The chapel is to the left and rear of this picture, and once adjoined both main entrance and private apartments, in a position similar to that at Caerhays. The central gate now leads through to an inner courtyard and to the door of the hall.

The Cotehele entrance arch was not primarily defensive, but designed to impress, with splendid heavy roll-moulded groined arches.

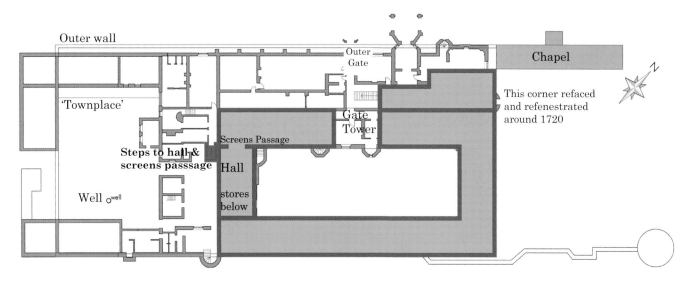

The 1547 building, as amended in the early 18thC, is here shown placed over the 1907 plan, which is in grey.

We also know from the Hearth Tax returns of 1663/4 that Caerhays had 23 hearths or fireplaces. This considerable number puts Caerhays in the top dozen largest Cornish houses, only Godolphin, Port Eliot, Lanhydrock and Cotehele having many more hearths. Caerhays must have been a large house rivalling the greatest in the county.

However, more has survived of this Caerhays than just written description. The new building of 1808 was said to have been built on the foundations of the earlier house. In fact, because the rebuild of 1808 raised the level of the ground around the old ground floor and retained the old ground floor, the reused earlier lower floor remains as the cellars which still exist below the raised platform for the new ground floor. The lawns and boundary walls around the house also appear to bear marks of the former lower floor.

Much of the existing hall wing therefore remains above and below ground, built to dimensions similar to many other buildings of the time and at right angles to the slope. It had a string course around the building, just above the ground floor which can still be seen at the join with the current small south west yard. It is also possible to identify other features such as the service or screens passage, decorative stonework, a hall arch and a basement window in what is now the cellar. The cellars retain the medieval porch to the rooms beneath the hall. This blocked entrance porch in the cellar still retains the arm length deep holes to each side of the doorway. These holes were for wooden door bars which could only have been inserted as the early house was built. Over the lobby and cellar doorway were the external steps up to the hall. These steps are now under the short corridor to the Georgian Hall; the slabs of their top landing still form part of that corridor floor. Throughout the existing building is much re-used cut stonework which include pieces of roll moulding. These contribute to the impression that the house was one of status and complex masonry. Evidence in plan, stonework and surviving features show that a considerable part of the 1547 building remains, including at least one wing which it is possible to measure and which appears to have been the site of the first hall.

The early house would also have had parlour or family wings.

The hall overmantels at Trerice, Cornwall, (top) and at Collacombe Barton (West Devon) both date from the 1570's. They give some idea of the internal plasterwork and decoration possible at Caerhays. However, surviving description suggest that the decorative sculpture and plaster at Caerhays was more splendid than these examples.

These were usually at the higher end of a building and at Caerhays were possibly up hill and towards the north west. It is also possible that the extension south east of the cellar block, the seaward side of the 'Rabbit Warren', was a Tudor extension.

## The Chapel

There had long been a chapel at Caerhays, and it is known to have been there in 1512, when Sir William Trevanion left to his son and heir, Hugh, a mass book, altar cloths and silk curtain for 'a chapel' that was at the house, not the church.

The description ascribed to Borlase from around 1720, tells of a medieval chapel set to one side of the main entrance gate. It can be assumed that a chapel was close to the family quarters of the buildings and within the walled domestic precinct. On the 1802 plan, a long narrow building stretches out north-east from the house. This block fits the description we have for the chapel and would place it at the conventional family end of the site in a position similar to that for chapels at other houses of the time. This location suits the description of the north wall as having decorative windows and meets a requirement for an altar at the east end. This site is just east of what is now the library.

Borlase described a north facing wall with four great windows, their glass taken up with heraldry showing the arms of related families. This glass showed off family connections to those with power and wealth in Cornwall and Devon and included the arms of Edgcumbe, Petit, Arundell, Courtenay, Carminowe, Hillersdon and others. There were also references to Episcopal power, a picture of a bishop, a possible female saint and various family coats of arms. The glazing included the arms of Philip of Spain and Queen Mary, which would have dated from 1554-1558 and were either added later (as were the arms of Elizabeth on the inner gate), or suggest that the mid 1550s was the date for that work. The glass must have given the family and their entourage much to look at during services.

At first glance, the plan for the chapel is confusing. Although the width is about what one would expect, the building seems overlong. However, a chapel with four great windows to one side would require a building about 9 bays long. If each bay were of 6 feet, a length around 54 feet overall could be suggested. Scaling the 1802 plan gives a building length of between 54 and 60ft. This matches both plan and description.

The central extension to the north which looks like a porch is also in an unexpectedly central position and, if a door, would require an entrance outside the domestic precinct. However, comparison with other chapels of the time suggest this was a stair tower.

Chapels were often completely separate, an independent block attached to the other buildings of a house, so a building built just outside the private apartments was normal. The little detached chapel at Lyte's Cary in Somerset is a good example of a chapel still surviving from that time. In Cornwall, a large number of house chapels are known to have existed. These include Cotehele, where the chapel was first recorded around 1411 and then renovated between 1485 and 1530. Cotehele was also designed to have a priest living on the first floor, and like Lyte's Cary, had a 'squint' through which family members could view the service. Trecarrel, a great house famously left

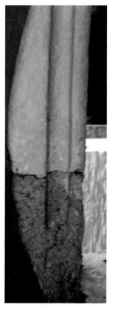

A granite 16thC roll moulded door jamb with decorative pyramid stop. It has been reused as a lintel to a c1815 opening to the undercroft at Caerhays.

unfinished, has a chapel which is now some distance from the surviving hall block, but which it is thought would have been right next to the parlour wings if all ranges had been finished. Trecarrel chapel was first mentioned in 1405 and was rebuilt in the early 1500s. Other Cornish examples include a detached chapel at Erth Barton on two floors and the substantial chapel at Shillingham, rebuilt in 1514, and set against the parlour wing of the great house. These few examples suggest that the position, design and layout of the chapel at Caerhays were in fact conventional. A date of 1420 for the first build, with renovation a century later, would be similar to that at other sites.

At Caerhays, the north extension seems likely to have been for a stair since, as with other chapels of the time, there may have been a priest's room on the first floor to the west. Although many chapels had a private or family end, often with a separate entrance or private window, the family door at Caerhays was perhaps in the west end, close to the parlour wing of the house. The chapel would have been divided in two by a chancel arch. The chancel to the east, although open to the family, would have been closed to the congregation.

Use of the chapel was noted through the years. One of the most memorable events was probably the 1748 marriage that took place in Caerhays chapel between John Byron and Sophia Trevanion, the grandparents of the poet Byron.

Although Byron family records suggest that the chapel was *'in ruins'* by 1809, there was a tradition that the chapel survived the 1808 demolition. CS Gilbert wrote in 1820 *'..that the whole of this [chapel has]been carefully preserved by the current proprietor'*. This tradition was applied to that room presently called the Georgian Hall. However, the Georgian Hall has no east end, is not shown on the 1802 plans, is not on early paintings, and surviving physical evidence does not support an early build. It seems more likely that the Georgian Hall was built as a servants' hall after the 1808 rebuild had taken place and was further altered and the window increased in size around 1880.

The site of the old chapel must be sought north east of the present castle.

## Alteration and extension c1690-1720

Although we know that there were at least two later plasterwork and decorative phases during the 16thC, the house seems to have remained little changed between 1547 and the years after the restoration in 1660. We know that it was described as a 'mansion' in 1646, a word that seems to have been used only to describe substantial estate houses with tenanted rather than worked farm land.

The Trevanion family retained control of some so-called 'rotten boroughs' and continued to be of status and importance in county affairs, as members of parliament, and as sheriffs. There were marriages to rich heiresses which could have helped fund alteration. Such small royal grants as were given to the family for the expenses and death of Colonel John Trevanion in the civil war would also have helped. It is therefore likely that there were alterations after the Restoration since the family would have thought the building old fashioned and in need of updating. Although we have no evidence of such alteration

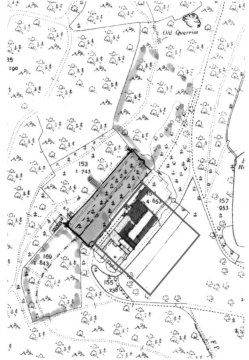

The area outlined in purple shows the extent of the 1547 precinct, which included house, garden, chapel, bowling green, pond and 'town place'. The precinct appears to have been a carefully designed equal sided square. The area coloured green shows the 'new' walled garden from circa 1700. Note the central water supply, terraces and viewing mounts. The areas dotted in green may also have provided walks for the 1700 garden.

between 1603 and 1702, it is therefore likely that Caerhays was given a makeover during the long tenure of Charles Trevanion, from 1643 to 1702, but after the restoration of Charles II in 1660.

John Trevanion took over from his father in 1702 and lived until 1740. It was said that he much rebuilt and altered the house and gardens at Caerhays although we know little of the detail. Around 1720 Tonkin recorded that

*'Mr. John Trevanion has been three times elected knight of the shire for this county, He has bestowed a great deal of money in buildings, gardens, &c., on this place but as there is nothing of regularity observed it may be more properly called a decent romantic seat than a complete habitation; and yet although it faces the south, yet it lies too much under a hill, and is therefore cold and damp in winter'.*

The comment implies that because renovation retained the form of the old courtyard house, it was difficult to add a regular façade. However, we have a small sketch in the corner of the 1802 plan which suggests that the north corner (the area roughly under the existing library) was modernised and given that new façade with the regular larger windows admired at the time.

John Trevanion also improved the gardens, and spent heavily on the grounds. It is wonderful to discover that the walled garden from 1700-1720 remains on site. This is the terraced and walled garden immediately by the north west of the present house. The lines of terraces, two corner towers and doorways still exist, finished in a way typical of the building styles of the period. The two corner turrets are typical of ornaments and viewing platforms in garden design throughout the 17thC. It is still possible to see in the northernmost corner that there was a staircase, lit by narrow slot windows. The stair probably led to a battlemented flat roof, intended as a platform from which to look over the gardens and landscape.

The 1802 plan also shows a semicircular projection at the east of this enclosure, which appears to have been a viewing mound, a classic late 17thC feature. A further platform at the south west end would have provided great views clear over the house to the countryside and sea beyond. Both viewing platforms can still be traced, and portions of their supporting stonework remain. Never intended for other than decorative purpose, the towers, mound, walls and surviving traces of the layout are an extraordinary survival from a little known late 17thC or early 18thC garden.

Important to this garden would have been the need for water to reach the various terraces. Just north of and in the centre of the wall to the garden, an adit was driven into the side of the hill. At the end was excavated a deep clear pit of water, from which water was then piped to both a central water feature and to supply the gardens. Although altered in the late 19thC, that adit still remains today, a

A drawing of Caerhays House as it was in 1802. This shows a steep sloping site with entrance at first floor level. The high, remodelled block on the north east corner is nearest, the corner of the Tudor quadrangle is to the left, the higher hall block is behind to the right.
*(The illustration is from T Corfield's 1802 survey)*

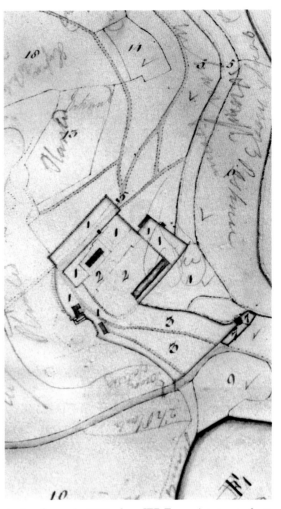

A plan drawn in 1802 when JTB Trevanion came of age shows the medieval courtyard and the late 17thC garden layout. It has been marked in pencil with proposals for later landscape schemes.

dark tunnel always full of beautiful clear water.

There were also 17thC terraces below the house. These can still be discerned on the ground, but have been masked by the ground works and desired drama of the 1808 design. They included a bowling green, ponds and rectangular enclosures, which probably long predate 1700 and fall neatly within the rectilinear precinct which could, like the 13/14thC precinct at Godolphin, be of much earlier date and form.

The late 17thC garden was thus to both sides of the house. It almost certainly extended to the south west and to the north west and is likely to have enjoyed the careful designs and walks that were typical of wealthy formal gardens of the time. The early gardens of Caerhays need further examination.

Also added at this time were new stables and a series of other outhouses. These are shown to the south, with what may have been a new drive down to the beach. C S Gilbert remembered them in 1820 as *'...at an agreeable distance on the southern side, and [having] a stately cupola and clock'*. They can be seen to the southwest of the house on the 1802 plan, although there seems now to be no trace of these buildings on the ground.

In 1753, a legal agreement for *'Mansion house of Carhais'* (sic) gives details of outbuildings, which themselves suggest a considerable establishment. The listing of the *'new sixteen horses stable'*, together with the *'coach house, stables, granary and culver house'* also suggest that there must have been earlier sizeable stable blocks. Other items listed include a *malt house and cole hole, dog kennel and pigeon court, the old stable in the grove, the flower garden, spalier hedge garden and kitchen garden, the new wilderness, malt house grove and John Eddy's orchards, nursery near John Eddy's orchards, cherry garden, garden top the orchard meadow, garden above the ash hill in the Grove, the orchard beyond the ash hill near Lower White Stiles, the new orchard including the nursery, the nursery near the White Style stable, the Nursery in the Helland stable, Gidle Orchard, Park Grove as far as the gate into Churchtown field, the present park Lawns..'.*

This list gives some idea of the extent of the gardens, nurseries and orchards, and the outbuildings in the early 18thC. We can work out where some of these gardens were, and it seems that they may have covered much of the hill around and beyond Caerhays, as well as including the historic precinct below the house and the walled gardens above it. To the seaward side of the house, it is still possible to trace the marks of the Tudor precinct and the 17th/18thC gardens.

It seems that the gardens at Caerhays were laid out in a manner similar to other gardens of the time. Towers like those at Caerhays exist at other late 17th and early 18thC Cornish gardens. The garden at Menabilly was, around 1722, reorganised to provide formal walled enclosures, with a viewing mount beyond one corner. The new house at Pentillie Castle, commenced in 1698, had courtyard gardens laid out with corner and intermediate viewing towers, some of which still exist. Antony, rebuilt around 1722, has a formal garden with decorative corner towers.

There are many examples of such designs in Devon, Somerset and beyond and Caerhays does not seem to have been behind in following the fashion for replanning gardens and grounds. Caerhays must have been an impressive house in extensive gardens.

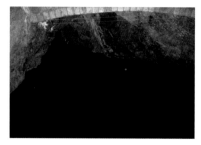

The 17thC water supply

Left:The entry to the old adit and well
Right: A doorway to a garden tower

The early 18thC walled garden wall, doors and windows

One of the garden towers without the long lost top section

## Designs for a new house in 1808.

When the old building was knocked down in 1808, it was said that the new building was built on the foundations of the original. In fact the old building was only partly removed and the new castle was built on to the ground floor of the old house. This is masked by the fact that, in order to make a higher more impressive building platform of greater drama, and provide a drier site not so close to the river bottom, the entire site was raised. The new house was therefore built at what had previously been the first floor level of the old house. This makes it much more difficult to imagine the land contours and site of the old house. It is sufficient to say that the cellars of the present house were the ground floor of the old house.

This relevelling of ground around a house was common at the time, not just to add drama to a location, but to allow entry on the principal floor, make elevations appear more ordered and to hide the less attractive service areas at the original ground level. Raising the ground around a house was carried out in Cornwall at Boconnoc, Pencarrow, Port Eliot, Menabilly and Pentillie Castle, to name but a few.

The new house designed by John Nash was built on a higher platform with better views both from and of the castle. The original design seems to have been for a modest-to-large villa, but with rooms of impressive scale and format. The adjoining plan of the proposed house reconstructs what may have been the original design. This design is supported by drawings from Neale and Willement, both thought to date from around 1815-1818, before the project was finished. The Neale drawing seems likely to have been based on an early concept or proposal sketch, since it shows a large area of black shaded ground between the house and the onlooker. This black shaded ground is not shadow, but instead emphasises the amount of fill necessary to raise the original ground level to create the house platform. It is this fill which now hides the buildings around the original service courtyards of the old house. The illustration, however, suggests some well-court buildings may have survived at first floor level. It is not certain that the eventual building followed the designs that these pictures suggest.

Whether or not the picture is an ac-

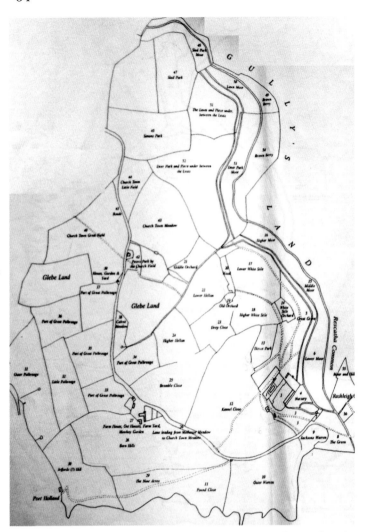

A tracing of the 1802 map showing the names of fields.*(Colson Stone)*
1. House, Outbuildings and Town Place
2. Lawn in front of the house, pond and Bowling Green
3. Main house Grove  7. Mill House, Town Garden and Mill Pond
13 House Park (thought to be a reference to the pre-1500 site uphill)

A drawing by Neale, published in 1818, thought to have been copied from the proposals made to the client before completion of building work. The area coloured black shows the fill needed to cover the old ground floor and level the site. In this original design the entrance porch stands clear of a diagonal sight line when arriving on the south east drive.

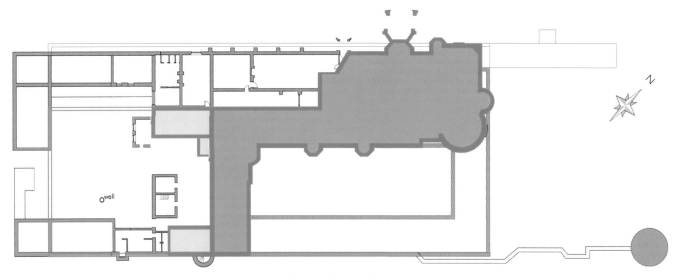

A reconstruction of John Nash's original design.
The 1907 plan is shown in grey and the area edged in red represents the medieval building.

curate representation of the Nash design, it is clear that the whole hillside elevation was focused on exaggerating the drama and importance of the porte-cochère; it was perhaps for this purpose that this view was drawn. Nash planned a diagonal approach emphasised by graduated building blocks to strengthen the arrival at and drama of the porte-cochère. In this drawing, the house is unencumbered by the later servants' hall and by later extensions. These later infills represent the greatest change to Nash's plan and may also have contributed to Trevanion's problems in financing the changes in land levels and the cost of building boundary and retaining walls.

John Nash designed a considerable number of country houses, including many castles. Almost none of these now survive. Even his own castle at East Cowes has made way for new housing. However, Nash's Castle at Caerhays remains true to the original design, a mass of different shapes against the skyline, with an asymetrical layout that disguises what was really not a big house. The use of angles, projections, levels and towers of differing proportions is both interesting and confusing. It may be that the differing towers and irregular plan were intended to suggest antiquity and development through the ages. It is more likely that the motivation for the design was dramatic. Caerhays is a fine piece of scene setting.

Moreover, it is not often noticed that there was in the long elevation facing the sea a careful regularity of plan by Nash, with two

An engraving, probably by T Willement and published in Neale, 1818. This is also a drawing thought to be done before building was completed. Note the small size of the external turret nearest the viewer, and that the walls, different in execution, cannot be viewed in this manner.

A water colour by H H Drake drawn before 1840. This may show the finished building. Note the lower height of the wing to the left, later raised by the addition of a second floor.

smaller turrets in the centre flanked by equal length blocks each side.

Caerhays was described at the time as radically innovative and exciting. This comment was intended to apply to the whole design, but can also be taken to apply to one or two building methods which were not traditional. For instance, it is possible that the roof was of shallow, light construction, covered with tarred paper rather than slate. According to Edward Twycross, writing in the 1840s, the '*quoins and parapets [were] composed of china stone, so called from being used in the manufacture of British porcelain and being a mineral production peculiar to Cornwall.* Porcelain battlements seem a bit unlikely, but the report suggests that the house had a reputation for having been built using 'new' construction methods.

Other commentators included JP Neale who wrote in 1818: '*[Caerhays] presented with considerable correctness the features of the semi-castellated dwelling of our ancestors; and very scientifically harmonizes with the picturesque wildness of the surrounding scenery*'.

CS Gilbert wrote in 1820 that the '*new edifice [was] on a very superb plan, which, from the fanciful additions that have been made from time to time  can scarcely be considered as yet completed... The appearance of Carhayes [sic] House from the ocean must be considered as an object of uncommon interest, particularly on dark tempestuous nights when the lights glittering through the narrow casements of the towers are of considerable service to the steady helmsman as he guides his vessels through the waters of the English Channel.*' This last passage of purple prose tells us more of Mr Gilbert and the expectations of his readers for romantic prose rather than accurate description. Before the Williams cut, it seems unlikely that you could see Caerhays from the sea.  What this passage really emphasises are the romantic ideals and manner in which the castle was designed and thereafter viewed.

Thus, Samuel Drew in 1824 described Caerhays as '*..the singular castellated building erected on its site. This house which is said to display much taste in its architecture and to bear many marks of artificial antiquity has been erected at vast expense.  It is still unfinished, but its view is interesting, and it seems admirably adapted for the residence of splendour and the exhibition of hereditary magnificence*'.

These comments suggest a cautious admiration, but also confirm that 16 years after work started, the building was not, by 1824, yet finished. Nevertheless, Caerhays Castle was a magnificent project and a great credit to John Nash.  The photographs of Caerhays give some idea of the drama realised by John Nash.

Four pictures show that the castle remains the design of John Nash.

## Decay and abandonment: 1839-1853

Caerhays is shown on the tithe map of around 1841/2 and on the auction particulars of both 1842 and 1852. The auction plans are both similar, although there is some minor variance. This may be due either to poor surveying or because squatters or farm tenants had, by 1852, erected one or two small sheds. The 1852 plan shows more service buildings than those conceived by Nash and it also appears that the servants' hall (the current Georgian Hall) had been added.

Although Nash's conception of a romantic castle villa survived, the contents and removeable structure did not. The Revd. Willimott reported that by 1852 the house had been 'robbed of all moveable fixtures, bells, bellwire, lead from the roof... '

A castellated early hopper at Caerhays

Caerhays: 'A sketch by Dr H H Drake, St Austell'; Litho by Weld Taylor, Printed by C Moody High Holborn
Note the gothic arch, the old cottage, the central drive entrance, schoolhouse and mill.

It had been said of Trevanion's Caerhays that '*the staircase was ... lighted by a large stained glass window with armorial badges of the several Dukes of Cornwall and the various heraldic devices of the house of Trevanion. There [were] also said to be other fine painted windows in some of the other rooms together with many "excellent" pictures and portraits of members of the Trevanion family and of the ancient houses with which they have been aligned'.* (Twycross) The Nash house was also said to have incorporated much decorative glass and other work from the medieval house. However, all stained glass and portraits had gone by the time of the second auction. The contents and furnishings had not survived.

## Urgent repairs: 1853-1858

Although Michael Williams bought a house whose plan was not dissimilar to that of today, the house was in poor condition, the roof had failed, water ran through the rooms and there was little glass in the windows.

The immediate works carried out were therefore to repair or replace the roof, refit the interior and provide more accommodation. There was formerly a plaque on the house referring to the restoration by Michael Williams in 1856. These works may have included the addition of a second floor to some wings which changed John Nash's stepped roof line. In addition the service areas were extended with works in the outer courtyards and courtyard

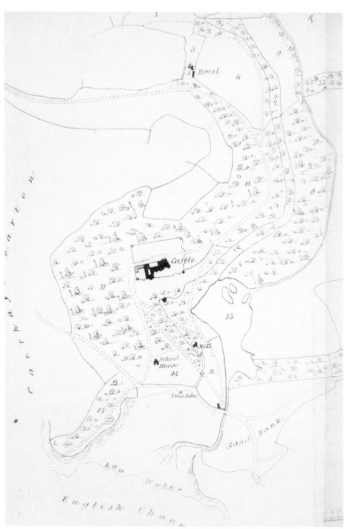

Part of a map in the auction details
for Caerhays from 1842;

rooms.

The 'book of plans' from 1853 has one drawing on which has been drawn the lines for the 'great cut' carried out in 1858 to allow a view of the sea. Some of the spoil was moved to the edge of the bay and piled on the dunes to the seaward side of the road and some may have been carried to the edge of the lake to the north east. It was also at this time that the new zig-zag road was cut in the rock on the road from Tregony to Porthluney.

## Victorian alteration and extension

In addition to changing the levels and carrying out practical improvements in the service yards, JC Williams filled in the space between the servants' hall and the porte-cochère with two large rooms. These provided a large, high, spacious billiard room with two fireplaces and a museum for the display of his mineral and other specimens.

JC Williams also added a second floor above the old hall to provide a complex of staff rooms in what is now called the 'Rabbit Warren'. The servants' hall was improved and the north gable provided with an upward addition to the window to accentuate a chapel suggestion. It should also be noted that the merlons, or battlements, of this gable run happily at the diagonal!

These works were carried out by J.P. St. Aubyn and appeared to have been more or less complete by 1881. J.P. St. Aubyn is famous for work on many country houses, including St Michael's Mount, and in particular for his work renovating church after church through Cornwall. Sadly, no plans or records of his work for Caerhays have yet been found.

Changes continued in the years before the First World War. In 1910, further bedrooms were added to the first floor on each side of the clock tower in the yard. The kitchens and laundry were provided with new equipment. Other extensions also took place in the service yard, together with further more distant service blocks such as a new dairy and the new generating house.

Few changes in the external appearance of the building were made after 1881. Although alterations have come and gone, they have not been material. The present house would be recognisable, and is very similar, to that seen by a visitor in 1881.

Part of a map in the auction details
for Caerhays of 1852.

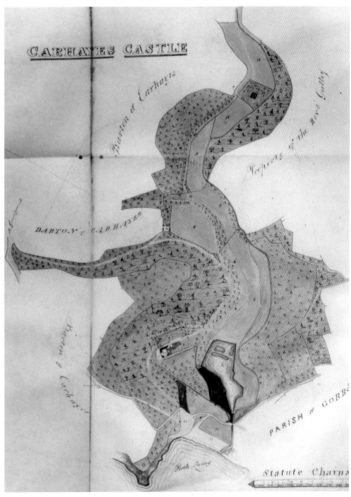

W Smith of Manaccan prepared a book of maps in 1853 for Michael Williams. The proposed 'cut' was later coloured in brown, together with an area where spoil was to be placed.

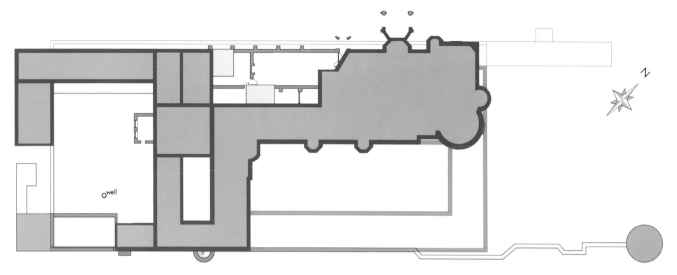

The building plan at the time of purchase by Michael Williams in 1853
The 1907 plan is shown in grey and the medieval building is shown in red.

## Landscape Alterations

To the medieval rectangular precinct, some 50 acres of garden or pleasure gardens had been added by 1740.

From 1808 onwards the existing gardens and landscaping were disregarded, and an entirely new garden planned to provide a dramatic backdrop to the new castle. The lines added in pencil to the 1802 map show ideas for the alteration of hedges, boundaries, or ground levels, and for laying out the landscape with plantations, shelter belts and walkways.

Plans prepared in 1853 also show pencil lines added when Michael Williams started to re-landscape Caerhays, a process that continued under JC Williams. These pencil marks on the early maps provide a fascinating insight to the alterations to the garden.

Despite the centuries of gardens and landscaping at Caerhays, and although it is possible to trace the different phases of the garden, there is no doubt that the overwhelming present impression is of a garden created by the Williams family in the second half of the 19thC.

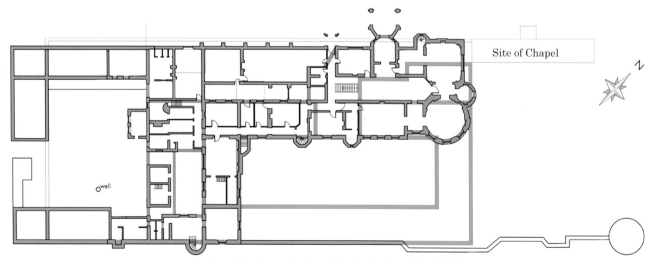

A plan of Caerhays Castle at the beginning of the 20thC.
The early medieval building is shown in red

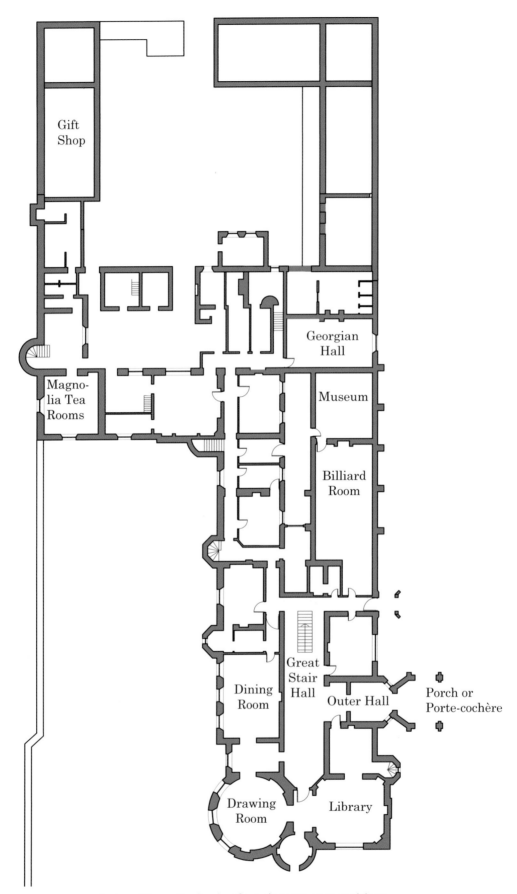

Gift
Shop

Magno-
lia Tea
Rooms

Georgian
Hall

Museum

Billiard
Room

Great
Stair
Hall

Dining
Room

Outer Hall

Porch or
Porte-cochère

Drawing
Room

Library

A plan of the castle showing the main rooms open to visitors

# Chapter 7
# A Tour of the Castle

Caerhays Castle remains a family home, occupied by the Williams family all year round. This means that Caerhays is alive, and a house for the living rather than an inert or sterile museum like many other historic houses. Modern clutter from everyday life stands with items collected over the years. Caerhays has not been manicured or restored for a visitor's pleasure but provides a look at the history of generations of the Williams family, in their home. As with any family home, visitors will remember that this is a private house and that there may be some restrictions during a visit.

This chapter describes the rooms open to visitors, who can join a tour of the ground floor from the 'Porte-Cochère'. This entrance is an elaborate stone archway that provides protection against the weather for guests alighting from horse drawn carriages or from the motor vehicles of today. Although cars could still use the arch, the family remembers the very early car which burst into flames here, since when cars have been encouraged to pass outside.

Two assumptions are often made when looking at Caerhays. First, when seen from the beach, the house looks enormous, but is not. In fact, the house was designed as a large villa, although with decorative turrets and gothic romantic add-ons. It is a tribute to the skill of John Nash that adding angled extensions, turrets and changes in level and façade give so false an impression of its size. Despite additions over the years, the house is still not as large as its front façade implies.

Although it could never be described as a small house, the main block has only five rooms on the ground floor, set each side of the high central hall. The other wings are really only one room wide, and much of the space to the rear of the house is taken up by three courtyards, one entirely enclosed within the house itself. In reality it is a large country villa rather than a stately home or castle. The architect, John Nash, intended to show off the power and wealth of the Bettesworth Trevanions with the castellated exterior. The interior is rather more modest.

The second thing to appreciate is that the original contents of the house were auctioned and sold from 1839 onwards. When the Williams family took on the restoration of the building, everything had to be provided save for some fireplaces, the staircase and a few oddments. The furniture, furnishings and paintings were all acquired by the Williams family in the 1870s and 1880s after rebuilding of the house was completed. Some of the family paintings predate their purchase of Caerhays and used to be rotated around the different Williams family properties in Cornwall. Other paintings were bought for the castle through a New York art dealer. There was no specific theme to the collection, which was assembled for pleasure although, as can be seen, the family clearly bought wisely.

The notes that follow are intended to give an impression of the rooms visited and provide a background to their use in family life.

## Outer Hall

The porch opens through double doors to an outer hall intended to lead the visitor through to the glories of the inner hall.

Above the fireplace is a self portrait of John Opie, a famous Cornish artist. Born at Stithians in 1761, he was buried in St Paul's Cathedral in 1808 alongside his friend Sir Joshua Reynolds, who once described him as 'The Cornish Wonder'.

The Outer Hall

## Inner Hall

This is the centrepiece of the building designed by Nash. It has a light and airy feel which is a feature of his work. Early in his career Nash designed and worked on three prisons in Wales. Although the great hall at Caerhays has similarities with other large houses, it has been suggested that the drama of this galleried long space, and its 'light and airy' feel, was learnt when he designed for incarcerated prisoners!

The wallpaper dates from the 1880s. Recently, the stair carpet has been replaced by Behar Carpets, better known for the refurbishment of the fire damaged carpets at Windsor Castle. The colours and patterns are as close to the original pattern as modern techniques and our skilled designer could achieve.

Looking at the ceiling far above, visitors can appreciate the problems of heating a house like Caerhays. The house was originally heated by a coal boiler with under-floor flues and vents. In the 1950s this had to be replaced. However, re-using the iron radiators with a resited oil boiler was not only of uncertain efficiency but also prohibitively expensive. Instead, night storage radiators were used to heat the whole house. They do not provide real warmth but, in rooms with infrequent use, prevent the build up of mould. They also avoid that cracking of plaster and woodwork which can result from excessive heat.

First sight of the Inner Hall

Caerhays is not a cold house but it can be a very damp one, as is the case in most Cornish houses near the sea. As children, the addition of another jumper was the order of the day, but one soon gets used to the temperature! Visitors from countries with full bore central heating and double glazing have been known to complain a lot.

In the hall, the main fireplace has an ugly (but essential) night storage heater, although, by the time you read this, it should have been replaced with an open fire.

It is probable that the underlying structure of this two storey hall always gave problems. Charles Williams was asleep in his pram here when a chimney stack fell through the gallery to the hall floor. Spare a thought for the luck that ensured that the writer and his pram were not damaged!

The Gallery over the Inner Hall

The paintings too are affected by the top light of the gallery. Not only the glare but the heat of the sun can cause flaking and fading. To reduce this, the refurbishment of the lead roof has had to include special glass which filters out the ultraviolet rays. This glass was also overlaid with a further layer of film to ensure no further damage occurs. Most of the pictures on display on the first floor have been removed. Those that remain are in need of restoration. The pictures on the ground floor of the main hall include:

The Main Staircase

'Over the Hills and Far away' by Sir John Millais. This is many people's favourite. Millais painted only about 20 landscapes. Each of these required considerable effort since the canvas had not only to be set up in a purpose built hut on the moor, but then took three months to complete. Each day, Millais would walk several miles to reach his canvas, carrying his shotgun in pursuit of black and red grouse. You can tell how long the canvas took to paint, because a close look shows the grasses and heathers at different stages of flowering.

'Chelsea Pensioner' by Frank Holl
This is to the right of the Millais.

'Lioness Defending Her Cubs' by John Swann
This is to the left of the fireplace. It is a dark night-time painting. Only recent cleaning has revealed all the lion cubs.

The North end of the Inner Hall. leading to the library.

'The Blacksmith' by Eustache Lorsay. This, which is outside the library, was painted in 1859.

'The Lady and the Dogs' was the product of collaboration between two artists. Andsell painted the lady and Firth the dogs.

'Country scene with sheep' by Verbokhoven

## The Library

This octagonal room is full of character and colour. It was always intended to be a comfortable family room, and the angled walls focus the room around the fireplace. The bookcases were cleverly built within the thickness of the wall. One bookcase, to the left, was built within a doorway to the adjoining garden room library.

The library represents many of the interests of the restorer of the castle, Michael Williams and his son, J.C.Williams. There are books on minerals, exploration and travels, on Cornwall and a range of specialist subjects. However, one suspects that many of the large dull tomes were 'shelf fillers' rather than a sign of great scholarship.

The Library

The garden library next door houses the records of the Chinese plant hunting expeditions, and was certainly much more used. Most of the books contain annotations in pencil from J.C. Williams.

The portraits of JC and his wife, Mary Christian, hang either side of the fireplace. Their features can still be recognized in The Williams family of today.

On the piano sits a picture of the earlier Charles Williams, and his wife Mary, alongside a picture of the early motor vehicles at Caerhays. AF 25 was the 25th vehicle in Cornwall in an era when most early vehicles were buses and lorries. The number plate, but sadly not the Rolls Royce, remains in the family ownership today.

The 1906 Rolls Royce Light 20 tourer, originally owned by JC Williams
Picture courtesy of Bonhams

The semicircular leather sofa may look somewhat battered in appearance today, but when the present Charles Williams was born at Caerhays, this was where Dr Hugh Colson, a great family friend, spent the night. He had several gin and tonics to hand while awaiting the moment to assist with the birth. It is said that his father switched to champagne by breakfast time and it was quite a party!

The Coronations of both George VI and Queen Elizabeth were attended by Charles Williams (1886-1955). As was customary, guests could take their chairs away with them, presumably by later collection rather than as they left the ceremony at the Abbey!

Finally, the bare light bulbs in the ceiling are worth looking at. They are the trophies and reminder of the early installation of electricity. Electricity was still a rare novelty in country houses before the First War. At Caerhays a special engine house and workshops were built for the generators and batteries. The current was DC rather than AC and the supply of electricity variable. Having too many lights switched on reduced the light from each. Chandeliers required more electricity than was available and would have been wired to two switches for power saving. In order to maintain a reasonable level of light, a walk through the house meant you had to switch the lights off behind you ensuring an eerie progress.

However, such bulbs were a great step forward from candles and paraffin lamps, and quite a status symbol, which may be one of the reasons that the bulbs were designed to be bare and seen.

They are, of course, impossible to replace (except with a long bamboo and great patience) when they expire. The engine house has long since been replaced by connection to the 'company mains', and the Engine House itself is now a holiday let.

The comfortable sofa in the library

Chairs used by Charles Williams at the coronations of George V1 and of Elizabeth 11.

## Drawing Room

It was in this room in 1853 that the Reverend Willimott recorded that ducks were living, when the derelict house was for sale and visited by Michael Williams. The room is circular. The doors, the windows, even their glass, the mirrors and some of the furniture are also curved to match with the design.

Curved glass remains unusual, and expensive. When I was about 8 years old, my father was giving a golf lesson to my brother on the lawn. The use of full sized clubs seemed to make disaster certain. Despite my cries of warning, the ball flew through the top of the drawing room window and lodged in the venetian blinds. A neat round hole was left in the glass. Even in the 1960s, the pane of glass cost £200 to replace. My mother was deeply unamused.

From the three windows of the drawing room you can see the sea, a view that was impossible when the house was first built. When the first house was built on the site, French, Spanish and North African raiders were still a threat, and so you did not want to be visible from the sea. The view was achieved by cutting through and removing a chunk of hillside. Looking out, it is possible to work out how much earth has been removed by following a line from the top of the hill to the left, known as the Nobby, to the tree line on the right. This view, very much in the picturesque traditions in which the castle was built, remains an empty landscape because the summer crowds on the beach remain hidden. It is a stunning seawards view, but looking the other way and catching a glimpse of the castle from boats passing Porthluney is still difficult.

The drawing room walls are covered in silk damask which dates from the 1860s. It is fraying and shredding in places and needs protection from sunlight at all times. One day it may reach the top of the list of things to repair or replace.

The Drawing Room

The water colours on the walls are of various Scottish scenes by Sutton Palmer. They add to the general feeling of quiet relaxation which this room always seems to have.

If you look closely at the carpet you will see signs of the many Pekineses that my mother kept. One was an albino and enormous character called 'Miss Puffkins'. 'Miss Puffkins' was also the security code name used for the Queen Mother's visits to Caerhays.

Between the drawing room and the dining room is an ante room. Looking out of the window towards that hill called the Nobby is a blue cedar planted by HRH Prince Charles, Duke of Cornwall. Prince Charles was once a frequent visitor when in his early 20s and, when my father first joined the Duchy Council, royal visits were informal affairs. At that time the Prince drove himself, would go to Caerhays Church and occasionally bring friends. However, later on, as the years passed, the entourage might number 20, excluding the security men. Although a royal visit was undoubtedly always a 'great honour and privilege', it was also a very considerable expense!

## The Dining Room

The dining room is a room that is still used every day. As was once common there are two tables, the second, a small and more friendly one in the corner, is used for breakfast.

The room has always been central to life in the house and provided a fine setting for food and company. One surviving oddment from another era is the screen set above a chair, which was meant to deflect some of the heat from the person whose back was close to the fire. Sadly such a fire seldom seems to reach those sitting on the other side of the table. The centrepiece of the dining room table is a handmade silver replica of a Mevagissey fishing lugger, FW1, made by the Mevagissey fishermen, and presented to Charles Williams on his 21st birthday in 1907, an acknowledgement of family support for local fishermen.

The room used to be somewhat longer, until the far end was altered to make what had been the Butler's pantry into a family kitchen.

The Butler ruled from that pantry until the 1970s, and was important in the life and memories of the family. In the first Charles Williams' time the butler, who kept a parrot in his pantry, would watch for very low tides from the small window, so that he could then collect a lobster from a small pool near Cormorant Rock.

During my childhood, adolescence and for almost thirty years Maurice Blandford was butler at Caerhays. He was confidante to my mother and an exceptional character. He was completely trustworthy, a wonderful friend, and utterly camp. If he disliked guests, vegetables might end up in their laps. If there was a risk that he might miss 'Coronation Street' or 'Come Dancing' on the television, soup plates would be whipped away when the spoons were still in the guests' mouths. In his dotage, Maurice strongly disapproved of shooting lunches since they meant a lot of work. To overcome this, the trick was to give him two large gins beforehand, but also to ensure that there was never a third gin until after the cheese.

My own childhood at Caerhays was much more informal and the display laid out on the table is therefore closer to common use before 1955, when Charles Williams died.

The portraits in the dining room include two portraits by Sir Joshua Reynolds and five by John Opie.

The same visitors book has been in use for over 100 years. It has had some impressive signatures

Maurice Blandford holding a portrait of his father, who was gamekeeper and gardener at Caerhays for over 70 years

'The Shepherd Girl' over the fireplace is one of Opie's best works. 'The Helston Beggar', also by Opie, is far less beautiful, and perhaps suggests a threat one would not wish to meet on a dark night.

'Mrs Cayawardine', by Opie is to the right of the fireplace and shows the portrait of a lady in disapproving grey. It seems that no matter where you sit at the dining room table her reproachful eyes remain fixed on you. Before we were married, my wife found Mrs C's searching looks quite troublesome at meals and especially so at breakfast. 'Hobnelia and the Snail' is a portrait next to Mrs C. It was said that the movement of the snail helped her choose the winner from her would-be suitors.

Family portraits include those of John Williams (1753-1841), his wife Catherine Harvey (1757-1826) and their second son Michael Williams (1784-1858). Michael Williams, who bought Caerhays five years before his death, is shown as a young man. All three pictures are thought to be by Leakey. Other family portraits include Elizabeth Davey, mother of JC, and a portrait of Elizabeth's father, Humphrey Davey.

## The Great Stair.

From the dining room, a tour returns to the inner hall, and on past the staircase. The staircase was a clever piece of design by John Nash, since it provides drama and grandeur within a narrow space. However, the decoration is probably different from that which he originally intended.

A different decorative scheme can be seen in a small painting which we purchased recently from Christie's with the help of our friend Alistair Sampson. The watercolour was done in 1818 by Thomas Willement, FSA, ( 1786-1871). He became the leading stained glass painter of his day and was appointed Heraldic Artist to George IV. It shows coloured glass provided and mouldings around the stair that are not there today. It also emphasises the drama of the new house, and was probably painted when building was not yet finished. The picture was intended to help sell stained glass windows to Bettesworth Trevanion so this painting was in effect part of the quotation. We assume that either the work was never carried out or was smashed or removed after the Trevanion bankruptcy.

## Other paintings.

'The Stag at Bay' by Landseer, above the stairs, is not only enormous but rather horrific. It is certainly not a painting for 'bunny huggers' or those against blood sports. Nowadays this type and style of painting is unfashionable and consequently underpriced.

'Sir Walter Raleigh's Wife' by Salter is on the right. She is shown, after his execution, pleading for the return of his lands. She was unsuccessful. In its way this is as disturbing a painting as the Landseer.

A ballroom scene which hangs to the left of the stairs may be considered still more cruel. This shows a court jester forcing a cat tied to his back to smoke a cigarette. Near to this, 'Hampstead Heath' by John Linnell is positively benign by comparison.

An early proposal for the glass and decoration of the main stairs, painted by Thomas Willement.

## The Original Billiard Room, now the Museum

This wing of the house was designed by JP St Aubyn and added in the early 1880s. This was a time when it had become fashionable for billiard tables to be used by the men after dinner. The room is top lit and of magnificent size. At both ends there are chairs to sit in warmth and comfort around a fireplace. Although originally designed as a billiard room, the use was swapped with the room next door, which was originally designed as the museum. The original billiard room, still confusingly called 'The Billiard Room' is now full of interesting objects from the past, together with one of the cases which display some of the mineral collection.

The Billiard Room arranged for house tours

The collections on view provide an array of memorabilia. They include picnic hampers, cookery books, kitchen utensils, garden tools, ancient toys, some of which are over a hundred years old, and a decaying stuffed rabbit which has been retrieved by generations of household dogs.

There is one cabinet with minerals and specimens from the rocks of Cornwall and around the world. They include all sorts of curiosities, and a lump of rock with a diamond which looks most uninteresting. However, most of the pieces glow and sparkle with colour. There are some splendid samples here, and the house is said to hold some of the best specimens in England. More details of the minerals are given in chapter 14. In the cabinet on the left is a lump of crystals which came from Arkansas. Many Cornish miners emigrated to the USA in the 1860s and 1870s and, in one particular mine in Hot Springs in Garland County, a set of charges opened up a cavern full of these crystals, some of which survived the blast.

A fine fireplace in the old billiard room

The most interesting of the costumes and uniforms may be the hand stitched wedding dress which is over 265 years old. With the dress was a note written by Michael Williams in September 1806. This explained that it had belonged to his great grandmother, Salome Young of Netherex (née Martyn), 1721-1745 who married in 1745.

The paintings in the billiard room are a mixed bag, which include: ' A Welsh Mountain Scene' by Benjamin Leader, who was known as the 'chocolate box' artist, is over the fireplace.

'Playing at Soldiers at Cobham' by Mr & Mrs Ward was exhibited at the Royal Academy in the 1850s. The ladies, or camp followers, appear to be doing the washing but probably also performed other 'duties' for the soldiers. Note the roped stones or 'turfs' holding down the thatch of the small cottage.

A dress from 1745 bears the note: *'This dress belonged to my great grandmother, Mrs Young of Netherex and was probably her wedding dress. She was Salome daughter of Mr Thomas Martyn; was born in 1721, married in 1745 and died in February 1806. Michael Williams 14 September 1827'*

To the right of this picture is 'Under the Vines' by Johnson which captures the Italian lakes with great clarity.

Other pictures include further family portraits, among them a striking portrait of Charlotte Williams as a child with a dog, and portraits of John Williams and of his wife, Catherine Harvey, which are slightly different from the portraits hanging in the dining room.

'HMS Acasta at the Battle of Jutland', commemorates the death during the war of the Williams heir. The plaque mounted below this picture remembers Colonel Spencer who, in retirement, cleaned and restored all the paintings in the house.

'Horses and Jockeys' is one of the most interesting of paintings, as it is one of only three survivors from the Trevanion era. Its survival is almost certainly because it was riddled with shotgun holes, and so not worth either selling or stealing. It hung for at least 100 years out-

Charlotte Williams 1855-1944

side the kitchen. It is said that the last Trevanions used it for target practise with their guns after a drunken dinner. It is assumed that the second horse in the picture, which took the brunt of the shot, failed to win the race, so losing the Trevanions the money they had bet and the money they had hoped to win. It was cleverly restored by Colonel Spencer. Although it is said the colours are those of Horace Walpole, the identity of jockeys and horses remains a mystery.

The room also contains a display cabinet showing a small selection of shells. These have been chosen from the large and outstanding collection of specimens from around the world. Most of the collection, still in boxes, is not on display, We hope that this collection, thought to be important, may one day be catalogued and assessed.

In the far corner of the billiard room is a secret door, which leads through to the Museum.

## The Museum, now the Billiard Room

In the museum, the billiard table is the first thing you see because, as explained above, the mineral collection and billiard table have swapped rooms.

My parents played snooker most nights since my mother was a firm believer in 'exercise' after dinner. The scratch marks on the edge of the table were made by spaniels who were encouraged to pinch the odd ball when progress in the match was slow or tedious. This often appalled visitors who did not properly understand 'house rules'.

The room is dominated by a picture of a Chesapeake Bay Retriever on what is clearly Caerhays (Porthluney) beach. The dog is exquisitely painted with each individual hair picked out and is similar in execution to a Stubbs painting of another Chesapeake retriever at Belvoir Castle. As was often the case, the important bit was done by one good artist and the rest of the background, as here, completed by someone else.

The story goes that the owner of the dog, Bettesworth Trevanion, had invited the wealthy Miss Burdett Coutts, his aunt, to visit Caerhays with a view to a financial arrangement which might have saved the family fortune. All was going well until her 'favourite' footman was bitten by the Chesapeake. Miss Burdett Coutts then drove off in high dudgeon and so ended Trevanion's last hope of escaping his creditors. Whatever the truth in this story, someone had humour enough to have the dog painted.

In the corner is the High Sheriff's uniform worn by J.C. Williams, and then, in 1968, by my father. Most members of our family would struggle to fit into it today, and it would not have fitted my cousin, Michael Williams, when he was recently High Sheriff.

Most of the antlers in the museum and the billiard room are from Glen Quoich or Strathvaich. Glen Quoich was a family house in Scotland which was demolished to make way for a hydro electric dam and lake in the 1950s.

The last stalker who worked for the family, George Stoddart, could describe in great detail many of the individual stalks made by my great uncle Charles in obtaining these heads. There are also one or two heads shot by the present Charles Williams. The best was a 19 stone 4 pound stag from Strathvaich and was then equal to the heaviest weight of any stag shot at this forest.

The pictures include Burncoose House in the 1960s and one of

HMS Acasta, at the battle
of Jutland, 1916

Horses & Jockeys:
a late 18thC painting.

One of the cabinets of rare shells.

Trevanion dogs on Porthluney beach

The modern Billiard Room
with a selection of stags' antlers

Glen Quoich Lodge. More interesting is the photograph of a shooting party at Glen Quoich with the Prince of Wales (later Edward VII) and his beautiful mistress, Mrs Keppel. Apparently the Prince was a very poor shot and the deer were actually driven to butts rather than being stalked in the normal manner. It is said that on one occasion he missed the lot, so one of the equerries had to bag one 'for' him on the way back to the lodge.

On leaving the museum room, you cross a narrow courtyard which was once enclosed as a vegetable store. Before the extension for the Billiard Room and Museum were added in the 1880s the far side was the exposed front of the house, as designed by John Nash.

Glen Quoich Lodge

## The Vase Room

This long narrow room was once known as the 'Vase Room', and used for preparing flowers for the rooms and tables. Now, it is used for the magnificent display set up by my mother. This must be a unique and considerable collection of baths and potties, with every sort and type of useful contrivance.

My mother always maintained that there was little difference between one's behaviour in infancy or old age and that the only issue was whether your legs or mind went first. Since she has spent the last years of her life in a wheelchair while my father became one of many sufferers from Alzheimer's, the potty collection is one of her best jokes. She really did enjoy setting it all up!

After this display, the back corridor has a picture of Gnaton Hall near Plymouth which was owned by Charles Williams, but which is today the home of George Lopes. As George often reminds us, the Williams family crest is still to be seen built into the walls of estate cottages.

The display of potties and water carriers in the Vase room.

## The Georgian Hall

This wing was converted into the Servants' Hall in the 1860s. Before the First World War there were reputed to be over 20 live-in staff in the adjacent wing of the castle known as the Rabbit Warren. It would of course be wrong to suggest that the name arose from any connection other than as a complex of small rooms.

The Georgian Hall, with its large 19thC fireplace, is used to host some 80 sporting lunches every winter. Around a thousand people a year enjoy the estate's hospitality in this room. It is also the setting for weekly Royal Horticultural Society lectures in the spring and corporate events in the summer. Although a working room, it still retains family touches.

My mother refurbished the room in 1995 for sporting and business entertainment and it was then re-named the 'Georgian Hall'. It was called this for two reasons.

Firstly, it was opened by George Falmouth (Lord Falmouth), who was then Lord Lieutenant of Cornwall, at a particularly convivial sporting lunch.

Secondly, the third Trevanion painting to escape the bankruptcy, which depicts George IV aged 59, was cleaned, restored and now, resplendent, hangs here. In my childhood the painting was covered in bat and owl excrement and looked beyond repair. The original hangs in Buckingham Palace and another copy is in The Vatican. As George

The gothic window in the
Georgian Hall

got older and more vain so his portraits depicted him as younger. Many of his portraits are almost identical and, apart from the face, much of this picture was probably completed by a painting workshop.

There are plenty of other conversation pieces in this room, perhaps necessary when so very many people who do not know each other will meet here. These include:

The gothic window itself, which was extended upwards, probably in the 1880s. In 2009 the entire window was taken apart and repaired, so that it should be good for some years yet.

The tapestry above the sideboard was sewn by my mother over several years.

Most visitors to the Georgian Hall ask about the framed section of wall pockmarked with holes. One enquired if this was part of some new collection of modern art. During the Second World War the room, like much of the house, was painted in blackout colours. This patch of wall once housed a dart board used by the 24 evacuees from the East End of London who lived at Caerhays during the war. We have collected signatures from those who have returned, including the playwright, Harold Pinter, and these will one day be combined with the framed wall.

A tapestry sewn by
Mrs Julian Williams

The painting of my father standing in the drawing room is by the famous wildlife artist Roger McPhail. Roger painted this from one visit (and three or four gins) and a few photographs. We could not afford the extra cost for him to paint the landscape bit through the window, a decision which was, on reflection, a big mistake.

Just by the door are pictures of the 'Caerhays Castle'. This train used to run on the Great Western Railway and was made in Swindon. A replica of the train was presented to my father by his friend Pic Howeson who once ran the Mevagissey model railway.

The original train had curved heavy cast iron name plates to each side. These came up for sale recently at £35,000 a side. A total cost of £70,000 for the two plaques seems an incredible amount when compared with the tiny cost at which we could get full size cast iron replicas. Appalled by the figure for the original cast iron, I am afraid you will not see the name plates at Caerhays!

The steam engine which proudly carried the name 'Caerhays Castle'.

After leaving the Georgian Hall, there is a short corridor which runs over the steps that, in 1547, led up to the old Hall and the 'screens passage'. A tour of the castle then ends in the inner back yard, where are the licensed Magnolia Tea Rooms.

# Chapter 8
# John Nash, The Architect of Caerhays

## His Early Career

John Nash has been called the great architect of the Regency period. He remains one of the small number of architects from the last two hundred years whose name is still familiar.

John Nash is perhaps best known for the Pavilion at Brighton, for laying out Regents Park, Regent Street, planning Trafalgar Square, for early work on Buckingham Palace and for Marble Arch. He is famous for his friendship and work with George, both when he was Prince Regent and as George IV. Sometimes seen as a great town planner, he also integrated architecture with landscape design, and completed a large number of private houses around the country.

John Nash was born in 1752. His father was originally a millwright from Neath in Wales and probably worked in London as a skilled tradesman. John was almost certainly brought up in Lambeth and when about 14, he was articled to the noted architect Sir Robert Taylor, for whom he worked for nine years. He then married and shortly after left Sir Robert's practice. He seems to have been impatient to make money for himself and started his own speculative building development in Bloomsbury Square, London.

Sadly, neither marriage nor development succeeded. Although there were two children of the marriage, Nash claimed that they were not his, but had been 'imposed' on him. He not only started divorce proceedings, which was an unusual and difficult procedure at the time, but was declared bankrupt. His trade was declared as 'carpenter, dealer and chapman', a phrase that does not sit with what we know of his apparent station and work. Nevertheless, the bankruptcy seems to have been sorted fairly soon and, although he was stripped of his property, he was declared a free man in 1784.

He then moved to Wales. Later on, to cover up the problems of his early life, Nash liked to suggest that he had inherited a lot of money before he was thirty, and that it was with these funds that he had 'retired' to Wales. In fact, he went to Wales in response to an advertisement for the rebuilding of the roof of St. Peter's, Carmarthen. It was in Wales that he received in 1787 the news that the first stage of his divorce had come through. His private life had clearly been unusual and remains a bit of a mystery. It is not certain that the final legal stages of that divorce were ever settled, since they may have been blocked in the House of Lords. We can only assume that his first wife

John Nash 1752-1835
An 1831 bust by William Behnes, enlarged by Cecil Thomas. The Portico of All Souls', Langham Place. *Image by David Castor*

Marble Arch: first erected at Buckingham Palace

died, since his later second marriage would have otherwise been biga-mous. It was also in Wales that his building consultancy commenced and that he established himself as a designer. For about five years he earned commissions from both private and public clients.

This work was boosted when he met Humphrey Repton in 1792. Repton was already active in landscapes and architectural schemes for country houses and needed someone with architectural experience. John Nash worked with Repton for several years, acquiring much business through the connection. This connection and his increasing business enabled Nash to return to London around 1797. However, the Repton friendship did not last much past 1800, when they fell out. This was probably because Repton, who was not always the pleasan-test of men, complained that Nash did not pass over a sufficient share of his fees.

By the mid 1790s John Nash was in his mid forties. He had a reasonable life with country house commissions, was making money and apparently leading a contented and happy existence. However this life was about to change dramatically. It really isn't certain how and why this happened.

Nash, now 46, married a young lady, the daughter of a wealthy coal merchant. It has been suggested that the young lady was in fact the mistress of the Prince of Wales and that Nash, who, in the words of one commentator, "may have been in a certain respect unfitted for marriage", was merely an 'official' husband. Certainly, the carefully worded reports of his two marriages suggest that John Nash had an unusual personal life. The second Mrs Nash also appeared with three children, whose father, a hop merchant from Worcester, was a cous-in of Mrs Nash. The children, of whom she appeared guardian, were brought up in the Isle of Wight. They bore the name Pennethorne. James Pennethorne appears as one of Nash's young assistants several years later, and eventually took over Nash's practice. Ann, the daugh-ter, lived as a companion to Mrs Nash after John Nash's death.

This private life confused people at the time and is not clear now. It has even been suggested, although it is unlikely, that a child or two might have claimed the Prince Regent as father. Sadly for scandal, there seems to be no evidence to support the insinuations.

However, it is certainly remarkable that in the year of his mar-riage Nash suddenly acquired great wealth, a substantial house in London and land in the Isle of Wight. He became a close friend of the Prince and was offered possibilities in politics and in business. Although his increase in status and wealth may have been prosaically due to successful property speculation, or to money inherited from his wife's father, the sudden rise in his fortunes attracted comments hint-ing at hidden contacts. In the words of one writer: 'He speedily ob-tained a large and lucrative connection'.

In any event, John Nash had obtained in 1806 a well fee'd post as architect to the Woods and Forests. This post was the start of al-most thirty years of work, not only for Government but also for the Prince of Wales. Although his private life may be obscure and frankly intriguing, the work he then achieved ensured that he will forever be associated with the Royal Pavilion, the development of Regents Park, Regent Street, the buildings at Carlton House and other London work. He is justifiably called one of the great town planners and one of few in Britain who saw some of his plan carried out.

All Souls, Langham Place

The Brighton Pavilion
*Picture courtesy of Brighton Corporation.*

Mall Galleries, Carlton House

Carlton House Terrace

## Changes in Taste

The interest in the romantic, the gloomy, the gothic and the picturesque started in the 1760s and is conventionally associated with the designs at Strawberry Hill for Horace Walpole and the literary taste exemplified by Walpole's own 'gothic' novel.

The turn of the 18thC saw changes both in society and in design. The industrial revolution was changing the make up of society, as were political theories and the effect and influence of a long war with the continent. Increased leisure time for gentry women, who were no longer tied so closely to the operation of a house, meant there was a new audience with more leisure for novels and for sensation. Scott, an imitator of this earlier fashion, wrote a series of novels to meet the public's interest in the sublime, in decay, in romance and in terror. There are many examples of this 'sensibility', itself a new use of the word and of interest in the gothic. Byron, a Trevanion cousin, was and is one of the best known examples of romantic adventure in both literature and life. Jane Austen herself wrote a skit, 'Northanger Abbey', on the gloomy and gothic romance which had become so prevalent. This was a period when respectability and sensibility combined with a wish for excitement and romance. The gothic sensibility required life to be sublime, romantic, dark, gloomy and overpowering. Decay, grandeur, fear, terror, novelty and sensation were all 'in' words of the time.

Some sections of society had rebelled against the formalism of the previous classical years. The setting of the house in a landscape, the views of the house and the views from the house had suddenly become the primary interest. The landscape had become a more important element than the formality of a building.

Some of the nine individual and eccentric designs for Blaise Hamlet

Leisure, education, money and a changing middle class ensured great change in the period between 1780 and 1830. It might be easier to compare this with the changes in taste and fashion that occurred in 1960s Britain. That decade had labour saving devices in the home, the mini-skirt, free music and generations whose attitude to society was completely different from that of preceding years.

The 'sensibility' of Nash's time was combined with the desire of the new class of industrially wealthy to demonstrate through the antiquity of their homes both their respectability and status. This social movement, combined with an interest in an unresearched and historically ill-focused concept of 'antiquity', provided the background to the castle's design.

East Cowes Castle, Isle of Wight in 1824. Note the walks and gardens which may also have been provided at Caerhays.

## Nash's Building Style

Nash is usually called a Regency or Georgian architect, although some commentators have suggested that he is best seen as the first of the Victorian architects. Because he doesn't seem to fit in the same bracket as Georgian, Palladian and Classical designers or with contemporaries such as Sir John Soane, it is probably simpler to suggest that he was just the great Regency architect. John Nash was the epitome of a change in taste from the ordered classicism and architecture of the previous 80 years. His buildings did not always follow the rules of classicism and many were meant to suggest an interest in the picturesque.

Kilwaughter Castle, Ireland

It is difficult to summarise his style since he was capable of designing all sorts of different fashionable items. Most interiors, however, ended up with classical elements which suited the more conservative living tastes of his clients.

He also cheerfully combined elements from different traditions. All Souls Church at Langham Place, built in 1822–1825, managed to combine a gothic spire, classical rotunda and Corinthian columns with cherub heads. It was much disliked by politicians and public alike at the time, but is now one of the most admired single pieces of architecture in London. Another complex of styles was the Brighton Pavilion which he converted from a fairly straight forward villa by Henry Holland to an extravagant mixture of balconies, Chinese pagodas, minarets and Indian domes.

His principal works range through Italian, Greek, gothic and Palladian styles. One of his most charming but little known achievements is the hamlet at Blaise Hamlet, where a number of small houses still stand as a perfectly romantic picturesque little village.

Although it has been suggested that his work is so disparate that it is difficult to get a 'handle' on him, much of the work is actually rather similar. Cronkhill Villa, allegedly in an Italian style for instance, is very similar in plan form and indeed in exterior to the gothic Castles that he designed. It is only differentiated by wide eaves and one or two brackets as opposed to a battlement or two. He had an affection for render, perhaps one of the reasons he hit early financial problems, which was used throughout. His so-called Tudor building at Longner Hall in Shropshire is rendered and clearly from the same stable as the Italian villa or the gothic castle.

Much of the work of his practice was actually carried out by assistants, and he was notoriously cavalier in checking or worrying about their understanding or detailing of his ideas. His designs were also, as is the case with every architect, subject to the requirements of the client. Clients too often override an architect's instructions. For example, some suggest that Luscombe Castle was ruined by the gothic bay added to the original scheme, which appears to unbalance the entire composition. This bay was probably not a John Nash addition, but built as the result of a client's direction.

The layout of his houses, no matter what the design, followed a fairly recognisable pattern involving one large dramatic often round unit and two or three great reception rooms accessed from first a great porch, an outer hall and then, in the larger buildings, a long inner, often dramatically galleried hall. Service wings and ancillary buildings were often set at an angle so that the building, although more inconvenient in use, could appear larger and more dramatic. It has been suggested that his early experience of designing for three prisons in Wales contributed to his liking for such galleries. I think it more likely that the galleried hall was simply part of the requirements of the time for sensational even if impractical space.

Much of his most public surviving work is in London, in the terraces and buildings designed around his great Town Plan. These are sometimes criticised for poorly thought out use, space and abuse of the classical elements and poor detailing. That may be so, but they remain some of the most easily recognised features of London, and set the mark for a century of great town houses, parades and streets.

It is probably right to end with a picture of his own house and office in Dover Street, since one can assume that, for his own offices, he would choose a style he preferred above all other. This building had deep and complex string courses and cornices, balustrades, four or five

John Nash's house and offices in
Dover Street, London

different window styles, and paired columns. The overall impression might have been confusing, but it certainly has style, many recognisable Nash features, and combines different architectural elements.

## Problems with Specification and Detail

Since Caerhays is known to have had problems in its construction, it is interesting to find that John Nash had a reputation for poor specification. It is difficult to know whether this sort of dispute was par for the time or whether his work was below the standard of others. Early in his career, he was required to design and build bridges. None of the small number attributed to him have survived and one collapsed within a short time of being built. He was seen as reasonably honest for the time, in his dealings, although much of his work encountered problems. Although building estimates have always been difficult, Uvedale Price was in 1798 warning Sir George Beaumont not to trust Nash's estimates and to 'get some other person to execute his designs'. Although early projects sometimes came in on budget, this became increasingly unlikely as he neared old age.

The gallery at Caerhays

New techniques can also be a source of difficulty or expense and John Nash was always ready to try new techniques. He used both hidden and exposed cast iron structures to provide frameworks at an early project at Attingham. He used cast iron structures to support the framing of the domes at Brighton; he was happy to experiment with tarred paper roofs. These uses were not necessarily 'thought through' or successful.

Despite his early training in an architect's office, he was casual about working out how things were to be fitted together and although his drawings show real skill he seems to have relied heavily on his assistants and associates to actually carry out the detailing. He is recorded as being remarkably relaxed as to whether or not his assistants carried out his wishes.

Problems with detailing are known even in early contracts. At Kilwaughter, for instance, the gothic windows turned out to be small pieces of built up wood or frets stuck outside the windows with joints that were not properly joinered and which therefore fell apart. He used tarred roofs without perhaps worrying too much about the long-term problems which these might present. The difficulties that the mastic on the domes of the Royal Pavilion at Brighton had in keeping out the water are well known. He also had problems at Caledon in Northern Ireland. This great house was altered, extended and provided with domes to the new wings. These domes had leaks right round them. The client no doubt thought it excessively expensive that Nash suggested that all the stucco should be taken off the domes to look at the leaks. Nash then went on to defend, either charmingly or naively that, although the buildings might be damp "*Caledon with all its charms has not the climate of Italy but that providence considering fruitful soil, a greater blessing than a dry house, has given you a horrid atmosphere*". This is a charming way of telling a client that he should enjoy a leaking roof!

Gothic detailing below the gallery landings at Caerhays.

Kilwaughter was another house with a tarred paper roof. This type of covering was probably chosen for its light construction and because the low pitch allowed the roof to be hidden behind the battlements. However, it leaked and the roof was lost. It was not just that some of his building details were ill-considered but also that he changed his mind. He probably also encouraged his clients to change their minds as building continued so that he could improve the picturesque and unusual elements of his design.

At his own castle at East Cowes he was said to have enjoyed making many changes. Indeed a commentator at the time (Brannon) wrote that changes are "certainly not calculated to ensure the greatest amounts of domestic convenience".

It is not difficult to find instances of dispute between any architect and client but such differences should not overshadow the work of John Nash. He should be remembered not only for the glory of his work in London and the drama of his work in Brighton but also for such splendid projects as All Souls Church, Langham Place or Carlton House Terrace. He achieved a great plan for London, and laid out a garden city, centred on Regents Park.

Although we may criticise the details, the overall appearance of his schemes are what we remember. Nash achieved architecture with landscape. He did not place a house **in** the landscape, but made the landscape part of the architecture. He wrote of Regents Park that it had "the attraction of open space, free air and the scenery of nature". These are appropriate words for a description of Caerhays Castle.

Luscombe Castle, Near Dawlish, a sketch showing the porch.

Luscombe Castle, Near Dawlish
*Picture courtesy of Robert Bargery*

## Country Houses

It seems clear that John Nash was a particularly good companion. Pictures show him with a small head, a little snub nose and twinkling eye. He seems to have got along with people and to have been considered really good company. Among the portraits of John Nash are one of him as a youngish man and one in old age. Both show a man who looks like a good dinner companion. This must have contributed to his gaining, during his working life, 64 country house commissions.

Caerhays is the only project of his which survives in Cornwall. However, not far across the border with Devon is Luscombe Castle. This little castellated house at Luscombe, on the south Devon coast, was designed in 1800 for the banker Charles Hoare, to whom he had been introduced by Repton. Originally intended as a small villa, it was not a classical house but a house designed as part of a picturesque landscape and with terrific views through the windows. Luscombe is important because it gives a good impression of what may have been Nash's concept for Caerhays. There are many similarities, not least its design as a relatively small, but dramatically laid out, villa with round tower and porte-cochère.

The designs at Caerhays came towards the end of Nash's life in country house design. Although he continued his practice for a further twenty years, these years were devoted chiefly to schemes in London and to the work for the Prince Regent.

## Nash at Caerhays

In 1808 John Nash, now 56, was an important figure in London and a friend of the Prince Regent. It is not therefore surprising that he should be asked to design a new house at Caerhays for John Bettesworth Trevanion. John Bettesworth Trevanion was the son of the man who had been Chancellor of the Duchy of Lancaster and therefore his London connections presumably ensured that Nash was a natural choice for a splendid house to establish a new status.

This watercolour was prepared by Thomas Willement, sometime before 1818, perhaps to show off proposals for the stained glass. Probably arranged through Nash, it gives a good idea of Nash's original concept for the hall. Not all the gothic tracery was carried out.

By this time he had already completed a number of projects and buildings whose exteriors and interiors shared more perhaps with stage sets and drama than they did with utility and traditional construction. He was also popular with clients, not just for his pleasant personality, but also because he gave clients what they wanted.

In many ways Nash's approach at Caerhays is summed up by lines in the 1794 gothic novel The Mysteries of Udolpho, by Ann Radcliffe: *The grandeur of the broad ramparts and the changing scenery they overlooked excited her high admiration; for the extent of the terraces allowed the features of the country to be seen in such various points of view that they appeared to form new landscapes'.*

The Porte-Cochère at Caerhays

His early connection with Repton may have helped John Nash become one of the best exponents of the picturesque and encouraged him to include the landscape within the architectural plan. A good example at Caerhays is the single tower set out to the northeast, which helps frame the views both from within and outside the house.

Caerhays remains one of the last and also the most successful of his country house castles. In this case, an essential part of the plan was to raise the proposed site so that the views could be improved. The earlier house survived but the land was raised around Caerhays so that the old ground floor became underground.

A view of Caerhays that gives some idea of the landfill necessary to provide the new castle with a higher building platform than the original house.

The earliest print we have of Caerhays is probably a design sketch rather than a finished building since at the date of the drawing it seems unlikely that the whole building was completed. This picture, drawn by JP Neale, shows two important concepts.

First, without the servants' hall and later 1880 extensions, the arrival at the porte-cochère is much more dramatic. Secondly, the picture shows in black the extent of the landfill which Nash and Trevanion planned. This area of fill around the old ground floor would raise the house to provide a better viewing platform and dramatic situation. Nash's castle has a porte-cochère with great entrance, a wonderful long hall leading to only three splendid and two lesser rooms. The hall is not a processional room but more an access or circulation space which with its high roof is essentially dramatic with a stair leading through the structural wall to give access and drama on the way to the first floor.

Caerhays Castle about 1818, a drawing by JP Neale, engraved by T Mathews. This picture was prepared long before the castle was finished and may have formed part of proposals to the client. The ground coloured black shows the area of fill and raised ground.

John Nash appears to have been a charming man and great manager. He was also a competent politician and will always be admired for his works in London. He is also to be admired for Caerhays Castle, although the failures in and cost of construction, together with the extensive landscape works, were alleged to have contributed to the Trevanions' failure. It was said of John Nash in later life that "no estimate he gave for a royal building ever had the slightest relation to what the treasury would be expected to pay", a comment that may have also applied to the works at Caerhays.

It has always been thought that extravagance in the new building at Caerhays contributed to the fall of the House of Trevanion. However, it does not seem that this alone could have ruined the Trevanions. Lough Cutra Castle, Co Galway, was built shortly after Caerhays and was similar to John Nash's castle at East Cowes. The work was constantly altered and expanded by both architect and client and costs rose to 40% over budget. The increased total for the larger Lough Cutra, including considerable earth works, was said to have been around £70,000. Caerhays should have cost much less, and such a figure was

The South Lodge

only a small percentage of the Trevanion wealth. Although, therefore, we can suggest that Trevanion extravagance and Nash design changes may have made Caerhays an expensive building, it seems unlikely that Nash can be blamed for all failures in the Trevanion finances.

## Other Designs at Caerhays

In addition to the main house, John Nash prepared other designs for Caerhays. Since all records have gone, we have to rely for this assertion on map evidence, historic word of mouth and the absence of claims by the Williams family.

It is thought that Nash's office designed two new cottages and outbuildings at 'The Hovel', which were erected sometime before 1841. Although the cottages were altered later in the 19thC, they still retain much of their original Nash design.

We can assume that he had a hand in the landscaping and theatrical dramatisation of the land between the sea and the house.

The design of the lodges may also be by him, although they may not have been built or finished until later. The Higher or Top Lodge on the west was erected by Michael Williams around 1858, when he also made the drive from the lodge to the house. This lodge is said to have been built from designs by Nash, although the large square windows sit unusually with the remainder. The Top Lodge is both picturesque and satisfying, although the north tower beside the arched opening is so small that it could only serve as a garden tool or rubbish shed.

The Lower or South Lodge was erected soon after construction of the main house started, when Trevanion was moving the coast road towards the sea. Maps show that that building was smaller than it is now. It was therefore probably extended by Michael Williams in 1858. Although the outer gateway has tiny arrow slots, it has neither the appearance of a work by Nash nor is it as robust as normal Victorian gothic. It does not seem to fit with either a defensive building or to add landscape splendour or drama. It is not really very satisfying. If the lodges are indeed John Nash's work, then they show little concern for historical interest or realism. They may instead represent fifty years of committee work, rendered charming by the passing of time.

Although the road bridge by the coast is dated 1910, this too was probably a rebuilt John Nash design that formed part of the Trevanion landscape work. Finally, John Nash's office was probably also responsible for the gothic arch that once ran over that coast road before the road was zig-zagged by the Williams'. This arch still stands, lost in undergrowth.

John Nash died in 1835. His architectural and planning achievements, together with his reputation as an articulate and witty man, gained him a monument in London. It is right that he should be remembered there, and right that Caerhays Castle remains as one of his few surviving castles, a castle that is and was the best, and most successful of his romantic castles. Sir John Summerson described Caerhays as 'an operatic performance'. It is better than that. It is a great piece of architecture in a planned landscape. Today it is the most satisfying, magical building.

Caerhays is a tribute to John Nash.

The North or Top Lodge

The North Lodge, from inside the gates.

The gothic arch by Nash that crossed the coast road, seen from the west.

The north-east tower at Caerhays

# Chapter 9
# The Curious Case of the Paper Roof

When the last male Trevanion died in 1767, the estate passed to the children of his sister. There was then, it seems, a long period when the house was rented to tenants until it was taken back by the young heir, shortly before his decision in 1808 to rebuild the house. One of the tenants at Caerhays was related to Sarah Loveday Gregor who, sixty years later, wrote down her memories of Caerhays and other houses.

She describes how Mrs. William Gregor had: " ... after her marriage .. resided at Carhays, an old gentleman's house long inhabited by the Trevanions whose heir (through a female) was then a child of the name of Bettesworth. [He] afterwards replaced the plain old-fashioned place of his ancestors by a most inappropriate castellated mansion, which, (having been erected by Nash, who thought more of plan than of execution) was absurdly roofed with papier maché, a new invention of the day. ... Mr. Nash was certainly <u>not</u> justified in recommending [this] to an inexperienced young man in a country so proverbially wet as Cornwall. The consequence was that when this roof, cracked by the sun and penetrated by wet, ceased to protect the interior, there were no means of mending it....Thus, after assisting to choose the site, I lived to see the new house a desolate ruin for many years, till falling into other hands through the no less striking ruin of the family, it seems destined to be again renewed and inhabited."

One might assume that the description of the new house as 'absurdly' roofed with papier-maché was a jokey way of describing the poor quality of the construction. It is therefore surprising to discover that the comment had some truth and to gain thereby an introduction to a little known corner of architectural history.

In the late 18thC many owners and builders experimented with new ideas and methods of construction. This was not only because of an interest in the new, but also of attempts to find cheaper methods of building. This was particularly important as many builders had direct interests in the financial success of their projects. Not all these new ideas were a great success. Although there was success in new inventions for the improvement of mining in Cornwall, it is difficult to track new ideas in building construction and easier to find that new construction ideas had failed. In Cornwall alone, two architects spring to mind whose inventions lost them much money.

Charles Rawlinson of Lostwithiel (1729-1786), who built the south wing of Boconnoc and a new gallery wing at Port Eliot, also

The picture of a new villa with shallow paper roofs and overhanging eaves, is from J C Loudon, 1812. It also includes a 'pleasant prospect', with sheep and the dramatic arrival of chaise and horses, so providing sentiment, prospect and drama in one go.

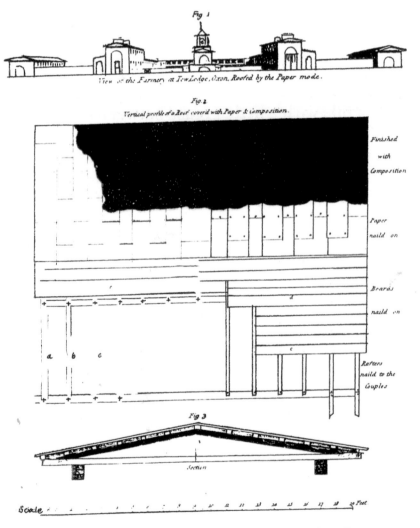

Plans and section for a paper roof at The Farmery at Great Tew:
*"An account of the Paper Roofs used at Tew Lodge, Oxon"* by J.C.Loudon (1812)
*Both illustrations provided through the courtesy of Dr Malcolm Airs.*

published a patented method of timber and slate roofing, whose title started *"The directory for patent slating...."*. The book title alone is 127 words long. Rawlinson was determined that his patent slate roofing would not only be less expensive, but also more durable than traditional methods. It wasn't. The roofs at both Boconnoc and Port Eliot appear to have failed.

John Johnson (1732-1814) architect of many country houses, surveyor of Essex, and designer of much at Port Eliot, lost in 1778 the court case about his own patent stucco. This stucco, or render, appears not to have been either entirely original, effective, or good value.

The period preceding and during the building of the new house at Caerhays was therefore one of experimentation, with trial of new products and systems. It may have been inevitable that a novel form of light tarred paper roof should be suggested for the new Caerhays by an imaginative specifier of new ideas for an enthusiastic young client.

## Early Use of Tarred Paper Roofs.

Paper roofs seem to have been first used around 1770. Their use continued into the middle of the 19thC.

Tarred paper was first used on larger buildings since it required a lighter construction and could cover bigger spans more cheaply. The construction was therefore used for stands, farm buildings, industrial buildings as well as for some houses. In 1778 for instance it is said that pitch paper was used with gravel. Apparently "house covering paper" was one of the products of the paper mills in North Riding in 1775 and Yorkshire had many factories making a specialist paper for use in roofs. Research suggests that the nearness of paper mills may have been important in the use of tarred paper. There are plenty of accounts of use in Scotland, and in areas of England such as Yorkshire, Devon, London and the Home Counties. Tarred paper was accepted by insurance companies as an adequate and proper roofing material. Such roofs did not require a more expensive premium.

New techniques always have a certain attraction. Tarred roofs would have been of interest to many, and widespread use would have made the idea familiar and acceptable as reasonable and sensible. The respected architect Henry Holland seems to have used the method in the 1790s and the specification there described is similar to that of later uses.

The reference to papier-maché in Sarah Loveday Gregor's journal may have been influenced by later developments in papier maché, including mid-century use of that material for prefabricated houses. In fact, the material had long been used for walls and was eventually also used on roofs. In 1772 for instance, laminated sheets of paper had been treated with linseed oil to produce waterproof panels. At Caerhays, however, it seems that the roofs were likely to have not been of papier maché, but, rather, of tarred paper.

## A Specification.

Although there are several descriptions of such paper roofs, it does not seem that there was one standard or widely used specification. All roofs used various compositions of tar/pitch, with sand. All roofs were more shallow than normal. Some seem to have been pitched at 20% but many were at 10%. When compared with the normal pitch of around 35 degrees or that of 55 degrees on older houses, it was alleged that great saving could be achieved. Not only did a shallow roof offer a reduction in the overall area when compared with a pitched roof, but it also had benefits from the lightness of the timber for a lighter construction. There was some debate about the cost of tar, but general opinion supported the view that tarred paper roofs were less expensive that traditional roofs.

The most accessible specification is that set out by J.C. Loudon in a book "An Account of the Paper Roofs used at Tew Lodge, Oxon in 1811". J.C. Loudon is now best known for writing encyclopaedias on gardening, agriculture and villa architecture. He is also credited with being the man who invented the concept and perhaps the term 'landscape architecture'. However his early life was in advising the landed gentry on improvements for agriculture, land and buildings. The buildings at Tew Lodge were part of the establishment for his own agricultural college. As can be seen from the tiny elevation in the drawing and from the cross section of his proposed roof, this was quite a splendid building.

## The Paper, Tar and Laying

We are not sure what type of paper was used. There are many different descriptions of the way in which it was laid, but no precise detail of from what it was made. One report suggests that any strong coarse paper would do. The usual paper that was used was probably almost a thick parchment. There were also many patent remedies for applying the covering mixture to the paper, some of which now read as an imaginative witches' brew of unusual ingredients.

The shallow roof pitch had thin rafters which were joined by horizontal laths. Over these were placed boards ¼" thick nailed to the backs of the laths. There even seemed to have been arguments as to whether or not the boards needed to be continuous in order to support the paper. The paper was then laid across the roof in horizontal courses, overlapping, nailed to the boards and then covered in a coat of pitch. One report suggests that the final coating should be finished by being rolled to ensure that the tar was well attached and possibly impregnated into the paper.

The paper was supplied in small sections, each piece measuring up to 2ft square. Each sheet of paper would have been laid in courses which overlapped in the same manner as slates. The roof therefore became one with two layers of paper, which formed a single even pitched surface about 1/8th" thick. It had a blue-black appearance.

Very often sand, forge dust or smithy ashes or other dusts were laid over the top of the tar in order to reduce the tar's likelihood to melt and run away in the sun. In July 1817 in the Gentleman's Magazine the paper and tar roof was recommended as "a texture which completely resists every description of weather for an unknown length of time... extensive warehouses... churches and farmhouses... have been so roofed for more than fifty years without requiring any repairs. As the roof is not made to rise more than 2" in a foot, the timber required is trifling, when compared to any other mode of roofing as now practiced."

Not only were there apparent advantages in cost and timber sizes, but this roof became popular at a time when the setting of a building in the landscape and the art of the picturesque had become pre-eminent. The dull blue-black finish was praised as being appropriate to make buildings look old, or pleasant, or attractive. We may find it difficult to accept that a shiny black roof was attractive but there was a real fashionable admiration for this technique. The key point for buildings like Caerhays was the shallow pitch which would allow the roof to be hidden behind a parapet or battlements. For grander houses larger spans were possible. The new roof did not require the heavy timbers, lead or stone used in an earlier age. An architect interested in new techniques and required to meet a budget for the construction of a new building would certainly have looked at the importance of such a tarred roof.

## John Nash, Caerhays and Paper Roofs.

Caerhays is said to have had such a paper-tarred roof hidden behind the battlements. John Nash was always interested in new ideas, and one of his earliest jobs used cast iron bearers to support a raised roof. Before Caerhays, John Nash designed a castle for the Agnew family at Kilwaughter Castle in Ireland in 1803. This is known to have had a sand and tar roof, although it is also recorded as having collapsed. Tar and paper roofs by John Nash are not well recorded, but it is possible that they were used wherever he had battlements or a parapet.

John Nash also specified such a roof for Buckingham Palace, which was intended as a new home for the Prince Regent. This work took place late in his life, suggesting that he still had faith in tarred paper roofs. However, the Nash work was marred by almost casual specification and changes in mind and it seems that the roofs at Buckingham Palace failed early, which may have contributed to the dissatisfaction of Parliament for John Nash's work and one of the reasons for his dismissal. By July 1838, the 'composition roofs' of the Palace were specified for replacement in copper or in lead.

## Problems

All descriptions of a paper roof suggest that the roofs should run well clear of the eaves so that the water can drop away from the roof. Records show that such roofs, when maintained, could indeed last well. Some roofs have lasted as long as 200 years. However, if a tarred paper roof on very light timbers were used behind battlements, a wide lead lined valley would be essential to prevent water getting to the ends of the slight timber joists. In the absence of such protection and of regular maintenance, accumulation of water or leaks would very quickly rot out the ends of the joists, causing the roof to collapse.

Another difficulty may have been that the tarred paper itself required constant attention. There is an entertaining account of such a roof at Ammondell in Scotland which was carried out some time shortly after 1812.

"A.D. Minto persuaded [the owner] to adopt a new sort of roofing...[of] paper covered with pitch. Whenever any flaw occurred which was as often as there came any extreme heat or frost or heavy rain, the laundry maid had to be sent up with a hot iron to iron the peccant places in the roof which was then supposed to be as good as ever. Perhaps it was but it was never very good".

In 1856 reports of Chevening House in Kent described use of

a patent "composition or cement", invented by Earl Stanhope in 1776 which *"although the cement enjoyed at one time a considerable fame and although several great buildings elsewhere, Buckingham Palace for instance, were covered with it, invention did not thrive in the house of the inventor. Although patched and soldered and mended again and again and again [the roof at Chevening] still let in rain in various places to the great damage of the ceilings and the discomfort of the inmates below".* Eight years after it was first applied, it was changed for patent asphalted felt.

Paper roofs became popular not only because they were 'new' and a product of new technology but also because they promised a budget roof, and because such a roof answered a new taste for the picturesque and colour schemes of the time. When properly used with projecting eaves, they were also thought to provide depth of shadow and to emphasise or frame the elevations.

They fell out of fashion first because a tax was applied to paper which made them more expensive, second, because lack of attention at the eaves meant that the timber structure was particularly susceptible to water damage, third because they were used in inappropriate positions and without maintenance and fourthly, simply because better and improved systems had been found.

By 1830 there seem to have been few who proposed a tar and paper roof. However, some twenty years earlier it seems that Caerhays had, behind its battlements, a shallow lightly timbered roof, covered with paper which was in turn covered with a thin layer of tar and perhaps sand. The failure of this roof may have been a factor in the difficulties of the Trevanions with the house. It seems certain that lack of maintenance permitted water to get to the lower end of the very light timbers behind the parapet. The failure of a light timber structure may have been the reason that the house so swiftly fell into decay between 1840 and the time of the Williams' purchase. The weaknesses of construction were probably always a problem for a tar and paper roof. By 1850 the relatively new roof at Caerhays was said to have collapsed to such an extent that the house was ruined.

Ducks were said to be preening in the drawing room.

# Section Three
# The Families who have owned Caerhays

10    The Trevanion family                          97
11    Trevanion Disaster and Sale                   109
12    The Williams Family                           117
13    John Charles Williams 1861-1939               127
14    Plant hunters in China                        137
15    Charles Williams and his successors           147
16    The Williams Mineral Collection               151
17    Recipes from Caerhays                          159
18    Caerhays Today                                 165

The Trevanion Coat of Arms

The Williams Coat of Arms

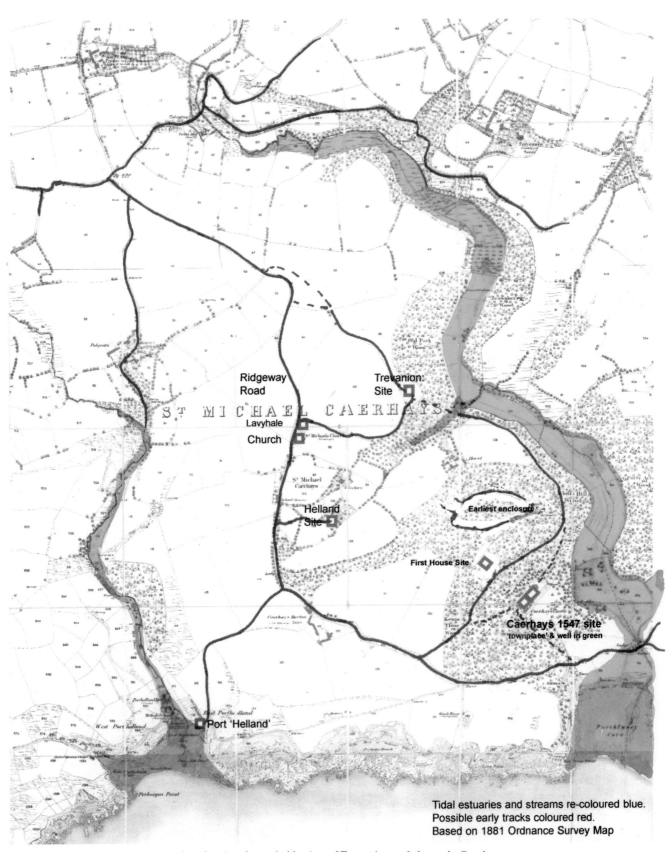

A plan showing the probable sites of Trevanion and the early Caerhays

# Chapter 10
# The Trevanion Family

## Early ownership and a legal dispute

Caerhays was not mentioned in the the Domesday Book of 1086, which could mean either that the area was under the control of the church or that the Caerhays area was then part of the large estate of Brannel. The early history of the holding at Caerhays is considered in the review of medieval landholdings.

By the early 13thC, 'Karyshays' was an estate or manor mentioned in legal documents, with John Fitz Ralph (who died in 1242) being known as its Lord. His son, Ranulph Fitz John was probably the Lord of Blanch-Minster, and also Lord of Week St Mary and Stratton (towns with castles in north Cornwall), and of the Isles of Scilly – an important man. One of his daughters, Margery, married Sir Oliver Arundell a junior of the great Arundells of Lanherne. Their son, Ralph Arundell, had his inheritance of Caerhays withdrawn by his mother Margery in 1287, which, with Portalan and Pengelly (now East and West Portholland), went instead to Roger and Emmeline de Inkepenne. To clear stewarding debts, Roger then, in 1289, passed his Caerhays properties over to his master, the Earl of Cornwall. When the Earl himself died in 1299 the property went to the Crown.

Ralph Arundell appealed to the courts for the return of his property after Roger de Inkepenne forced his way into his house at Caerhays and stole from his coffer not just silver cups, but also, and presumably significantly, a number of deeds and muniments. Ralph succeeded, regained Caerhays, married Elizabeth Seneschal and left the place to his son, another Ralph, who although an Arundell, seems to have called himself Petit; in 1379 he ensured that the manor of Caerhays (together with the two Porthollands) would pass to his daughter Joan and her children.

## The arrival of the Trevanions at Caerhays

The Trevanion family was named from a now lost settlement north of Caerhays, close to or even within the medieval deer park. The name Trevanion was said to mean a 'dwelling in a hollow'. The probable site of Trevanion is a large level plat below the surrounding land, but has steep slopes, almost cliffs running down to rivers on two sides. In the early eighteenth century Thomas Tonkin wrote that the site was still detectable, but only because 'the footsteps of two or three ways leading towards it point out the former situation.'

The Trevanions had been of rank for several generations, serving in Cornwall and Devon as rectors or judges.

Following a childless first marriage to John Trevarthian, Joan Arundell re-married Robert Trevanion of Trevanion, a man whose brother was the knight, Sir John Trevanion. It was the children of Robert and Joan, who had married around 1390, who inherited the Caerhays estate.

The wood edged and frying pan shaped site of Trevanion

The Trevanions were by now among the leading families of the west country. Richard, son of Robert, was Knight of the Shire of Cornwall at the 1407 Parliament at Gloucester and in 1420 at Westminster. He was not just active in the county but also a player on the national stage until his death in 1426. He had also married Joan, a daughter of Otho Bodrugan of Bodrugan, a family who were at the time the most powerful in Cornwall and lived at a now vanished 'great house' a few miles to the east. The family continued to serve in parliament and to marry well. John, son of Richard, served as MP for Lostwithiel in 1433 and married Jennet Treffry of Place at Fowey. Until they were stolen, the church at Caerhays had a helmet and short sword that was said to have been worn by William Trevanion at the battle of Bosworth in 1485 at which it was also said that he was made a 'knight banneret' by a grateful Henry VII. Trevanion was active in The Wars of the Roses and on the same side as Sir Richard Edgcumbe of Cotehele, the great man of Cornwall at this time. Sir Henry Bodrugan was pursued by them to his cliffs from which he 'leapt' to a boat and escaped to France.

The politics and allegiances of the time are confusing. It is sufficient to say that the Trevanions came through this period well. The historian Hals was more specific, saying that;

'they have flourished, at Caryhayes and Trevanion in great fame, wealth, and reputation in their country... and... had bestowed upon them by their princes, ... the lands of several rebels and traitors, forfeited by attainder of treason, ... in the York and Lancaster wars, and in Flamock's, Arundell's, and other Cornish rebellions'.

The period of the early Trevanions was described in 1838 by Davies Gilbert in delightful prose. It describes the Trevanions' fortunes around both 1500 and in the Civil War.

'The ancient and respectable family of Trevanion has experienced the vicissitudes arising from civil dissensions. In those times [the 14th & 15thC], it is quite clear that the love of plunder and eagerness after confiscations must have been the sole motive of action on either side.... Trifling as have been the causes of domestic as well as foreign wars, no one can believe that, in the absence of all contested political principles, men could be found who would deluge their country with blood for the sake of seating on the throne an individual whose name was Edward instead of another designated as Henry, on the frivolous pretence, that, had England been a farm and its inhabitants farm stock, one of the parties possessed claim through females superior to the other ...

In such a conflict three families ... from Cornwall were engaged, Bodrigan, Trevanion, and Edgcumbe ; and when Richard III obtained sovereign power, ... Bodrigan endeavoured to seize the property of Edgcumbe, with little respect as it would seem for the life of the Possesor; but in the final struggle at Bosworth Field, where Henry Tudor put an entire end to this contest for power under the guise of property, by seizing the whole to himself, Trevanion and Edgcumbe had the good *fortune to appear on the winning side. [They] subsequently availed themselves to the utmost of belligerent rights against Bodrigan, as he had attempted to do before against them... His property was divided between the two families opposed to him...*

*At a subsequent period [the English Civil War] when wars were levied in support of principles, and when men of honour and of virtue engaged on either side, as their early prejudices, investigations, or accidental experience induced them to believe that one or the other would prove most conducive to the public good, the Trevanions were less successful. They asserted their conviction in arms - that the country would be best governed by concentrating hereditary power in a single man... and Mr. John Trevanion, bearing a colonels' commissions, shared in the military glories of the western army, and fell under the walls of Bristol.*

*His father experienced the mitigated fate of those who were vanquished in this contest by compounding for his estate; and when after a long interval, his friends came again into power, and succeeded in placing at the head of affairs the son of their former chief, those immediately surrounding the seat of government possessed but slender means, and still less inclination, to risk their own safety by indemnifying those at a distance who had suffered in the Good Old Cause."*

## Wealth, status and a great rebuild

Sir William Trevanion, said to have been knighted at Bosworth, was further knighted in 1508, when he was Sheriff of Cornwall and his son made an equerry of the king. He had married Anne, daughter of Sir Richard Edgcumbe, thereby combining two rich and powerful dynasties. He also benefited from receiving in 1504 some Bodrugan estates at Newham and at Restronguet. He must have felt sure of both his position and his wealth. He was Sheriff of Cornwall in 1503, 1508 and 1516 and died in 1518.

His Will of 1512 left detailed instructions for his tomb, although nothing of that tomb now remains. The Will also, as was common, left guidance to his wife. This included the stricture that she should '*dwell at Carihais*' with his son Hugh so long as she remained unmarried '*so that my son may be by her better comforted and ordered in good courses*'. Parents have always worried about their teenage children.

Sir William's son Sir Hugh I was born in 1500, and was a leading man in the county during a troubled period. Sheriff for Cornwall in 1527, 1532, 1542-3 and 1552, he, with Sir William Godolphin, carried out commissions for Henry VIII. He was of similar age to the king, with whom he seems to have been friendly, and jousted with him regularly in London. He commanded the king's ships in the French wars and attended the marriage of King Henry and Anne Boleyn.

In 1539 he was one of those who surveyed the coastal defences in preparation for war with France and was rewarded with the office and lovely titles of *escheator and feodary* of the Duchy of Cornwall. He was also made the constable of Launceston Castle, where he would have secured the cash received through his other offices.

However it was not all plain sailing. Cornwall was a long way from London, and the Trevanions, like many other great names, behaved more or less as they wished. It must therefore have taken some guts and court connections to get Hugh Trevanion to the Star Chamber in 1543, where he was accused of '*procuring, abetting and comforting*'

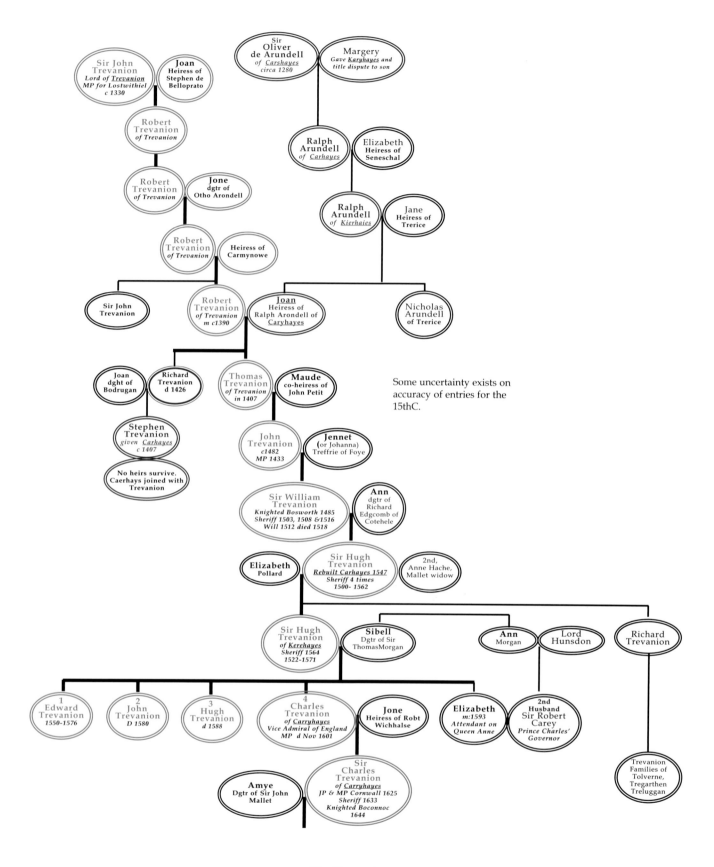

The Trevanions.
This family tree shows the descent of Caerhays from the Arundells of the 13thC,
transfer through marriage to the Trevanions, and the Trevanion family down to the second Sir Charles Trevanion.

a group of six riotous men, *'arrayed with swerds, bucklers, daggers, bowes, arrowes and other wepyns'* in forcing John Arundell from his tenement at Helland (a farm that lay inconveniently between Caerhays and the church and Trevanion park) and then taking possession of it. Witnesses denied that there was riotousness and that Sir Hugh took possession, but it is noticeable that neither Helland nor the Arundells (presumably scions of the family that preceded the Trevanions at Caerhays) were mentioned again in the documents of that place.

With the enormous increase in his wealth and an assured position in the top flight of great families, it was inevitable that Sir Hugh would wish to aggrandize his house. There is a surviving Trevanion rent roll from 1546, when the place was described as 'that capitoll mansion house, barton and demesnes of Caryheyes'. Not only was there clearly a great mansion house, but the 15 foot long roll was important for its listing of the manors and the rights to which the family could claim.

From such descriptions as we have, that house would have rivalled many great houses further up country, with its heraldic sculptures, decorative plasterwork, wall hangings and chestnut panelling. It was said to have been completed in 1547.

Between 1539 and 1571 Trevanions were appointed Escheator for the crown by the Lord Treasurer, thereby being responsible for holding Inquisitions into estates of those deceased who were reputed to hold land of the monarch. This was another position from which the holder could expect to make large sums. We also have details of a complaint in 1550, when it was reported to the court by Sir Hugh Trevanion and John Trelawney that *'one of our houses was badly spoiled'* in the 1549 rebellion. This gives some evidence of the continuing need for a house defensible against riot, although it is not certain whether this refers to Caerhays. Finally, in 1552 Sir Hugh sat on that commission for Cornwall which inquired into what remained of the revenues and assets arising from the dissolution of the monasteries and church possessions. This sort of enquiry was usually reckoned to make the commissioners considerable sums.

Sir Hugh died in 1562, not long after having the stained glass installed in the chapel at Caerhays. The glass and the decorative sculpture of the house highlights the difficulties of political loyalty and the pragmatic approach of this and many other families. After spending the prime of his life supporting Henry VIII's anti-Catholic policies, he displayed in his chapel the royal arms of those arch-Catholics Philip (of Spain) and Mary. Despite this protestation of loyalty, the arms of the anti-Catholic Queen Elizabeth were, shortly before or after his death, added to the entrance to the house.

## Court connections.

The central figures at the Royal court were knit closely by marriage connections. These connections proved most useful over the next sixty years for the Trevanions.

Sir Hugh's son Sir Hugh II only enjoyed his inheritance for 7 years; he was Sheriff of Cornwall in 1565 and died in 1571. However, his marriage to Sibell Morgan gave him a brother in law who was Lord Hunsdon, Queen Elizabeth's first cousin. Hunsdon was trusted by the Queen and a man of great influence. Sir Hugh had four sons, Edward, John, Hugh and Charles, who successively held Caerhays between

1571 and 1601. The boys' uncle, Richard, continued the family's public duties until Charles, the youngest of four sons, was able to take over.

Charles, MP for Grampound in 1584, was a man of importance. Richard Carew recorded that in 1599 Charles, who had been Sheriff of Cornwall in 1596, controlled the sixth largest of eleven regiments in Cornwall, containing five companies, 500 soldiers, 190 muskets and 130 *calivers*. In 1600 Charles, along with other gentry, was involved in investigating complaints that boats were being prevented from reaching Lostwithiel by weirs, fish gathers, stakes, kiddles, and floodgates erected by the people of St Winnow. In 1601, the year of his death, as vice admiral of Cornwall, he had to impress 200 sailors and deliver them to Plymouth. In an unusually kind tribute written after Charles' death, Richard Carew described him as '*a Gentleman, through his vertue, as free from greedinesse, as through his faire livelyhood, farre from needinesse... and that in conversing with the worst sort of people (which his office oftentimes enforceth) he can no more be disgraced, then the Sunne beames by shining upon a dunghill will be blemished.*'

Charles had had a younger sister who became most influential at the court of King James I. That young sister, Elizabeth Trevanion, had been sent away to marry an older man who was warden of the Marches of Northumberland. She eventually married, for the second time, Sir Robert Carey, the future Earl of Monmouth. Sir Robert's memoirs have ensured that he remains one of the most glamourous and likeable of Elizabethan adventurers. He was charming and poor but well connected, indeed his father was Lord Hunsdon, a son of Henry VII and Anne Boleyn's sister. Sir Robert was famous for riding for three days to tell James I of Queen Elizabeth's death and thereafter he and his wife were central to the court of James. His wife Elizabeth (née Trevanion) was lady in waiting to Queen Anne, and Sir Robert was governor of her son, the future King Charles, who seems to have been largely brought up by Elizabeth. Such connections were magic. The story of Sir Robert and Elizabeth Carey enlivens any reading. The Careys survived endless court intrigues and lived long. A stunning life sized portrait now at Montacute House shows them with their three children in a picture painted around 1617. Elizabeth Carey (née Trevanion) must have been an interesting and exceptionally capable lady.

Sir Charles, son of Charles, was Vice-Admiral of the south coast of Cornwall. He was Member of Parliament for Cornwall in 1625 and appointed Sheriff in 1633. In 1642 he and son Jack declared for the King and after that son had been killed Charles was knighted by the King at Boconnoc in September 1644. At the end of the Civil War Charles was fined £665 10s 8d for his delinquency in supporting the King and in February 1648 was included among a group of 'malignant gentlemen [who] speedily meant to disturbe ye peace of ye country'. He died before the monarchy was restored.

Colonel John Trevanion, the elder son, known as Jack, was one of the Royalist heroes of the Civil war and one of the principals responsible for the resurgence of royal fortunes called 'Success in the West'. Born in 1613, he married Anne Arundell of Trerice in 1634 and was Member of Parliament for Grampound in 1639. He raised a regiment of 700 volunteers for the King and fought from Braddock Down in east Cornwall all the way to Bristol. He played a crucial role in the successes at Windmill Hill, Launceston and Stamford Hill in company with his close friend Sir Nicholas Slanning, but was killed in 1643 at Bristol and his regiment was decimated in their attack. Sir Nicholas Slanning died alongside him. Jack Trevanion was described by Clarendon as the quieter of the two, 'a man of good understanding, great courage, but of few words, yet what he said has always been to the purpose.' A popular verse of the time explained:

> The four wheels of Charles's Wain,
> Grenville, Godolphin, Trevanion, Slanning, slain.

Colonel John Trevanion's picture was included as a heroic figure in an 1816 engraving taken from an earlier drawing. This shows him with flowing locks, armour and sash.

The years following the restoration were years when the family might have been said to have 'kept their heads down'. They made largely fruitless attempts to recover the money spent by them on the King's behalf. On Charles'death his grandson, Colonel Jack's son Charles, held Caerhays for around 45 years till dying 'on the night of a great storm', 26th November 1703. Two other sons, John and Richard had naval careers and a third, Hugh, lived at Newham. Charles was MP for Grampound from 1661 to 1679.

The Trevanions were in the 16th and 17thCs among the county's top half dozen families, providing many Sheriffs of Cornwall, as well as Justices of the Peace and Members of Parliament.

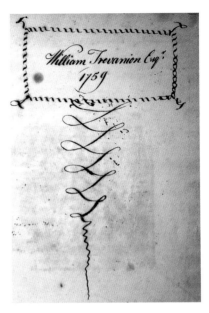

The Trevanion cookbook
of 1759 (see chapter 17)

## Renovation of the house and gardens

John Trevanion, who inherited in 1703 led, a quieter more 'gentry' life, and was less concerned with 'big' events. He maintained the standing of the family, and was Member of Parliament for either Tregony or Cornwall in 1705, 1710 and 1713. Tregony was what was called a 'potwalloper' borough, a name that referred to voting rights being apportioned to a fireplace. Although this sounds as though voting might go to residents, landlords built those houses for the vote, and Tregony was a very rotten borough, with two seats in the Com-

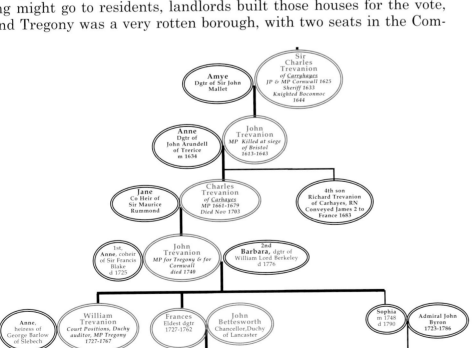

The Trevanions.
From Sir Charles Trevanion to the last male heir, William Trevanion, who died in 1767.

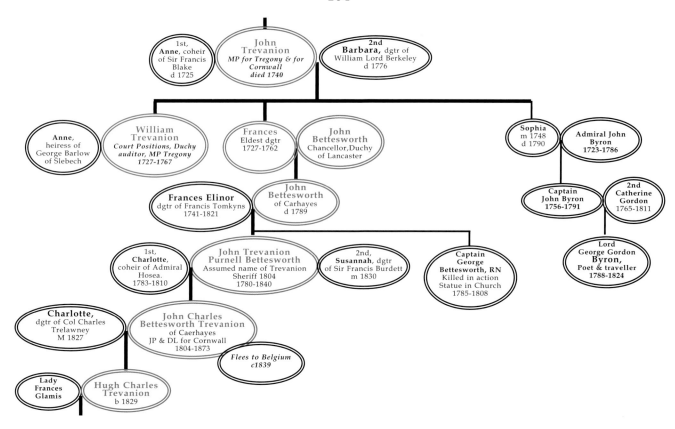

A family tree for the Bettesworth-Trevanions from 1767-1840

mons, one of which was under Trevanion control.

John Trevanion married twice. His second marriage to Barbara, daughter of Lord Berkeley of Stratton, produced three children, William, Frances and Sophia. He lived at Trevanion for nearly 40 years and made extensive improvements to the house and gardens at Caerhays before his death at 73 in 1740.

These improvements are thought to have included laying out formal 1700 style pleasure gardens and modernising the house by the addition of rooms to the north west corner and the addition of regular fenestration to that corner. He also built some fine stables.

We can imagine him living fairly quietly but in comfort and 'high gentry' style. He must have loved the house because in his Will, his housekeeper at Caerhays, Mary Polsue, was left an annuity so long as she remained there to look after the house and furniture. His Will also stated that 'every person who… shall be from time to time be entitled to possession of my capital mansion…. shall sufficiently maintain, support, and uphold the houses, gardens, walks and park at Caerhays, and leave the same so well and sufficiently repaired, maintained and upheld to the next person…'.

His son William, who became auditor of the Duchy of Cornwall, married the heiress Anne Barlow of Slebech in Pembroke. The only picture that survives of William is a drawing of him being dragged from one Oxford college to another by a muse, leaving his sad friends behind. The picture is full of classical allusions and shows him in flowing drapery. William died in 1767 at the age of 40 and without issue. His wife took her fortune back to Wales and remarried. William Trevanion was 'the last of his race'.

The monument to
William Trevanion

# The Bettesworth-Trevanions

William Trevanion may have been the last in the direct male line, but there were plenty of other family members still remaining. It was to secure the inheritance for this wider family that William had set up complex will trusts, although it was these trusts themselves which became the problem for the future of Caerhays.

William had two sisters. The younger of the two was Sophia, who in 1748 was married in the Caerhays House Chapel to her cousin Captain John Byron; £12,000 went with the marriage. Sophia seems to have been a beauty with sex appeal, of whom it was said that *'Men would have willingly run thro Fire'*. In later life she was a friend of Mrs Thrale and of Dr Johnson. Mrs Thrale assessed Sophia as the second most worthy lady of her acquaintance. John Byron was one of 18thC England's heroes, known as 'Foulweather Jack'. He had been born in 1723, a son of William Byron, 4th Baron Byron. Later made an admiral, he is a character whose adventures are still read today. He had joined the Royal Navy as a Midshipman in the service of the Royal Navy and served on *H.M.S. Wager* in Lord Anson's Circumnavigation. The *Wager* was wrecked and from 1743 to 1748 Byron was a castaway. His book about his time as a castaway was published in 1768. He died on 10 April 1786 at age 62. It was his grandson who became George, Lord Byron, the poet, adventurer, traveller and eccentric, a man whose life must have addled the ambition of his cousins.

It was through William's eldest sister, Frances, that the Trevanion inheritance passed. Frances had, in 1667 married John Bettesworth, whose family were from Sussex and who was Chancellor of the Duchy of Lancaster. Their son, another John, seems to have lived at both Caerhays and London. He died at Caerhays in 1789, leaving five young children, the eldest boy being then only 9 years old.

This was John Trevanion Purnell Bettesworth, who we for ease call JTPB. To the JTPB name he then added the Trevanion surname on coming of age in 1801.

The year in which he came of age probably brought to an end almost fifty years of neglect at Caerhays, which appears to have been let out from 1753, perhaps first when William Trevanion was at Oxford and certainly for many of the remaining years of the century. The tenants who occupied the house included the family of Loveday Sarah Gregor, who, some fifty years later, wrote dismissively of the condition of the house. Although they no doubt stayed there on occasion, or between tenants, the Bettesworths do not appear to have lived at Caerhays, but rather to have milked it, the estate accounts being managed for some time under the direction of Francis Polkinghorne and Charles Rashleigh, either as neighbours or trustees. The account book for 1779 to 1788 has survived and as is the case with any list of expenditure, it is the smaller details we now find interesting. The income from rents and 'tin dues' was spent on administering the manor court, paying high rents, house repairs, 'bound stones', the carriage of furniture, repairs to park palings, shooting certificates and so on. More telling is that the largest entries for expense appear to be for the purchase and carriage of port, sherry and claret. This wine account was considerable and amounted to many times the amount spent on maintenance. There were also bills for 'forfeiture', that is, for absence from events in Cornwall, and bills for 'board and tuition for 'master Bettesworth' (£17-4-0 in 1786 and 18gns in 1788). Some items hint at

Sophia Byron, at the time of her marriage in 1748, in a white silk dress and wearing garlands. The pastel is now attributed to William Hoare of Bath. Reproduced by permission of the Byron Trust

Admiral John Byron
by Sir Joshua Reynolds c1749
Byron set out in the 'Dolphin' to the South Seas in 1764, and became Governor of Newfoundland in 1766. In 1778 failure in the West Indies to intercept the French contributed to the defeat of the British in the American War
*Photo: Isla Tyrrell; Reproduced from original portrait at Newstead Abbey with permission of Nottingham City Museums and Galleries*

financial difficulty. These include the £50-11-0 paid for three lottery tickets in March 1788 and payment of arrears of the Land Steward's salary for 2 years and 3 months in the sum of £57-15-0. This figure should be compared with just one of the bills paid that year for wine, in the sum of £52-3-4. This figure must be seen in the context of the Land Stewards salary of around £20.00 per annum. Drink, lotteries and absentee management suggest that the downfall of the Trevanions started in the second half of the 18thC.

On coming of age in 1801, JTPB was a young man in a world of gothic romance, a new world of change. Like other of his contemporaries, he wanted a modern but imposing house. He may also have wished to emulate the romantic ideals of his cousin the poet Byron and live up to his younger brother, George, who was captain of a frigate by the age of twenty, and killed in action at twenty-three in 1808. A dark life-size statue of him stands in the Trevanion aisle of Caerhays church.

In 1807, John Nash was commissioned to draw up the designs for the ostentatious show of wealth and taste that helped the Bettesworths on their road to bankruptcy.

Captain Bettesworth
Killed in action 1808

Nash's wonderfully fantastic castle is really a large castellated mansion, its entrance front with port cochere (for sheltered decanting from coaches), encouraged a dramatic arrival. The south east side and the main rooms have wonderfully extensive views over the park, lake and on to the cliffs of Gorran, and is also the side that makes people gasp when they first see it. It was always intended to be seen, to display Nash's genius and Trevanion's wealth and ambition.

It is fortunate that this rural masterpiece survives – it could easily have been swept away just decades after it was built, standing empty and unloved. Many of Nash's other country house castles have now gone, including East Cowes Castle, the house he built for himself in 1798 on the Isle of Wight. His Luscombe Castle near Dawlish, begun in 1800, does however survive, in a beautiful Repton landscape. It prefigures much of what we see at Caerhays.

Despite early political position, social success and a great inheritance, JTPB Trevanion appears now to have been a tragic figure. He had been made Sheriff of Cornwall at just twenty-four in 1804 and was elected as MP for Penryn in 1807 and had married the heiress Charlotte Hosea. of whom there is a picture in the National Portrait Collection. However, her early death in 1810 and the death of her little girl seems to have thrown him. He remained unmarried for 20 years, which was not common practice at the time. It would seem that the second marriage may have been an attempt to marry money, and save his estate. It is also puzzling that, contrary to many other gentry families of the time, we have little record of attempts to develop the considerable mining rights which he held over an astonishing 40,000 acres. Nor is there evidence of other development of the directly held land which amounted to some 3,500 acres at Caerhays, with further holdings elsewhere. It may be that the land was so tied by family trusts and entail upon future generations that his hands were tied.

One of three surviving Trevanion pictures: George IV, found hung high and blackened, in the staff quarters.

## The Last Trevanion at Caerhays.

The life of JTPB Trevanion at Caerhays comes through to us in the remnants of gossip and reminiscence.

There are stories of his battles to complete the house, of continuing legal arrangements in relation to his complex inheritance, of law suits against and from others. Known as 'Squire Trevanion' as he became older, he seems to have become a bit of an eccentric or 'character'. It is he who, irritated by the wild donkeys on the cliff, built or extended the 'pound', although since the pound appears to have been already in existence we prefer to suggest that he merely improved the building. The nervous amusement in the story of him being rolled in the dirt during a dog fight, also suggests he was held in some awe.

One of three surviving Trevanion pictures. Jockeys and horses. The painting of the right hand horse was damaged by shot.

We know he raced horses and bet on them. We also know that he had unusual 'great dogs', called 'pyranean wolf dogs' and that when he fled the house, he left six of his great dogs behind.

Some tales do not seem to fit with the character of a 60 year old and may therefore be apochryphal. There are stories of after dinner competitions to shoot out the eyes in ancestors' portraits. It is suggested that the reason only three pictures survived the ruin of the family is because those survivals had themselves been ruined or overlooked through damage. The picture of two race horses is said to have been ripped by gun shot, after the failure of the horse to win a race.

The Trevanion family had many wealthy relatives, some of whom had already given them aid. JTPB's aunt was a member of the Coutts and Mellon banking family, and was in 1837 the wealthiest woman in England. Angela Burdett Coutts went on to become one of the great philanthropists of the century, was made a baroness in her own right, and was described by Edward VII as, after his mother, 'the most remarkable woman in the kingdom'. One story is that Miss Burdett Coutts might have been persuaded to marry a Trevanion. Certainly she received countless offers of marriage, but since she spent 52 years living with her beloved companion, Hannah, and only married a young man when in old age and after Hannah's death, this hope seems to have been unjustified.

One of three surviving Trevanion pictures. A Trevanion dog and a dog with a stick on Porthluney beach

Miss Burdett Coutts, who had sufficient spare cash to solve any problem, was induced to visit Caerhays in the expectation that some small part of her fortune might save the family. Sadly, one of the Trevanion dogs bit her 'favourite' footman. The Trevanions laughed. She left in high dudgeon. The Trevanions had a picture painted of the dog. Several versions of this story exist, so there may be some measure of truth in the legend.

Finally, there are the stories of JTPB's last years, when he probably despaired of saving the house. We know that the house contents auction list included 1200 'choice bottles of wine', together with blood stallions and breeding horses, so we can imagine that horse racing and horse breeding were important to him, as were dinner and wine.

He left an heir, Hugh Charles, who was only 10 or 11 when the final crash came. Hugh Charles spent much of his life trying to protect his remaining estates and sort trusts, debts and the legal cases he had been bequeathed.

## Two anecdotes and watercolours

These anecdotes were written down by the Revd W Willimott, some fifty years after he had heard them, by which time they had no doubt already become embroidered.

## The fight with the mastiff

'Sometime before this the Squire and parson, not being on friendly terms, the parson was forbidden with his servants to use the drive through the Castle grounds. The Squire possessed a pyranean wolf dog and the parson a mastiff. The parson's man, John Whetter by name, thinking the Squire was away, ventured to pass by the Castle with the mastiff and was met by the Squire and his dog. The dogs immediately began to fight and pulled the Squire off his legs into a large bunch of brambles, where he lay unable to right himself and the dogs fighting on the top of him. The Squires language was anything but Parliamentary whilst Whetter tried to separate the dogs, whilst the squire chased them on with unsparing oaths and execrations'.

The fight in Caerhays drive between the Pyrenean wolf-dog and the Mastiff, in which squire Trevanion is pulled off the road into the brambles.

## Squire Trevanion and the asses

'I have often been asked why the pound was built on the hill by the coast road gate. I was informed that old Squire Trevanion built it in which to impound the donkeys which in his time were a great nuisance roaming about the parish; they used to breed on the Dodman and when forage became scarce on the headland, fed in the lanes adjoining. The squire riding on the beach at Port Luney on his pony mare was on one occasion attacked by a number of these Jack asses and had a difficulty in escaping: hence he waged war against them, built the pound and every donkey which could be caught in the precincts of the castle was put in it until rescued by the owner paying a fine; this was an endless source of contention but no one in those days was bold enough to withstand the squire's will'.

Squire Trevanion escaping from the asses.

*Willimott watercolours reproduced with permission of Vicar and Churchwardens of St Michael Caerhays.*

# Chapter 11
# Disaster and Sale

It is still not certain quite how the Bettesworth Trevanions managed to go to ruin so comprehensively, in so short a time. When the last Trevanion had died in 1767, and the estate passed to his sister for her son, the old house was tenanted, and the estates managed by absentee landlords. We have records of three manors being sold from the Trevanion estate to Sir William Lemon in 1786. There were other disposals of property in the late 1700s and in 1789, the stock, deer, even the furniture were all sold and the house advertised for let. Nevertheless there is little reason to doubt that this was still a large estate around 1801 when inherited by JTP Bettesworth, who assumed the surname 'Trevanion', when he turned 21.

It has long been said that building the castle ruined the Bettesworth Trevanions. Others have blamed the ground works he completed, which included moving a road, raising the house platform and the enormous walls built around the castle gardens. Neither the cost of castle or earth works seems to fit the bill. A larger castle than Caerhays built by Nash in Ireland cost much more than expected, the total coming to the enormous sum of £70,000. Caerhays should have cost rather less than that. It started, after all, as a relatively modest sized house, valued at a mere few thousand by the time of the auctions, forty years later. Although it seems he still owed £28,000 to one creditor, who was probably the builder, this is but a percentage of the apparent sum owing. Even had it cost as much as the £70,000, which the auctioneers stated as the building cost, that would still only have represented, had it all been still owing, a mere 20% of his liabilities when he fled the country. It is also possible that he had become enmeshed in lawsuits, since there are records of chancery cases which did not go well. One case may even have been about a failing roof. 'Entail', that legal curse for a family that ties up the present for future generations, may also have been one of his difficulties, and he may have been so restricted by trusts that he could not use all his capital. There seem to have been a good list of trusts and "entails" in his creditors.

JTPB Trevanion may have been an incompetent manager, or he may have chosen not to, in an era when trade was sometimes considered inappropriate. He does not seem to have made serious attempts to use the advantage that possession of 40,000 acres of manorial and mining rights gave him; he does not appear to have made or tried to make money. It might be, of course, that it was because he tried, and lost,

## CARHAYES CASTLE, CORNWALL,

*About four miles from Tregoney, five miles from Mevagissey, nine miles from St. Austle, and twelve miles from Truro.*

### TOPLIS AND SON

HAVE the honour to announce that they will SELL by AUCTION, on the PREMISES, **CARHAYES CASTLE.**

*The Residence of John Bettesworth Trevanion, Esquire,*

On Monday, April 22nd, and five following days, commencing each day at One o'Clock exact time, (under a Bill of Sale, and by order of the Sheriff of Cornwall,)

### THE COSTLY FURNITURE,

Comprising Drawing-room, Dining-room, Library, and Breakfast-room, Suites of Oak Tables, Sideboards, Chairs and Couches, richly carved in the Gothic style, Curtains of Merino Damask, &c., and Wilton and other Carpets, two six-feet Oak Bedsteads, and several with Mahogany Posts, with Morine and Chintz Hangings bordered, Goose Feather Beds and other Bedding, Wardrobes, Chests of Drawers, and Chamber Furniture.

A fine toned Piccolo Piano Forte, by Wornum, in Oak Case ; three finely sculptured marble Busts, by Behnes ; a few modern Paintings, Family and other Portraits ; a pair of Duelling Pistols, a Rifle, and two Guns, by Forsyth ; a curious Chime Clock, Bed and Table Linen, China and Glass.

*The Library of Books, composed of 1800 Volumes, the greater portion elegantly bound.*

### One Hundred Dozen of Choice Wine.

All the Fixtures, composed of Stoves, Bells, and Presses.

The FARMING STOCK and HORSES, including the *Blood Stallion* MARVEL, (by Muley, out of Lacesta,) five Colts and Filleys, two Brood Mares, three Saddle Horses, 45 Head of Red Park Deer, five Alderney Cows, 11 Oxen, 45 Sheep, a St. Bernard Dog and five others, a small quantity of Hay, Barley, and Wheat, and numerous Effects. May be viewed on and after Thursday, the 18th instant, and Catalogues of the Farming Stock and Books to be had gratis of MESSRS. COODE and SONS, and at the INNS at St. Austle, Truro, Tregony, and Mevagissey ; and Catalogues of the remainder of the Effects to be had (1s. each) on the Premises, and of the

**Auctioneers,**
No. 16, St. Paul's Church Yard, London.

ORDER OF SALE :—

On MONDAY...... April 22nd...The Farming Stock and Horses.
On TUESDAY.... April 23rd...The Library of Books.
On WEDNESDAY April 24th...Furniture and Linen.
On THURSDAY.. April 25th...Furniture, Guns, Paintings, and Wine.
On FRIDAY...... April 26th...Drawing-room, Dining-room, and other Furniture, and marble Busts.
On SATURDAY. April 27th...Furniture, Culinary Articles, &c.

---

# CORNWALL.

## Particulars

OF

## VALUABLE FREEHOLD ESTATES,

NOBLE MANSION,

### PRODUCTIVE CHINA CLAY WORKS;

COMMONS,

INCLUDING

### Minerals, Manorial Rights,

IN THE SEVERAL MANORS OF

*Caerhais, Treburthes, Grogoth, Tolgarrick, & Treverbyn Trevanion,*

CONTAINING A

### VAST EXTENT OF COUNTRY,

IN THE SEVERAL PARISHES OF ST. MICHAEL CAERHAIS, GORRAN, ST. EWE, RUAN LANEYHORNE, CUBY, CONELLY, ST. AULTELL ST. STEPHEN'S, ST. DENNIS, AND ST. MEWAN.

## TO BE SOLD BY AUCTION,

### BY R. COAD,

On MONDAY, the 13th day of JUNE, 1842, AND FOLLOWING DAYS,

AT LYNN'S HOTEL,

In ST. AUSTELL, in the County of CORNWALL.

*\*\* Printed Particulars may be had of Mr. COAD, at Liskeard ; and at all the Principal Inns in the Counties of Devon and Cornwall, as stated in the Advertisements.*

---

# CORNWALL.

### TREVANION ESTATES.

## Particulars,

WITH PLANS AND CONDITIONS OF SALE, OF VALUABLE

## FREEHOLD ESTATES,

NOBLE MANSION,

### PRODUCTIVE CHINA CLAY WORKS.

AND

COMMONS,

INCLUDING

### Minerals and Manorial Rights,

IN THE SEVERAL MANORS OF

Carhays, Treburthes, Grogoth, Tolgarrick, & Treverbyn Trevanion,

CONTAINING A

### VAST EXTENT OF COUNTRY,

IN THE SEVERAL PARISHES OF ST. MICHAEL CARHAYS, GORRAN, VERYAN, RUANLANHORNE, PROBUS, CUBY, CORNELLY, ST. AUSTEL, ST. STEPHEN'S, ST. DENNIS, AND ST. MEWAN.

## TO BE SOLD BY AUCTION,

### BY JOHN J. GUMMOE, OF ST. AUSTELL.

### In 125 LOTS,

ARRANGED TO SUIT THE CONVENIENCE OF PURCHASERS, (UNLESS PREVIOUSLY DISPOSED OF BY PRIVATE CONTRACT,)

AT DUNN'S HOTEL,

ST. AUSTELL, in the COUNTY of CORNWALL, On MONDAY, the 11th day of October 1852, And the following days. To commence at 10 o'clock in the Forenoon of each day.

*These Sales are made subject to such reservation, if any, of mines or minerals and rights of working the same, and to such rights of way and other easements, if any, as the Premises respectively are subject to. Descriptive Particulars, with Plans and Conditions of Sale, may be had on and after the 1st day of September next, of the said Mr. JOHN J. GUMMOE, at St. Austell aforesaid ; of Mr. H. RHODES, Solicitor, 9, Davies Street, Grosvenor Square, London ; of Messrs. HARRISON, TENNANT, and FINCH, Solicitors, 2, Gray's Inn, London ; and at the Principal Hotels in the neighbourhood of the Estates.*

**Caerhays for sale**

Left: An advertisement from the Royal Cornwall Gazette, April 1839
Right: Auction details from 1842 and 1852

that he got into trouble. It seems likely that it was simply poor cash flow and a shortage of funds that really spelt the end. This shortage was aggravated by the cost of the castle and the money he had to find for his second wife's dowry. Although gambling has long been thought to be a strong contender as the cause of the crash, it seems reasonable to suppose that financial ruin came about through a combination of all the different factors.

Whatever the reasons may have been for the catastrophic debt, they are reasons that we are now unlikely to discover. His bankruptcy and the subsequent sale of contents meant that few papers have survived to help us. Towards the end, the family had clearly given up. Their evening pastime seems to have been to shoot the eyes from family portraits.

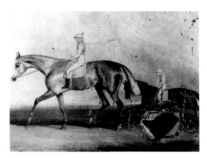

This painting is one of three Trevanion paintings that have survived at Caerhays. It is said to have been damaged by a pistol shot at the horse that lost a race. The horse may bear the colours of Horace Walpole, the 3rd Earl of Orford.

The financial difficulties under which the last Trevanion laboured are to some extent set out in the documents through which Michael Williams purchased the property. These documents must have cost a fortune in legal fees. They started by asserting that the deeds, the root of title and trusts, the settlement established at the death of William Trevanion in 1767 were all missing. The list and amounts of creditors is astonishing. The first creditor listed was the Bank of England, who had originally advanced £15,000, to which they had later added a further £5,000.

Trevanion had borrowed from his family and from his solicitors, who held mortgages for considerable sums. It seems the real crash came around 1833, when he was trying to raise sums as small as £200.00. It is in the following year, 1834, that the long list of annuities started to be registered. In addition to what might be called normal debts and mortgages, it seems that Trevanion had been settling with his creditors by granting annuities for repayment over a period of years, each being secured by mortgages on the entire estate. Even the most hardened banker must quail at the thought of 30, yes 30, mortgages having been established, with repayments each year which it was quite beyond his ability to pay. The creditors included James Gibbs, the younger, (possibly the builder) who was owed some £24-28,000 and died without recovering any money. Adding up the total of the mortgages, it seems Trevanion owed around £300,000. He still owned considerable acres valued by surveyors before auction at about three times that figure. Trevanion just couldn't pay the interest, and was probably restricted by trusts from sorting the situation out.

Trevanion seems to have put the place up for sale sometime before he left the country, but sale failed because his affairs were so complicated. This was still a period when arrest for debt meant a prison sentence in the Marshalsea, a London prison for debtors from which release was difficult. The Marshalsea, about which Charles Dickens wrote at length, was no laughing matter. Arrest for debt had to be avoided, and the only recourse for someone in Trevanion's position was to flee the country, where it was often still possible to receive remittances from an estate, and indeed to live a fairly comfortable existence.

Reminiscences of the Rev Willimott tell of a wild race between the pursuing bailiffs and Trevanion, aided by his solicitor. Trevanion fled abroad to die in 1840, bankrupt and disgraced, in Belgium.

## Auctions and legal cases

There was an auction of contents in 1839. This makes sad reading

# LOT 1.

# CAERHAIS CASTLE AND GROUNDS.

The FEE SIMPLE, in possession of a

## SUPERB MANSION,

Substantially built, and containing numerous well-arranged and commodious Apartments, richly

### ORNAMENTED WITH SCULPTURE IN WOOD AND STONE,

fit for the Residence of a Gentleman with a large establishment; together with extensive Offices of every description, forming a majestic pile of

### Castleated Architecture,

with beautifully diversified outline, surmounted with elegant towers and pinnacle, and surrounded by a moat and embattled wall. The whole of which has a very imposing appearance, and delightfully situate, commanding an extensive view of beautiful scenery, amongst which are the

### Gigantic Cliffs on the borders of the English Channel,

and the sandy beach of Port Luny, on the upper margin of which stands the CHIEF LODGE, an appropriate structure with a massive archway, through which is the Carriage Road to the Mansion, forming a graceful serpentine drive, with a gentle ascent. The rising back ground at the north west is well stored with thriving Plantations and stately Trees of ancient date. Opposite the eastern front appears

### THE DEER PARK, A ROMANTIC PIECE OF SCENERY,

enclosed with woodland, embracing the edge of an extensive Pond of exquisite form, studded with islands covered with drooping branches and aquatic flowers. Between the Pond and the Mansion are the Pleasure Grounds and Terraces, with Carriage Roads leading to various parts of the Property, consisting of Arable, Meadow, and Pasture Land, interspersed with fine Plantations and Timber of large dimensions, extending through a picturesque vale, with an eastern aspect, through which flows a winding stream of water. The whole of which is situate within the manor of St. Michael Carhais, in the parishes of Caerhais and Gorran, and divided into the following convenient Closes :—

| Ref. to Map. | Name of Closes. | Statute Measure. A. R. P. | Ref. to Map. | Name of Closes. | Statute Measure. A. R. P. |
|---|---|---|---|---|---|
| | | | | Brought forward | 142 2 25 |
| 1 | Walled Garden | 2 2 6 | 19 | Part of Ditto | 5 1 22 |
| 2 | Wood | 3 2 24 | 20 | Plantation | 2 3 1 |
| 3 | Orchard | 0 1 19 | 21 | Ditto | 1 3 29 |
| 4 | Garden | 0 0 11 | 22 | Ditto | 0 3 29 |
| 5 | Homestead | 0 0 25 | 23 | Ditto | 0 2 29 |
| 6 | White Stile | 6 1 30 | 24 | Ditto | 1 0 16 |
| 7 | Plantation | 0 0 26 | 25 | Ditto | 3 0 19 |
| 8 | Lower Meadow | 13 3 24 | 26 | Ditto | 0 3 27 |
| 9 | Higher Meadow | 3 1 11 | 27 | Ditto | 2 0 13 |
| 10 | Plantation | 1 0 7 | 28 | Ditto | 0 1 8 |
| 11 | Wood | 50 0 18 | 29 | Ditto | 0 1 13 |
| 12 | Castle and Pleasure Grounds | 2 3 22 | 30 | Ditto | 0 0 17 |
| 13 | Pond | 5 3 20 | 31 | Ditto | 0 1 3 |
| 14 | Cottage and Meadow | 2 1 2 | 32 | Ditto | 0 0 24 |
| 15 | Plantation | 3 2 1 | 33 | Ditto | 0 3 10 |
| 17 | Brown Berry Plantation | 14 2 18 | | | |
| 18 | Deer Park | 31 2 39 | | | 163 2 3 |
| | | 142 2 25 | | | |

Also, the Reversion in Fee, expectant on the decease of Dorcas Caweth Rowse, aged 27, William Rowse, aged 23, and Thomas Guy, aged 23, held by lease dated the 4th of January, 1827, for the lives of the said parties of Carhais Water Grist Mill, working three pair of stones, with every conveniency for making flour; together with a good Dwelling House and Outbuildings, now in the occupation of Joseph Rowse.

Reserved yearly rent, 1l.: heriot, 2l. The land-tax on the whole of this lot has been redeemed.

This page describing the house is from the auction catalogue of 1842

# LOT 1.

The FEE SIMPLE, in possession, of

# CARHAIS CASTLE AND GROUNDS.

The Castle (at present out of repair) is a

## MAGNIFICENT STRUCTURE,

built in the

## FLORID GOTHIC STYLE,

with spacious Apartments and Offices, decorated Hall and Library, grand diverging Staircase, painted windows, groined ceilings, and other embellishments.

The parterres and terraced walks are enclosed within an embattled wall, with turrets and handsome Gateways. The foreground slopes beautifully into a wooded Glen, through which are various undulating paths and drives traversing delightful Pleasure Grounds, Deer Parks, and woodland scenery, now skirting an expansive sheet of ornamental Water, fed by rivers and streamlets, winding through a most picturesque and romantic valley, and now leading the way under stately trees and thicket groves, till abruptly terminated on the summit of a beetling cliff, whence a splendid prospect is obtained of the English Channel and different bold promontories. The sandy beach and formation at the base affords every advantage for bathing, fishing, boating, or yachting. On approaching the main Lodge from the Mevagissey road, a glorious view is opened to the spectator,—in the foreground a Meadow, through which the river winds along its serpentine course to the adjacent sea. On either side are dense masses of luxuriant foliage, uniting across the middle distance, and emerging from the midst, the princely pile of towers and battlements looks out imposingly; its rich tint strongly relieved by the darker shades of trees, forming the lofty background, taking the Mediæval Lodge, sea, and cliff on the extreme left: altogether the whole presents one of the most enchanting scenes the mind can easily conceive. This charming Lot is situate within the Manor of St. Michael Carhays, in the parishes of Carhays and Gorran, and divided into the following parcels of land:—

| Ref. on map. | Name of Close. | A. | R. | P. | Ref. on map. | Name of Close. | A. | R. | P. |
|---|---|---|---|---|---|---|---|---|---|
| | | | | | | Brought forward | 87 | 2 | 6 |
| 1 | Castle and Pleasure Grounds | 2 | 3 | 25 | 13 | White Stile | 6 | 1 | 36 |
| 2 | Wood | 50 | 0 | 18 | 14 | Garden and Orchard | 2 | 2 | 6 |
| 3 | Plantation | 3 | 2 | 1 | 15 | Brown Berry Plantation | 14 | 2 | 38 |
| 4 | Cottage and Meadow | 2 | 1 | 2 | 17 | Moor | 4 | 1 | 28 |
| 5 | Pond | 5 | 3 | 23 | 18 | Deer Park Hills | 16 | 2 | 22 |
| 6 | Lower Meadow | 13 | 3 | 5 | 19 | Long Plantation | 11 | 0 | 25 |
| 7 | Higher Meadow | 3 | 1 | 21 | 20 | Orchard | 0 | 1 | 37 |
| 8 | Plantation | 1 | 0 | 33 | 21 | Polcarne | 5 | 2 | 26 |
| 9 | Wood | 3 | 2 | 7 | 22 | Willow Plots | 3 | 2 | 14 |
| 10 | Homestead | 0 | 0 | 25 | 23 | Lower Polcarne | 7 | 3 | 5 |
| 11 | Garden | 0 | 0 | 14 | 24 | Pond | 1 | 2 | 37 |
| 12 | Orchard | 0 | 2 | 32 | | | | | |
| | | 87 | 2 | 6 | | | 162 | 3 | 0 |

16 { Also, the Reversion in Fee, expectant on the decease of Dorcas Carveth Rowse, aged 37, William Rowse, aged 33, and Thomas Guy, aged 33, held by lease dated the 4th of January, 1827, for the lives of the said parties, of *Carhais Water Grist Mill*, working three pair of stones, with every conveniency for making flour; together with a good Dwelling-house and Outbuildings, now in the occupation of John Whiting. Reserved yearly rent, 1l. 2s.; heriot, 2l.

The Land-tax on the whole of this Lot has been redeemed.

This page from the auction catalogue describes the house in 1852 and confirms that he took almost nothing with him. It records some good horse stock, a lot of fine wine, and all his personal possessions.

A first unsuccessful attempt to auction the house was made in 1842. In March 1848 legal actions continued, listing the complex cases surrounding Trevanion affairs, noting the further sums owed and the assets and liabilities they had tried to ring fence by transferring to yet further trusts. There were difficulties with marriage settlements and with lands which might, or might not, form part of the creditors' claims. There were also accusations of conflict of interests between the parties.

The legal report makes interesting but confused reading. The Trevanion affairs were a dog's dinner and it is therefore not surprising that the second auction had to wait to be held in 1852, once some of the legal difficulties had been cleared up. There are interesting differences between the sale catalogue of 1842 and that of 1852. This last from 1852 hints at some of the decay.

*'The Castle (at present out of repair) is a magnificent structure built in the florid Gothic style, with spacious apartments and offices, decorated hall and library, grand diverging staircase, painted windows, groined ceilings, and other embellishments.'*

The Rev Willimott had visited the house in the year of his arrival 1852. He later recalled that the house then had been *'robbed of all moveable fixtures, bells, bell wire, lead from the roof* [he may not have heard of the papier mâché], *and when I first visited it, ducks were washing themselves on the drawing room floor.'*

In 1852, a sale of the house was achieved to a Dr Drake, acting for a Mr Fellowes of Reigate, in the pitiful sum of just £5000. This sale, due to 'the titles or power of sale being unsatisfactory', then fell through.

## Purchase by Michael Williams

Caerhays was finally sold a couple of years later in 1854 to Michael Williams; the Royal Cornwall Gazette of April 27 1855 reporting that the estate had cost Mr Williams *'about £50,000, which with other purchases invested by him within the last year or two will amount to upwards of £170,000...'* Michael Williams went on to repair and restore the house.

## The Last of the Trevanions

Although court cases continued for years, branches of the Trevanion family survived and may even have retained remnants of land and mineral interests in Cornwall. They never lost their sorrow at losing Caerhays; one or two promised to leave the estate money. It is said that descendants still live.

The last heir in the male line, Hugh Eric Trevanion, died in 1912, having probably committed suicide. One reason suggested for this was that he was being forced to consider marriage to a woman, when he preferred life with Albert Edward, who had been a petty officer on an ocean liner. We know quite a lot about his unusual life, because his overbearing and eccentric mother insisted on two inquests into his death. Despite the restrictions of the age and the restraint with which the case was reported, the inquest reports still make lively reading. Hugh Eric had lived an extravagant life, and his excesses were dutifully recorded by friends and family. He also happily wasted great sums of money, so perhaps he had inherited that cheerful defiance of financial responsibility from the Bettesworth line.

The seal of the last of the Trevanions.

# The Reminiscences of the Revd William Willimott.

The Revd W Willimott was about 27 years old when, in 1852, he arrived at Caerhays to become the rector.

*'In 1852 I was presented to the Rectory of St. Michaels Caerhays by Lady Granville of Dropmore, the last of the Pitts [who was the patron of the living]. I picked up from time to time certain strange stories respecting the last squire Trevanion who had fled from the castle [some] years before and, being outlawed, never returned.*

*His lawyer was Mr. E. Coode & Son of St. Austell who knew the difficulties the squire was in and kept a sharp look out from his office near the stable yard of The White Hart St. Austell for Bailiffs who might come from London by the coach to arrest the Squire. The ostler was in Mr. Coode's pay and informed him that two men who had come by coach had ordered a fly for Caerhays Castle; whilst these men were getting some breakfast in the hotel, the fly was ordered by Mr. Coode*

*to follow him down the hill out of the town. Mr. Coode was picked up and was driven rapidly to Rescassa and took up its place in a bye road overlooking the Castle. Mr. Coode got out and went down through the wood to the Castle, found the Squire and eventually persuaded him to leave the Castle for the fly waiting on the top of the hill. Some time had been lost by the bailiffs in getting another vehicle and at the last moment Mr. Coode persuaded Squire Trevanion to make his escape and as the bailiffs approached the Castle by the Portluney Road, the Squire and Mr. Coode went up the rocky path at the head of the pond and found the chaise ready to take them to St. Austell where they arrived in time to catch the mail coach.*

*They had the start of their pursuers by 2 hours and the squire got away, never to return.'*

A second story told of failure to steal the sole surviving fitting.

*'During the [many] years Caerhays Castle had no owner but the Court of Chancery, it was robbed of all moveable fixtures, bells, bell wires lead from the roof. When I first visited it, ducks were washing themselves on the Drawing room floor. At last there was nothing to carry away but the large bell in the stable yard. There was living at this time a very strange character at Penvor Gate...[who] when I knew him ... was an old, but very strong and robust man, [although] always on the watch for he lived in fear of his life being taken. One night, he heard a noise in the road outside his gate, lit his candle and went out to see. [There, he] stumbled upon a donkey down in the road with a cart propped up on one wheel, a shaft broken and the large bell of the castle lying in the road. The thieves who had stolen it made their escape and he trundled the bell into the ditch. In the morning he had it put up in his yard where it remained until the castle was restored some years after'.*

*Willimott watercolours reproduced with permission of Vicar and Churchwardens of St Michael Caerhays.*

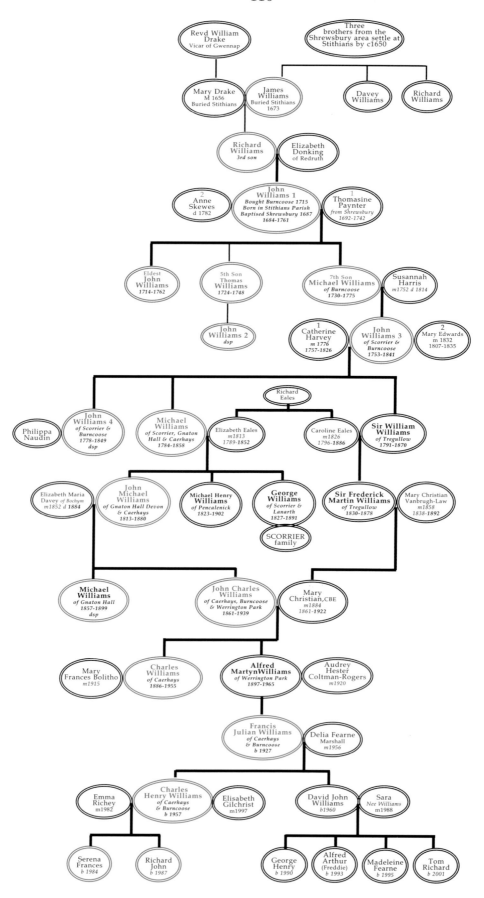

This family tree has been simplified for the story of Caerhays.
Many branches and descendents have been omitted.

# Chapter 12
# The Williams Family and the Purchase of Caerhays

The Williams family are thought to have arrived in Stithians, Cornwall around 1660, perhaps because there were new opportunities in mining through the abolishing by the Protectorate of the old mining restrictions. Their background and wealth are not clear, but they either had money, made some quickly or had rare skills, since they soon became the managers of mines. Although they seem to have had connections with Monmouthshire, attested by the survival of legal papers and by the similarity of their seal to that of the Monmouth Williams, the family had come from the Shropshire area, where still live their collateral descendants. Although living in Cornwall, they retained their connections with Shrewsbury, Shropshire. John Williams (1685-1761) was taken back to Shrewsbury to be christened in 1688, although this was three years after his birth in Cornwall. He also returned to Shrewsbury to marry Thomasine, a girl from there and it was in Shrewsbury that some of his children were married, despite his living in Cornwall. It seems that the family had long had Shrewsbury connections, and that this connection with Shrewsbury cousins was kept alive to the end of the 19thC.

Burncoose House in 1845

Having arrived in Stithians, they moved a few miles to Gwennap, a parish in which some members of the family still live. They are shown as having property in Stithians around 1650, and it is likely that James Williams was of some status when he arrived, as he would not otherwise have been able to marry a parson's daughter. Living first at Cusgarne, in Gwennap, they moved to Burncoose in 1715.

The Williams family have therefore been settled and working from Burncoose for 350 years, a period which puts the family amongst the few in Cornwall who have stayed at one place so long.

Burncoose in the late 20thC

The Williams family are notable for the number of children born to each generation, and the wide interests and success of so many branches. The family tree has been simplified to show the main line through to Caerhays. This does a disservice to the many different family branches and to their lives. A look at any part of this large family turns up stories of achievement.

The many branches of the Williams family have also long been involved in political or local government work. This commitment was not that associated with the empty representation of rotten boroughs, but rather the hard work associated with committees and management, whether in local government or the House of Commons. Public service

Burncoose today

has continued through to the present. Save for the case of Sir William Williams in the mid 19thC, the family has also been associated with an unwillingness to accept honours. Each generation has stories of shyness in this matter. In 1851 Michael Williams wrote 'Dizzy[Disraeli] offered me a peerage tonight', which he then refused. Another more recent offer of high honour is said to have been casually refused over the telephone.

Part of the modern fame of the family is as gardeners. An interest in gardens ran through all branches of the Williams family and many had fine gardens. At the end of the 19thC, the main Williams family occupied some 21 country houses in Cornwall and Devon. The list of their gardens is impressive and many, although now sold out of the family, are, like Caerhays, yet open to the public.

A chimney at the Dolcoath Mine

The historian of the Williams family is Colonel G.T.G. (Toots) Williams. His copious notes and essays cover over 700 individuals and their lives during the last 200 years. They attest to the wealth of interest and varied activities of the family in Britain and around the world. It is usually expected that every family history will record a few lemons. However, perhaps because they were so numerous, and the less successful less obvious, the family records few such underachievers, but rather appear for 350 years to have produced men and women of ability, of achievement and of business skills, who have shone in many different spheres. A history of the family's mining activities, their houses, families and business machinations over centuries of activity, would require a series of substantial volumes.

## Mining in Cornwall

Any story of the Williams family requires an overview of mining in Cornwall, since this was the background to their business success.

In the literature of Cornwall, mining and mining history is perhaps the best covered of all subjects. It remains a subject of intense interest among enthusiasts in the county; there are numerous historic and mining societies and many individuals have enormous knowledge of the mines, their history and the processes.

Mining developed from the working of tin and extraction from deposits of ore found in streams on or near the surface. This tin was associated with the combination of granite and sedimentary rocks and had for over 3000 years been combined with copper to make bronze.

Two illustrations of the abandoned engine houses which form part of the modern Cornish landscape

The most common of the tin bearing rocks is called cassiterite and, as surface deposits became rare, it could be seen in cliffs, or on outcrops of rock. From the middle ages on, the veins of tin-bearing metal were followed into the ground and this developed into mining.

The veins of metal bearing rock are called lodes, and although usually quite shallow, it remained difficult to get at them without having to drain water from the tunnels or 'levels'. The mining that was undertaken was not therefore like the opening of a quarry or the making of a big excavation. Quarrying did exist in Cornwall, but has been of lesser importance save for the Delabole slate quarry, for granite, specialised masonry and road fill. Mining in Cornwall meant the digging of tunnels or 'levels' to extract metal bearing rock. Cornwall is still covered by the engine houses and chimneys of mine after mine in the metal-bearing parts of the land. These are the obvious evidence of the many, many buildings which were required to process the metal.

The principal buildings were required to house steam engines which hoisted men and material from the mines as well as the engines

A wheel from a beam engine resited at the entrance to Dolcoath mine, Harriet shaft.

which pumped the water from mines to make them accessible. 'Stamps' were used to crush the rock into dust to enable the extraction of the metal. The hundreds of chimneys were used to draw air through the great boilers of the beam engines that powered the pumping, winding, stamping and processing machinery. In addition to engine houses, winding wheels and chimneys there were also acres of buildings for handling the products. These included complex runs to handle arsenic. All these buildings were built to serve and work on the rock dug out of the earth. Their extent is now often masked by undergrowth, leaving only the engine house and chimney to mark the sites. The buildings were backed up by mineral tramways and ports for handling the ore. Some areas of Cornwall retain so interesting a collection of early industrial buildings that in 2008 they were granted World Heritage Site status.

The Ruins of the Poldice Mine
The labyrinth of workings included copper ore, wolfram, arsenic and stamps for conversion of cassiterite ore to tin.
*Photo Courtesy Eva Krocher*

Although tin was always of importance, much of the later mining was for copper. There were also quantities of other minerals and metals such as lead, silver, zinc and wolfram.

The great phase of Cornish mining was really quite short, since it lasted from 1640 to 1880. This period also saw that development of machinery, of engines and of an engineering tradition in which Cornwall led the world, and whose inventions came to be applied for other uses across the Industrial Revolution.

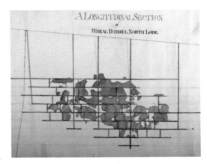

Wheal Damsel, a longitudinal section of the North Lode

Mining has given rise to an enormous body of literature whose effect is to rather over emphasise the importance of mining in Cornish history. It is true that the activity of mining supported both independence and loyalty among the miners, and that this almost tribal adhesion, together with a sentimental feeling for mining endured long after the mines themselves had closed. Of equal importance to the Cornish economy and to the Cornish character were the stories and funds that returned to Cornwall from miners who had emigrated as Cornwall's mines became less profitable. These emigrants, known as 'Cousin Jacks', have ensured that Cornish traditions in mining have been spread world wide.

The mines themselves were developed in accordance with late medieval business practices. Ownership of land did not necessarily include the rights to mine below the ground, these rights belonging usually to the manor or administrative district for the area. Funds were raised not by shareholders but by 'adventurers', who would put up the money and then enter into an arrangement with one or more 'managers' or agents to act for them. Adventurers and managers were men of importance.

Many mine buildings now lie covered with waste which has become a garden of wild flowers

Attempts to make money through the extraction of mineral bearing rock were made all over the Cornish landscape, by family after family. However, it was at Gwennap that the Williams family were active and this was a parish that was once described as the 'richest square mile in the Old World' during the late 18th and early 19thCs.

## John Williams 1 (1685-1761)

The grandson of the first Cornish Williams was John Williams, known as John 'the first'. John 1 not only seems to have married a lady with money, but made money either from 'adventures' in mining enterprises or as a manager and agent. He was also made manager of the Hearle land in St Day, which helped him become one of the

A tin sample from Williams, Harvey and Co Ltd, Mellanear

most influential of mine managers. In 1715, he bought the house and small estate of Burncoose, which was then either new, or was built by him. Burncoose is in the Parish of Gwennap and became the centre of the family's activities for the next three centuries. It still remains part of the Caerhays Estate today, and is now the modern home of the Burncoose Nurseries.

## John Williams 2 (Born 1714)

The second John Williams was appointed the manager of the Poldice Mine, was involved with the Mineral Lords syndicate and seems to have been of influence in mining circles. It was also he who got the 'Great County Adit' started. This 'adit' was a tunnel which helped drain the water from numerous mines in the principal mining area of Cornwall as mines were dug ever deeper in search of metal and mineral bearing rock. Although John Williams 2 had a reputation for showing no quarter in matters of business, we know little of his life, nor even the date of his death. He does not seem to have married or fathered children.

## Michael Williams 1 (1730-1775)

The businesses and estate therefore passed to John 2's brother, Michael, who was the 7th son of John 1. He lived at Burncoose having married Susannah Harris of Cusgarne, another family important in mining enterprise in Cornwall. Despite this inter-interest marriage there remain reports of competition with the Harris family, some of whose mills were cut off from water by the expanding Great County Adit, under Williams management.

## John Williams 3, The Dreamer (1753-1841)

John Williams 3, was born at Burncoose in 1753 and died in 1841 aged 88. Despite inheriting only £100 from his father, he turned out to be the leader in a remarkable line of 18th & 19thC businessmen. He founded the Williams mining, smelting and banking empire and in his heyday employed 10,000 people. He married Catherine Harvey, a daughter of one of the other great business families of 18thC Cornwall. Her portrait suggests she was a formidable woman.

He could claim to control the Gwennap copper belt and was said in the Parliamentary report of 1799 to have controlled 33% of the mines in Cornwall. He was also alleged to have under his hands 30% of world copper production. Even 25 years later, when there had been a glut of new mines, he was said still to control 20% of Cornish mines. He owned tin smelting works, sulphur mines, quarries, and was also a director of the Cornish Bank. He also issued three respected and uniquely guaranteed tokens, due to the shortage of copper currency. In 1803 he started his own copper smelting business in Swansea, and expanded the mining interests beyond Cornwall and Wales to deal with the New World. In 1804, during the Napoleonic wars, it is astonishing to find that the first shipments of foreign ores started arriving from Cuba, Mexico and Peru, countries that still seem distant today.

Although he competed with other great mining family businesses, he also worked with them. He had notable partnerships with the Fox family of Falmouth and with them was managed the

Wheal Kitty, St Agnes
An example of the detailed drawings made for mine workings

The site for Scorrier was bought in 1778 by John III, 'the Dreamer', who built the house as a 'count house' for the mining enterprises. Michael Williams II (1784-1858) converted 'Scorrier Office' to a house in 1845. On Feb 29 1908 the house was destroyed by fire, and rebuilt with concrete fire barriers. The photograph shows the house today. It remains in the ownership of the Scorrier Williams family.

foundry at Perranarworthal. The Williams family later bought out the Fox interests and changed the name to 'The Williams Perran Foundry'. It was also with the Fox family that John Williams built the Plymouth Breakwater, developed the harbour at Portreath and built his own tramway from his mines at Poldice to Portreath. From Poltreath, copper ore could be shipped to his own smelter in Swansea.

He also bought the land at Scorrier, built a large house there in 1778, and cleared and laid out gardens and woods. He became a man with an international reputation and visitors to Scorrier included both Louis XVIII and Charles X of France.

However, when in his 70s, around 1825, John decided to leave the family home. This may have been because the house at Scorrier was also the main office, that the 'copper office' was to be opened at Burncoose in 1826 and that a younger son Edward and family lived in West Devon. Perhaps it seemed a good time to hand over the business to his sons John, Michael and William. It also seems probable that copper mining and business possibilities along the Tamar were an attraction. His wife died in 1826, the year they moved to Calstock, so he then set up home with Mary Edwards, a young housekeeper who was only 19 at the time. He married her when she was 25, and he 56 years older. Their one child died at the age of four and he outlived his second wife. John, his two wives and the infant daughter are all buried in Calstock church. His older children were shocked and horrified at their fathers behaviour and worried that this might complicate the family inheritance. When he handed over to them most of his existing businesses, they changed the name from 'John Williams and Son' to 'John Williams Junior and Brothers'.

It is the more astonishing therefore that having bought the Manor of Calstock in old age and started again, he had, within a couple of years, some 600 men in his employ and was busy making another fortune. He built a village for his workforce, known as Williamstown, now part of Gunnislake. It was in great old age, that he built the breakwater at Plymouth, one of his most notable achievements.

John Williams 3 was a great mining adventurer and successful business man. Despite this, he is now remembered by the rather unlikely title of 'The Dreamer'. This is because, in 1812, he dreamt of the assassination of the Prime Minister in the lobby of the House of Commons. He had this dream three times in one night, in incredible detail, nine days before the assassination took place.

So extraordinary was the dream, so strong his impression of it, and so astonished was he by the news of the assassination, that he prepared 'attested statements'. The first was drawn up in the presence of The Revd Thomas Fisher and Mr Charles Prideaux-Brune and has been kept at Prideaux Place. Another account was put in the Times Newspaper, and a third was given to his friend Dr Abercrombie. Yet a further account was given to Mr Hill, a barrister and his grandson, rather later in life. All these records were practically identical, and some are very considerably longer than that noted below, which was written some years later. Details distributed at the time included his telling of the dream story to friends, and pages of 'corroborative detail' of London items that could not be known by John Williams. Whatever the truth of this mystery, it seemed extraordinary to people at the time, and so extraordinary that it seems worth repeating here, in the version retained within the family.

ILLUSTRATED CATALOGUE

Pumping & Winding Engines,

AND OTHER PLANT USED FOR MINING PURPOSES,

HORIZONTAL, FIXED, AND PORTABLE ENGINES,

CORNISH AND OTHER BOILERS,

GENERAL MACHINERY,

MANUFACTURED BY

WILLIAMS' PERRAN FOUNDRY CO.,

PERRANARWORTHAL, CORNWALL,

AND

1 & 2 GREAT WINCHESTER STREET BUILDINGS, LONDON, E.C.

ESTABLISHED 1795.

WILLIAMS' PERRAN FOUNDRY CO.

ELEVATION OF PUMPING ENGINE.

BUILT FOR ST. DAY UNITED MINES.

Williams' Perran Foundry Co.

PERRANARWORTHAL, CORNWALL,

AND

1 & 2 GREAT WINCHESTER STREET BUILDINGS, LONDON, E.C.

Two illustrations from a catalogue for The Perran Foundry, first started by George Fox and John Williams. It was taken over entirely by the Williams family in 1858. It closed in 1879.

This account was given by John Williams to Mr Tremayne at Heligan, who gave it to Michael Williams, elder brother of John Charles, in 1894.

## The Dream

Some account of a Dream which occurred to Mr John Williams of Scorrier House in the county of Cornwall, in the year 1812, taken from his own mouth and narrated by him at various times to several of his particular friends.[Written at Sandhill, Calstock, Cornwall], December 9th, 1837.

John Williams 3, 1753-1841
Portrait by Leakey

*"Being desired to write out the particulars of a remarkable dream, which I had in the year 1812; before I do so I think it may be proper for me to say that at that time my attention was fully occupied with affairs of my own, the superintendence of some very extensive mines in Cornwall being entrusted to me. Thus, I had no leisure to pay any attention to political matters, and hardly knew who at the that time formed the administration of the country. It was therefore scarcely possible that my own interest in the subject should have had any share in suggesting the circumstances which presented themselves to my imagination. It was in truth a subject which never occurred to my waking thoughts. My dream was as follows:-*

*About the 2nd or 3rd day of May, 1812, I dreamed that I was in the Lobby of the House of Commons ... A small man, dressed in a blue coat and white waistcoat, entered, and immediately I saw a person whom I had observed upon my first entrance, dressed in a snuff coloured coat with yellow metal buttons, take a pistol from under his coat, and present it at the little man above mentioned. The pistol was discharged, and the ball entered under the left breast of the person at whom it was directed. I saw the blood issue from the place where the ball had struck him, his countenance instantly altered, and he fell to the ground. Upon enquiring who the sufferer might be, I was informed that he was the Prime Minister who was also Chancellor of the Exchequer. I understood him to be Mr Perceval. I further saw the murderer laid hold of by several gentlemen in the room. Upon awaking I told the particulars above related to my wife. She treated the matter lightly, and desired me to go to sleep, saying that it was only a dream. I soon fell asleep again, and again the dream presented itself with precisely the same circumstances. After awaking a second time, and stating the matter again to my wife, she only repeated her request that I should compose myself, and dismiss the subject from my mind. Upon my falling asleep the third time, the same dream without any alteration was repeated, and I awoke, as on the former occasions, in great agitation. So much alarmed was I, and impressed by the circumstances above related, that I felt much doubt whether it was not my duty to take a journey to London, and communicate upon the subject with the party principally concerned.*

Catharine Harvey Williams
1757-1826 Portrait by Leakey

*Upon this point I consulted with some friends whom I met on business at the Godolphin Mine on the following day. After having stated to them the particulars of the dream itself, and what were my own feelings in relation to it, they dissuaded me from my purpose, saying I might expose myself to vexation or contempt, or be taken up as a fanatick. Upon this I said no more, but anxiously watched the newspapers every evening as the post arrived.*

*On the evening of 13th May (as far as I can recollect), no account of Mr Perceval's death was in the newspaper, but my second son, at that time returning from Truro, came in a hurried manner into the room in which I was sitting, and exclaimed, 'Father, your dream has come true, Mr Perceval has been shot in the Lobby of the House of Commons. There is an account come from London to Truro, written after the newspapers were printed.' The fact was Mr Perceval had been assassinated on the evening of the eleventh. Some business soon after called me to London, and in one of the print-shops*

*I saw a drawing for sale, representing the place and circumstances which attended Mr Perceval's death. I purchased it, and upon a careful examination, I found it to coincide in all respects with the same scene which passed through my imagination in my dream. The colours of the dresses, the buttons of the assassin's coat, the white waistcoat of Mr Perceval, the spot of blood upon it, the countenances and attitudes of the parties present were exactly what I had dreamed. I forbear to make any comment upon the narrative, further than to declare solemnly that it is a faithful account of facts as they actually occurred."*

This dream was of particular interest in the 19thC when spiritualism, table turning and matters of the occult became popular.

From 1810 on there were a number of attempts to challenge the Williams supremacy, to establish independent management and provide competing rail links, ports and smelters. The Williams family were not much affected by this until the early 1840s when their control over the Great Adit was reduced and more owners used their own agents rather than going through Williams companies. In the end the Williams' resigned the management of the Adit in 1853. In 1862, there were family disputes among partners which included the Harveys - and this affected the Williams' tin smelting interests. Although they continued with exceptional and indeed, for a time, increased influence, their mining businesses declined with the decline of mining for the whole county. From 1840, discovery of deposits in Australia and America had dwarfed those of Cornwall and broken the Cornish control of copper. By 1880 even smelting in Wales had been overcome by the overseas competition. The last great copper mines seem all to have been closed in the 1870s. The business interests of the Williams were, by the 1870s, a shadow of their former selves, but it was not until 1888 that the last major investment was sold by them.

John Williams 3 had four sons, all of whom developed different interests. This generation widened the family's businesses and saw them and their further relations established in a number of houses and gardens around Cornwall and Devon.

Although it was a large family, it seems to have been a reasonably close one, particularly as two of the brothers, Michael and William, married two sisters from the Eales family.

Richard Eales, 1759- 1852
Father of both Elizabeth (1789-1852), wife of Michael Williams 2 and of Caroline (1796-1886) who married Michael's brother Sir William Williams

## John Williams 4 (1778-1849)

The eldest son, he married a French Huguenot lady, Philippa Naudin, but had no children. Known as John the Quaker, he was an FRS, Fellow of the Linnean Society and respected scientist, naturalist and collector, with particular talents for plants and animals. He administered the Williams' businesses. Of great wealth when he died, he left everything to John Michael, which doubled his nephew's wealth.

## Michael Williams 2 (1785-1858)

It was John William 3's second son, Michael Williams, who fought hard to maintain the Williams supremacy in mining affairs in a changing world of great competition. The fortunes of mining and metal handling ebbed and flowed, but it is probable that the writing was on the wall for the industry by the 1850s. Nevertheless, Michael's competitive edge was helped when, in 1853, he became an MP, allowing him to fight competitors who had proposals for railways and mine transport. It is difficult to appreciate the influence he had on world

This couple is probably John Williams 4 and his wife, the French Huguenot Philippa Naudin.,

wide copper production. Much ore was taken to the works in South Wales by boat from Portreath. His influence in South Wales too was recognised by his appointment as High Sheriff of Glamorgan in 1840. He was also, at different times, Deputy Lieutenant of Cornwall and Deputy Warden of the Stannaries.

Michael Williams added to his estates first, Gnaton Hall in Devon and then, in 1854, Caerhays Castle. He was by now 69 years old and this was a big project for the restoration of a house that had proved difficult to sell and from the purchase of which earlier buyers had backed out. The house was in a terrible state, made worse by the theft of all moveable items from a property that had not been maintained and had been in the hands of an absentee bankruptcy court for some 14 years. Caerhays may have been in a poor way, but the price was advantageous since it reflected both this and the years of dispute over the title.

Michael Williams 1785-1858
Portrait by H Pickersgill junior 1854

The impression of theft by the dastardly Caerhays locals was so strong on Michael that when, after a visit to the work, he left his walking stick behind, he sent his footman all the way back from Trevince in Gwennap to Caerhays, stating that the local thieving inhabitants were not to be trusted. This was a considerable journey just to collect a walking stick, which would have taken many hours on horseback.

Michael's work included the alteration of the road along the coast, and removing a great hunk of hillside so that the sea could be viewed from the garden, drawing and dining rooms. It is said that this work was undertaken partly to give work to unemployed fishermen during the winter months and to miners during a mining recession. Since this was the removal of rock, not soil, it was a drastic piece of landscaping. Although Michael never moved in, restoration of the house was noted as being near completion when he died in 1858.

## John Michael Williams (1813-1880)

Michael's eldest son, John Michael, inherited Burncoose in 1861 and then, having lived at Pengreep, completed, furnished and moved into the refurbished Caerhays after his father's death. He had a reputation as 'the richest man in Cornwall'. His interests were not just in mining, but in the smelting business in Wales, in manufacturing, in banks and in property. He married Elizabeth Maria Davey, daughter of Stephen Davey of Bochym. John Michael Williams continued the repairs of Caerhays and repaired the church in 1864. He also fulfilled the positions and obligations of local politics. He enjoyed his country sports, but lost an eye in a shooting accident and in later life was always painted or photographed in profile.

The house at Caerhays was described by Polsue in flattering terms, when writing in the 1860s

*The ancient mansion was demolished in 1808, and the present magnificent structure was raised on its site. It consists of a large main body with lofty round towers and turrets, the whole being battlemented throughout. The new owners of this palatial seat have expended large sums in the renovation of the house and grounds; the former they have finished in a style of magnificence surpassing the original design in architectural*

Mrs Elizabeth Williams and her six children
on arrival at Caerhays c.1868:
LtoR: Michael, Elizabeth, dog, John Charles, Elizabeth Williams, with Florrie (born 1866), Charlotte, Clara

*beauty and correctness; and the whole have been thrown more open to the sea by the cutting down of an intercepting headland. The chief entrance to this highly interesting place is through a turreted gateway of corresponding character. The unique collection of minerals, formerly at Scorrier House, has been removed to Caerhays Castle, where it may be inspected at pleasure by the professed geologist, scientific persons, and gentlemen of taste'.*

The reference to 'gentlemen of taste' intrigues and amuses. However, to question visitors nowadays as to whether they are of sufficient taste to be allowed entry, seems unlikely to be allowed under the numerous restrictions of current legislation.

The 'Williams cut' seen from the castle.

## Foreign adventures and the Battle of Batoche

The Williams family was not of course restricted to those who lived at Caerhays. We tend to concentrate on one or two figures, forgetting that there were many others with interesting lives.

The Victorian age was full of campaigns or wars now little remembered; many involved members of the Williams family.

For instance, William Williams (1821-1846), 4th son of Michael and Elizabeth Eales, was one of few to survive the 1st Afghan War of 1841. He brought home from that campaign not only a shirt of chain mail alleged to date from the time of Ghengis Khan and now the property of the Edgcumbes, but also a large uncut emerald which had been in an Afghan turban, and which can be seen in the portrait of Mrs John Michael Williams.

Another Williams, a grandson of John 3, has a statue erected to his honour in front of the town hall in Port Hope, Canada. This was Arthur Trefusis Heneage Williams who lived at Penryn Park (sic), Port Hope, Ontario.

A hopper bearing the date 1868 records the date of improvements.

By 1885, descendents of French Canadian voyageurs who had intermarried with the Indian population, were known as the 'Metis'. This group, an independent group of trackers, hunters and traders, formed an association called 'Les Gens Libres' and became a competitor to the Hudson's Bay Company. Eventually there was a full scale war between the government and the Metis, who were good rifle men led by competent French leaders. The war culminated in the Battle of Batoche, an engagement which involved 2-3000 people with four days of rifle fire and hand-to-hand fighting, but only 25 or so dead from the two sides. The battle was won by the heroism of Lt Col Williams, whose charge broke the Metis defences. Lt Col Williams was known thereafter as 'The Hero of Batoche'.

## What good have the Williamses done?

In 1868, Frederick Martin Williams prepared a poster to support his election as MP for Truro. Frederick's character was not typical of the family's more normal modesty. The broad sheet was a large poster of dramatic intent which relied on old fashioned influence rather than political creed. However, it gives an idea of family activities and achievements, including some, like the Irish venture, that are now forgotten.

At the end of each question on the sheet was printed the magic answer, 'The Williamses'.

The 'Old Servants Hall' had the window altered and given a gothic top.

### To the Electors of Truro:

What good have the Williamses done?

Since Mr. Passmore Edwards, in his weakness, disappointment, and rage, has sought to blind the Electors of Truro, as to the good effected by the WILLIAMSES, it may be well to state a few plain and important facts bearing on the subject:-

John Michael Williams (1813-1880)

Who may be justly called the Fathers of Cornish mining ?

Who stand foremost as developers of the mineral resources of Cornwall ?

Who, when the Daveys abandoned Poldice and Wheal Unity Mines, came forward and preserved this field of labour for about 700 hands, and thus prevented a vast amount of poverty and suffering ?

Who, when Messers Taylor abandoned the Great Consolidated Mines, came forward and preserved employment for about 1,500 hands, and thus again drove back ruin and suffering ?

Who, when the United Mines were abandoned by a London Company, came forward and preserved employment for about 1,200 hands, once more repulsing the working man's dreaded enemy ?

Who, when the principal part of the present Clifford Amalgamated Mines were abandoned by the Messers Taylor, came forward and saved the concern from ruin, and the Parish from wide-spread poverty ?

Who came to the rescue when, last year, the St. Day United Mines were abandoned, and caused the undertaking, now employing over 1,000 hands, to resume working ?

Who, when in consequence of the low price of minerals, a serious number of shareholders deserted Clifford Amalgamated Mines, determined to prevent the stoppage of the undertaking, which is now employing nearly 2,000 hands?

Who were instrumental in the commencement or resuscitation of the following mines:-    Wheal Bassett, St. Agnes, Wheal Chance, Gwennap; Wheal Clifford, Gwennap; Gunnislake, Calstock; Wheal Maid, Gwennap; Wheal Trefusis, Redruth; Wheal Tamar, Calstock; Wheal Pink, Gwennap; Wheal Phoenix, Calstock; Wheal Duchy, Calstock; North Downs, Redruth; Wheal Jewell, Gwennap; Rose Lobby, Gwennap; Carharrack, Gwennap; Wheal Jewell, Gwennap; Rose Lobby, Gwennap; Carharrack, Gwennap; Wheal Providence, St. Erth; Trevabyn, St. Erth; Bodraveran, St. Erth; Carnon Stream Works, Perran; Pentire, St. Minver; The Union Mines, Gwennap; Treskerby, Gwennap; Great St. George, Perranzabuloe; Cardew, Redruth; Creegbrawse, Kenwyn; Wheal Calstock, Calstock; Poldice, Gwennap; Wheal Damsel, Gwennap; Wheal Spinster, Gwennap; The Wood Mine, Kenwyn; Wheal Cupid, Redruth; The Great Godolphin Mines, Breage; etc, etc.

Elizabeth, Mrs John Michael Williams, (Née Davey), wearing the famous uncut alluvial emerald once in an Afghan turban.    *H W Pickersgill, 1854*

Who, in 1748 projected and commenced and for 20 years prosecuted the Great Adit which empties into the Carnon Valley, an adit which has been the means of materially helping to drain 30 or 40 miles of the richest mineral ground in Cornwall, and in so doing has added millions sterling to our Counties products and given employment to thousands!

Who, directly and indirectly, created the great districts of St. Day, Carharrack, Lanner and Gwennap ?

Who made the miserable and poverty-stricken wilderness of Gwennap into a beautiful and productive district ?

Who, opened up the great Manganese districts around Launceston, near Exeter and in Warwickshire ?

Who embarked an immense capital in mining in Ireland, in Ireland's darkest days ?

Who resuscitated the now great Lisburne, Gogignan, and Nantymwyn, and other neighbouring lead mines in Wales ?

Who, directly or indirectly, are the means of an annual expenditure of many thousands of pounds in Truro and the District ?

Who should heartily support Mr. Frederick Martin Williams, the Conservative candidate for Truro ?

–The Electors of Truro.

Who made a fatal error when he foully abused the Williamses?

-Mr. Passmore Edwards.

Who must we justify and honestly reckon among the very best friends of Cornwall?

The Williamses

Michael Williams, with two dogs. 1857-1899.  The elder brother of JC, he lived at Gnaton Hall and Newquay.

Printed at the "Royal Cornwall Gazette" Office, Truro

Dated *(Hand written in ink)*          November 1868.

# Chapter 13
# John Charles Williams

It was under the ownership of John Charles Williams, known as JC, the second son of John Michael, that the castle, farm and estate buildings were improved and developed into the estate we see today. JC was a man of remarkable energy and foresight, but not, as other members of his family, interested in mining. He devoted much of his life to politics and selfless public service, holding positions as chairman of many bodies, including Cornwall County Council and was Lord Lieutenant for 18 years. Apart from his interests in gardens and horticulture, he was a keen follower of hounds, and an excellent shot. He rented a moor in Scotland from the 1880s, buying Strathvaich in 1925. His name is perpetuated by the large number of plants which bear his name. He was only 19 when his father died. His elder brother inherited the businesses but JC was left a large capital sum and Caerhays although the house was then still occupied by his mother. He married his cousin, Mary Christian, the 11th child of Sir Frederick Williams, in 1884 and, needing somewhere to live and to give himself independence and, perhaps, for the rabbit shooting, he bought Werrington Park, near Launceston, in 1885. This Jacobean mansion had been remodelled by the addition of a new façade and wings, all of which needed renovation and modernisation. It was therefore at Werrington that he got a taste for the improvements that became a continuous stream of work on cottages, farms and other buildings at Caerhays for the next three decades. He moved to Caerhays in 1887.

John Charles Williams

It was probably also at Werrington that his interest in gardens and plants was aroused. When he bought the place, there was apparently a large greenhouse used for orchids and orchid propagation. Although he does not seem to have developed orchids any further, it was they which gave him a life-long interest in plants and plant propagation. This interest was combined with the usual Williams business approach. When he moved to Caerhays, the first gardens were not laid out with the shrubs we see today, but with long beds of daffodils, for which there was then a new and emerging market. Some of the old daffodil beds can still be seen in the Caerhays garden today.

JC continued to own Werrington, but used it more as shooting lodge with farm and garden run with Caerhays, rather than as a residence. The gardens were developed, the greenhouses maintained and other species besides daffodils were developed. The greenhouses grew orchids for the Covent Garden market from 1922-1955. There

Mary Christian Williams

was not just a magnificent conservatory, but also a Chinese garden.

When a younger son, Alfred Martyn Williams (1897-1985), married in 1920, he was given Werrington, which has remained in that family since. A Caerhays footman, Henry Gilbert, was given to Alfred Williams with the house and promoted as butler. Henry Gilbert was a man of considerable character, who always maintained a poker face. GTG Williams remembers that, as a boy, he had been ferreting with Charlie, a groom. Later he was brought tea by the butler, who said, with his famous poker face, "Poor old Charlie, they found him down the quarry with his braces round his neck". This caused consternation to the young boy. As he left the room, however, Henry the butler continued: "It's all right, he was having a shit".

On another occasion Henry and his staff had to cope with a mob of cheerful Williams children who were using the fire hoses on them. It is easy to forget that the staff were part of the family community.

It would be wrong to forget that JC Williams had other houses and other interests outside plant life. In particular, he was devoted to Scotland and deer stalking. He rented a substantial deer forest in the Highlands of Scotland, Strathvaich, which he eventually bought in the 1920s. JC was MP for Truro-Helston from 1892 to 1895, but soon tired of national politics, although he remained a County Councillor from 1889 until 1931 and was Lord Lieutenant 1918-1936. Despite this public service, he was known for his dislike of London. When he gave up being a national MP, it was said that this might be because he wished to be with his children as they grew up and wished to do good work in Cornwall. It was also said that he did not like sitting up late and missed seeing his garden and flowers develop.

Although he carried out public duties, JC remained a very private man. He used his considerable wealth to fund projects for the public. This included giving 108 acres at Nare Head to the National Trust, and funding for the publishing by the CPRE of a wonderful survey of Cornwall, which is a fine and early example of conservation literature. Other projects included the heating for the cathedral in 1931 and anonymous provision of education and family holidays for the children of Cornish clergy. He was also the leader in the movement to provide playing fields for schools in the county. These were only a few among many other unknown acts, since the instruments of his generosity were strictly forbidden to disclose the source of any funds.

If local politics and business (quite apart from running four houses) occupied much of JC's time, the remainder was spent on his main passion which was gardening. After he left politics JC started to hybridise daffodils. A good number of his hybrids are still in commercial production today. Soon after the turn of the century JC became heavily involved in sponsoring and funding plant hunting expeditions to unexplored parts of China. This was the basis of what is still one of the country's finest plant collections. JC was, in consequence, one of the founders of The Garden Society and The Rhododendron Society. He corresponded with many botanists, including those at Edinburgh and Kew.

It was JC who started 'The Garden Book' at Caerhays. This diary has a page for each day of the year and three subsequent generations have continued to record events in the garden. The excitement of seeing in flower new species never before seen in Western Europe comes through very clearly in JC's notes.

An early photograph of Werrington

'Werrington's conservatory in its hey-day'

A royal and formal mine visit: JC sits with Edward VII

Trophies of shooting during a royal visit to Glen Quioch by Edward VII

Civic duty: A reception for Edward VIII when Prince of Wales

Despite a dislike of motor cars, he took an interest in them for getting around Cornwall and was an early user. He gave up hunting in 1906 to concentrate on public work and the car then became all the more important. JC registered his first car, a 20hp Wolseley, on 22 December 1903 only 14 days after the first registration of a car in Cornwall. JC's number was AF25, a number plate that is still in use by the Williams family. A Rolls Royce Light 20hp, number 40520, registration no AF274 , built in 1906 and then given the bodywork in the style, 'Roi des Belges' was delivered and registered in June 1907. This car was involved in an accident in 1922 and was then stored. After partial restoration it sold at Bonhams of London for £441,500 in December 2009.

Children were encouraged to dig their own vegetable patches;

Another car was a 1909 Rolls Royce 40/50hp, chassis 60934. It had, first, a specially mounted Rothschild of Paris Laundaulette and then in 1913 was re-fitted with a Hooper double Laundaulette. Although we admire the cars owned by JC, it is notable that to him they were a convenience and nothing more. He was known for his dislike of a motor car, because as he said, it went too quickly for him to see things in the hedges. Nor did he aspire to grandeur. His chauffeur felt that JC should not, as Lord Lieutenant, be driven around in an old 'Tin Lizzie' and pressed JC to get something new. When told that a new car had at last been bought, the chauffeur was disappointed to find that the new car was just another 'Tin Lizzie'.

Horses and hunting were always of importance

The cars at Caerhays were a source of pride to the chauffeurs.
The Rolls on the right may be the one re-sold in 2009.
The number plate of the central car is still in use.

A 'Hooper' Double Laundaulette on a Rolls Royce chassis for JC Williams, the photograph being dated September 1913

The 1906 Rolls Royce Light 20hp Tourer ordered by JC Williams in 1905 was restored by a collector and sold at Bonhams of London for £441,500 in December 2009.

Late 19th and early 20th century photographs of family activities, transport, farming, of the
numerous staff at Caerhays and of gamekeepers and pheasant rearing pens
Sitting in the Carriage (2nd down top left) are Mary Williams with Hester Jobson and baby

Although he had a profound dislike of publicity, JC was proud of his position and connections, a pride that was typical of the time. He had a book carefully written out showing the genealogy of the Williams family, together with the many cousins. In most generations there had been a number of children, and in aggregate this ensured that the Williams family and its branches were a numerous and close knit clan. The genealogical tree also showed how, through the Eales, to whom there had been two marriages in the 19thC, there was a direct female line of descent from William the Conqueror.

The report of a visit to Caerhays made on July 25 1901 manages to convey an almost reverential approach to the splendour of the castle. This was when the main building renovations had finished and so we can imagine the house as representing the height of Edwardian luxury. JC Williams had invited the members of the Royal Institution of Cornwall, of which he was president, to visit Caerhays for lunch. The visitors presumably arrived in a number of carriages.

*'From this point a long stretch of narrow, winding, sharp cornered road, often with high hedges, brought the excursionists to Caerhays Church. Another mile and a half, and the conveyances were drawn up at Caerhays Castle, the beautiful home, enriched by many art treasures, of Mr. and Mrs. J.C. Williams, who extended to their guests a simple and cordial greeting. The castle, once the seat of the Trevanions, was rebuilt early in the last century from designs by Nash, the architect who remodelled Buckingham Palace in 1825. ...The castle has a delightful, secluded situation, close to the seashore, in the neighbourhood of Goran Haven. Excellent luncheon (after 4 hours drive!) no speeches – merely a few words of sincere thanks by Mr. J.D. Enys FGS and Mr. Sylvanus Trevail [The famous architect and Cornish notable].*

*'A couple of hours were spent in viewing the house and grounds;*

An Edwardian Garden Party 1907

*and in partaking of tea. Some of the party examined the fine collection of Roman coins, part of the hoard found near by in 1869 of which 39 are in museums etc. [Others] studied the works of Romney, Millais, Opie & others. While a few accompanied Mr. Williams to view some of the rare plants for which he is so celebrated.'*

This report in the society's journal gives a good idea of the more formal social activity of that time.

JC's wife, Mary Christian, had her own interests and activities, gaining a CBE for her work during 1914-18. She died of diabetes in 1922, 17 years before JC.

They had five sons and one daughter, although two sons did not survive the First World War. Robert Williams, his second son, with whom JC had a particular bond, could not wait to join up and so with the enthusiasm common in that first year of the war, went to France in his own car and chauffeured a General. Joining the Grenadier Guards with a commission, he was killed at Loos in 1915 aged 27. JC's third son, John Francis Williams, a lieutenant in the Navy, was also killed in 1915, aged 26, while serving in HMS Russell. HMS Russell, a two funnelled battleship had assisted at the withdrawal from the Dardenelles, was mined off Malta and sank with the loss of 100 lives.

The First War changed the society in which JC had lived, not only through changes in staffing, through the loss of all his staff to war service, but also in social attitudes. It was also a time of continual distress and worry as the news came through of one death after another in the family. It was not just his own two sons, but also the children of his friends, his neighbours, his extended family, his staff and tenants who died or were injured.

John Charles Williams lived on at Caerhays for seventeen years after the death of his wife. In his long life at Caerhays, he experienced that dramatic change in country house living and social and business conditions that occurred between 1880 and 1939.

JC Williams oversaw a continuous stream of new and renovation building work. The illustrations give some idea not only of the work at Caerhays to estate buildings, but also of life in what was one of the great, and well staffed, houses of the south west. We know that the young JC enjoyed his hunting. He also took an interest in new developments, being one of the first to install electricity, building an 'Electrical Works' for the purpose. Much of the current village of Caerhays was built and provided with public facilities including schools and village halls; farms too were rebuilt and extended. Other work at Caerhays included dairies, the installation of a stunning drier in the laundry room, and the building of an electricity centre. This programme continued to the First World

A photograph taken at Caerhays of men going off to enlist for service in the First World War
*Back Row:* Arthur Rowse, George Blandford, William Michael, Stanley Burley, John Burns, Unknown, Brother Burns?, Charles Burns
*Front Row:* Herbert Michael, William Beard, Charles Harris, Charles Michael, Albert Paddy

A military band marching through the Top Lodge towards the house

This picture, hung in the billiard room by JC, was a reminder of the death of a son in the Navy: HMS Acasta at the Battle of Jutland

War, and is attested by a collection of early drawings, plans and building specifications.

However, there is little doubt that JC is best remembered not only for his love and work in his own gardens but for the work he did in developing plants and in hybridisation. Famous for his primary interests in rhododendrons, camellias, magnolias and daffodils, he was also interested in fuscias, birds, wild flowers and ferns as well as cultivated plants. The 'Terrace' or 'Chinese garden' at Werrington showed his buddleias at their best.

He was also really interested in hybridisation for new varieties. Hybridisation had started in England around 1840 with daffodils. It was a conference attended by JC in 1890 which seems to have won his interest. He developed daffodils from 1893, and in 1898 made his first cross. Some 40 new varieties of daffodil developed at Caerhays were shown at shows, although, in accordance with his reputation for anonymity, they were usually shown under a number without his name

His first rhododendron specimens seemed to have been developed from 1885. It was a remarkable tribute to JC that the first of the great Wilson's seeds from a new rhododendron to survive was named *Rhododendron williamsianum*. This was the plant that was to become the base for much future hybridisation.

JC was also interested in rhododendron hybrids making 20-30 crosses a year. By 1917 264 species and natural varieties of rhododendron were growing at Caerhays.

Many of his famous specimens were from SW china, and Caerhays was famous for the flowering of rhododendrons earlier than elsewhere in Britain. For his garden he set out and built shelter belts of laurel, bamboo and trees. His garden was based on those ideas heralded as 'wild gardening' in 1897, which represented a move away from borders and towards large decorated areas. JC was also patient during the time, often twenty years that it takes for new plants to seed or flower.

It may well be that, in the future, his notes on forty years of gardening may turn out to be the most enduring of his gardening achievements.

Billiards was an abiding passion - an 18thC print has been relabelled with the names of friends

Certificates and tickets from a trip on a Zeppelin bring a touch of fantasy to Caerhays.

More garden diary with notes and attached ephemera.

The garden book, a daily record which has been kept up ever since 1897.

J.C.Williams was a collector of books and had both fine bindings and unusual books of reference. This shows an illustration from: 'The Kin Shan, or Golden Island, China, its Scenery, Architecture, Social Habits etc., Illustrated'

Rhododendron davidsonianum Caerhays Pink Form

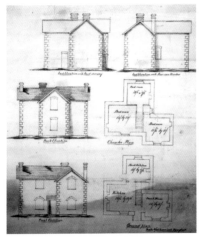

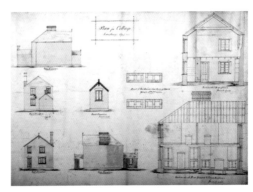

Part of the plans for a single cottage with decorative chimney, bargeboards and porch, drawn in April 1899

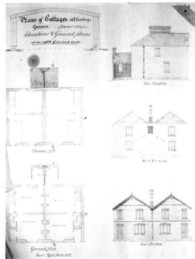

A design for a quirky t-shaped cottage with three rooms on each of two floors. The drawing is marked with a building cost of £295.

Plans for a pair of semi detached cottages at Caerhays

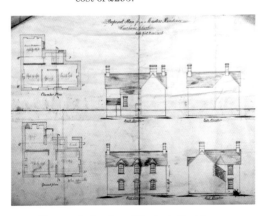

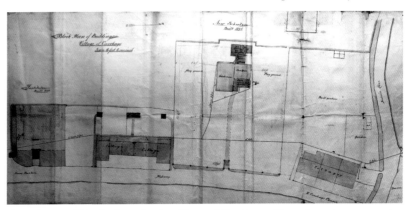

Proposed plan for a Master's Residence, Caerhays Schools

One of several block plans for the village of Caerhays. They show the progression of additions to the village, including the 'Institute' of 1893, the new school of 1895, and 2 blocks of cottages with 6 and 3 units respectively. A further plan shows more cottages in 1895.

Noah's Ark - the cattle shed in the park built by JC Williams to a design of February 1893, above, still stands today.

New buildings were intended to be sensible, attractive and meet what we would now call conservation standards

Many of his friends were gardeners, whether professional, famous or amateur. They included Professor Bailey Balfour of the Royal Botanic Gardens in Edinburgh. EH Wilson visited in July 1911 to see his buddleias at their best and he was on good terms with other plant hunters, arranging lectures and visits for Forrest and Captain Kingdon Ward.

JC's first presidential address to the Royal Institution of Cornwall was on gardening, and throughout his life he worked to develop a wide distribution of plants and flowers.

JC founded and fostered many of the links round Cornish gardens and was generous with gifts of seeds and plants, though often wishing that generosity to remain unknown. An early article on his gardens in The Garden magazine managed to avoid mentioning him save as 'an owner who was nameless and faceless'.

New buildings in Caerhays Churchtown, and at Pound, showing careful workmanship and individuality.

Although JC Williams 'won the gratitude and respect of his contemporaries' and was called the 'greatest Cornishman of his time', it is right that he should be recalled today through his affection for flowers and plants.

Rhododendron 'J C Williams'

'J.C. Williams'
(japonica x saluenensis)

Three plants named in honour of JC Williams

'J C Williams' (M. sargentiana var robusta x M. sprengeri 'Diva')

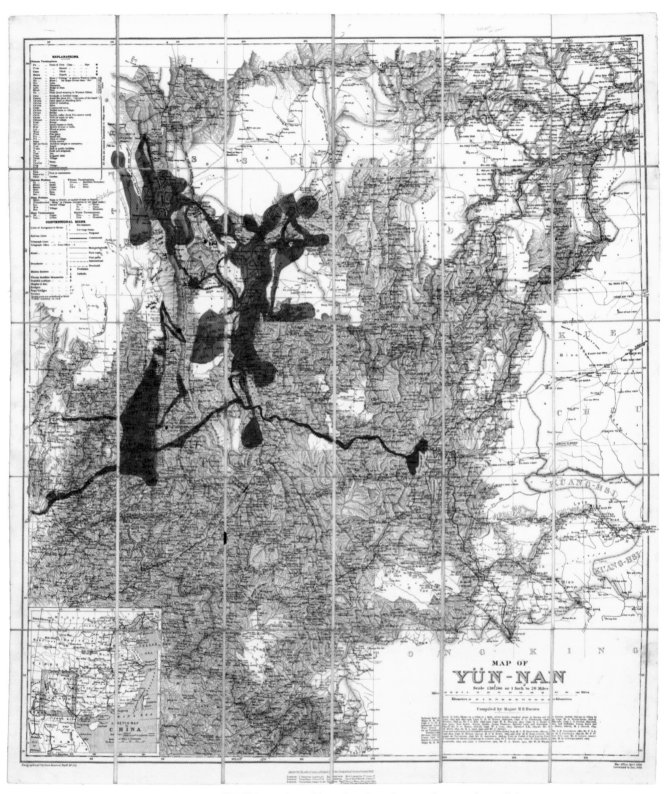

A Map of Yunnan in SW China, coloured in red to show dates and areas of expeditions.
*Collated by Major HR Davies for War Office 1906*
*Original scale 1 inch to 20 miles*

# Chapter 14
# Plant hunters in China

The history of any one house is often just that – the history of a single house. However, it is from that house that people have travelled the world, fought wars or enjoyed life. It is the connections to a wider society and world that can give depth to a history and a part of the interest of Caerhays has been the long association which it has enjoyed with botanic and plant development.

We may be accustomed to market gardens and garden shops but it is surprising to find small specialist nurseries and shops which, at the end of the 19thC, sold seed or information on foreign and exotic plants. Their products were found by 'plant hunters' who went out from Britain to record and bring back new specimens. This hunting was an extension of the late 18thC interest in analysing or recording species and the competitive finding of new varieties. Hunters necessarily went to unknown parts of the earth. In a modern world criss-crossed by planes, such places are no longer so strange and distant. The plant hunters, however, travelled in that great percentage of the globe which was little or never visited.

It is still possible to find libraries which stock large scale maps from before the First World War. In these maps, North India, Tibet, Nepal and Southwest China have large areas which are either just blank, or coloured purple to show the land is 'high'. Notes on the plans say that no knowledge of those areas is available. Imaginative recollection suggests they also had the phrase 'mountains and lakes liable to move'. That may not be true, but the blank maps give some idea of how much of our world was, around 1900, then unknown. Those areas were not only far from well travelled routes but also had peoples with differing and strange systems, social habits and allegiances.

For a time, Caerhays was central to the far off activities in South West China. J.C. Williams had already bought seeds collected in South West China when he started to finance such expeditions himself. The story of the expeditions and the scent of danger contrast with the quiet life of Caerhays after 1900.

Much botanic report concentrates on the recording of the plants and seeds found, but overlooks the adventures that were necessary to find the plant specimens. The first years of the 20thC were years when Burma and the unknown lands to its north and west were being opened up to travel. It was in 1904 that Britain made a little known and rather embarrassing invasion of Tibet under Brigadier Younghusband. One

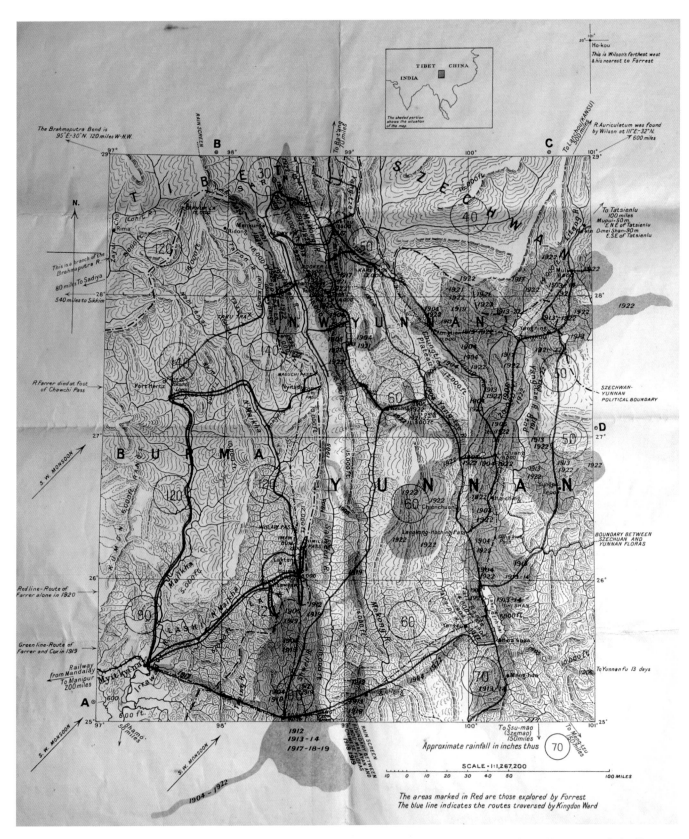

A larger scale map of Yunnan in SW China, which has been overprinted to show the dates and areas of expeditions not only by George Forrest, but also by R Farrer. A blue line marks the journeys of Kingdon Ward who operated from 1911 in the area George Forrest thought his own. The map also notes the nearest that the expeditions of Ernest Wilson came to that area frequented by George Forrest.
*Origin of map unknown: Caerhays archive.*

reason for that expedition was that Tibet and its adjoining areas were considered desperate unknown country. The plant hunting expeditions were taking place to the east of Tibet but also in areas that had never ever been visited by Europeans. Although most expeditions were well recorded and written up at the time, they still remain a relatively little known area of study.

Two plant hunters had particular connections with Caerhays.

George Forrest at the time of his first expedition

## E.H.Wilson (1876-1930)

Ernest Henry Wilson had the nickname Chinese Wilson because of his many expeditions to China, which was becoming known as a great untapped continent.

Wilson, brought up as a gardener in Gloucestershire, must have been of exceptional ability, because he quickly worked his way to botanic prizes and to jobs at the Royal Botanic Gardens at Kew. EH Wilson started traveling at the request of the nursery firm, James Veitch and Co, to find just one specific rare tree - the 'dove tree'. To us this sounds rather like an expedition to find a unicorn, but was for the botanists of the time an important issue.

On E.H. Wilson's first trip, he crossed the United States by train, sailed to Hong Kong and then went on up into China. He described this last section as "… it is a 600 Km walk away". He goes into no further detail, taking what must have been a lonely and dangerous adventure for granted. He spent two years in those isolated mountain valleys before returning from that first expedition in April 1902.

Wilson returned to continue his adventures. It was on the Min River in China on a third visit in 1910 that his leg was crushed by an avalanche of boulders when he was in a sedan chair; he set the leg himself with the tripod of a camera, before being carried back in a trek of three days to people who could reset the leg. It is the equable spirit in which this is reported that seems to me worthy of notice.

George Forrest: A formal picture of him as a young man.

It was following the trip made by Wilson to China, that, in 1903, JC Williams bought his first 25 chinese rhododendrons through the Veitch nursery in Exeter, with further purchases of chinese plants the same year This was to prove the start of a life long interest for JC in the plants and botany of the area. JC continued to purchase seedlings and products from Wilson's expeditions and Wilson's visit to Japan resulted in a complete collection of Kurume Azaleas being set at Caerhays by Wilson himself.

## George Forrest (1873-1932)

George Forrest made seven expeditions to the mountains of the east Himalaya range and his adventures were closely connected with Caerhays. He collected not only seeds and plant specimens, but also skins or the dried remains of butterflies, birds and small mammals. He recorded over 31,000 different plant specimens.

George Forrest was born in Scotland in 1873 and died in China in 1932. In his early life he learnt something of scientific analysis and recording while apprenticed to a local chemist. He must also have been an adventurer because when he suddenly inherited a small sum, he headed for Australia in hope of a fortune in the gold rush. He returned ten years later, having, it is said, found just one nugget. He had many adventures in Australia and talked happily about having travelled

George Forrest with his dog, in China

Eastern Flank of the Lichiang Range from camp at base of southern end, taken at an altitude of 9-10,000ft. Main Peak in centre hidden. June 1906

A side gorge of the Tali Range, eastern flank at 10,000ft looking west to backbone of range at about 14,000ft. Vegetation in foreground chiefly bamboo and rhododendron scrub. G Forrest 1906

Western Szechuan. Entrance to Chmochuen-ssu Temple, 3 miles outside North Gate of Chentu City, avenue of Cupressus funebris Endl. June 11 1908

Western Szechuan. Temple of Tao-ssu with Ficus infectoria Roxb., Min River, near Kiating Fu. May 5 1908. June 11 1908

Western Szechuan: Temple with bamboo and Nanmu Trees (Machillus Nanmu Hemsl.). Kuan Hsien. 2,700ft. June 16 1908

Western Szechuan. Hsuan-Kou. Typical riverine village of western Szechuan. 3,000ft. June 17 1908

Log of Tsuga yunnanensis Mast. 18ft 6in x 9in x 7in carried by one man over mountains! West of Kuan Hsion, June 19 1908

A page of photographs taken by George Forrest, selected from the enormous number of carefully annotated photographic records in JC Williams' archive at Caerhays.

hundreds of miles on horse-back, of living on what he had shot with his Winchester rifle from the back of his horse and also of times when he was near death from thirst when crossing deserts.

On his return, he was introduced to the Royal Botanic Garden, Edinburgh. It was the principal there, Sir Isaac Balfour who recommended that he go as a plant hunter to South West China.

A journey to South West China at that time involved sailing to Bombay, crossing the Indian continent, ignoring the problems of plague, and then using local boats for the next stage to Burma. The boats were extremely dangerous. Death from the failure or sinking of boats was as likely as a successful arrival. In 1886, Upper Burma was annexed to the British Indian Empire so that under the loose British control, you could travel right up the Irrawaddy river towards China, which was only some 35 miles from the river. But that 35 miles was only a mule track, which could take many days to pass. Passing on into China for weeks on end, the journey might average only 6 miles a day, and during such journeys guns were kept handy because of armed robbers, dacoits, or the local militia.

In a world where other plant collectors are murdered or vanish into the forests never to be seen again, Forrest said of one journey,

*'Heavy rain, flooded rivers, beastly roads, and fever... however with the exception of a slight depression at not being able to proceed I never felt better in my life'.* Some of his friends did not survive such journeys; one young European faced by a river with *'one of those horrible single rope bridges'* attempted to swim the river leading the mules, only to be dragged under and drowned.

The expeditions he undertook were adventures which few would now happily consider. The difficulties were many. He had to assemble people who would work with him and who could be trusted in a region that was unknown. The areas were mountainous with many deep valleys entirely covered with forests where isolated communities were exactly that, isolated and suspicious. The politics of the country were problematic. At one time, his life was in danger when warrior priests were killing not only foreigners but any local people who were suspected of having contact with them. During his first expedition (1904-7), there was a period when George Forrest travelled only by night, hid by day and nearly starved. His accounts of that starvation and of his recovery do not make pleasant reading. He managed to escape one place disguised as a Tibetan. He was plagued by diseases including malaria, by insects and, of course, by the sheer difficulty of crossing all the gorges, where bridges and tracks seemed unknown.

On his second expedition, China had been proclaimed a republic and in addition to the other problems endemic in the area, revolutionary troops, who Forrest called 'a band of undisciplined ruffians' were beheading people with no trial, which also meant there were mutinies amongst the people who worked with him.

Before one of the expeditions funded by J C Williams, there was discussion of the equipment to be taken. Apart from a number of guns and repeating pistols, there were oilskin coats and sou'westers, a camp bed, pillow, a rubber medicine chest and cases, axes and sheath knives and endless paper with which to make labels. Forrest also carried early photographic equipment and had to buy, wherever he went, sufficient tents, saddles and harnesses for any ponies he could find. Sadly, Forrest may record the day he shot his first wolf but never

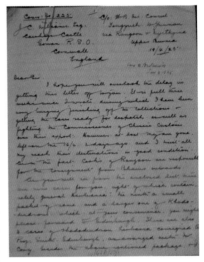

Part of one of many long letters to JC Williams from Balfour at the RBG Edinburgh

A letter from George Forrest to JC, dated 19 April 1905

A box of correspondence with George Forrest, from Caerhays

Western Szechuan: Tachien, one mile from the south. 8,400 ft July 23 1908

Western Szechuan: Men laden with 'brick tea' for Tibet. One man's load measures 317lbs avoird., the other's 298 lbs!! Men carry this tea as far as Tachienlu, accomplishing about 6 miles per day over vile roads. 5000ft. July 30 1908

Western Szechuan. View in ravine of the Tachien-lu River. This stream falls 4,000ft in less than 20 miles. 6,000ft. July 30 1908

The Lichiang Peak taken from the Lichiang valley. Altitude 8,500 ft looking north.Peak distant about 12 miles. May1910

The SW face of the Lichiang Peak, distant 3-4 miles. at 17,000ft the main peak being about 20,000ft. July 1910

Small lake on the summit of the Sungkwei Pass, looking NW with Rhododendron forest on left and oak forest on right. Sungirwei Range. 12-13,000 ft.  November 1910.

Another portion of Rhododendron Forest on the Sungkwei pass. 1910

A second page of photographs taken by George Forrest, selected from the annotated records at Caerhays.

wrote a proper record of his journeys. Those diaries and letters which have survived, tell of hazardous trips up cliff valleys, of problems with mule horses, of difficulties in persuading people to come with him, of persuading his team that they would not die from mountain spirits, of hearing that friends he had made had been slaughtered and their hearts torn out. The letters have a flavour of sangfroid: *'I had a very hot and dusty journey up from Bhamo and with my usual luck just missed trouble on the way...Kangnan...had just been attacked and looted by a body of brigands some 400 strong..[despite soldiers arriving to defend] them, a right good scrap ..included 12-14 soldiers dead and 2 couriers dead and one lying dangerously sick at some point on the road'*. There is no proper record either of the hours that must have been spent in cataloguing, preparing, drying and packing specimens for shipment to England.

Pages from specimen records, annotated by JC.

It is notable that single minded dedication to plants meant that he ignored, or did not report, much that would now be of interest. There is little information on his friends and the chinese he worked with so long, nor on how he established a wide network of collectors over a considerable area. He was single minded in his pursuit of plants alone. He wrote dismissively of Kingdon Ward, another collector, for taking an interest in other aspects of the country besides botany.

The photographs are many, and of fine quality. They are an extraordinary record and the albums of black and white or sepia pictures are labelled and detailed with great care. The records of plants were no doubt essential. However it is notable that there are relatively few pictures of the people with whom he spent time. A print of a man on a hill top is not only blurred but unannotated, and one has the feeling that little was of importance unless it included a plant with a latin name. The records include carefully typed analytical notes on plant types, but almost no reference to the fascinating culture and buildings of the country, now a lost world about which we would love to know more.

JC kept printed and bound record books not only of George Forrest's expeditions but also of his own plants and propagation, including such titles as 'Chinese Plants at Caerhays and Werrington'.

The adventures of Forrest in South West China are worth reading about and are given more detail in Brenda McLean's book.

Although it was JC's interest in plants that led to their meeting and to JC becoming the sole financier of Forrest's third expedition and although plants were the primary focus of this finance, their friendship and perhaps the excitement in these trips may have been as important as the scientific skill and success of the explorations. The impression one has from reports of the expeditions and from the correspondence of J.C. Williams, is that this plant hunting provided a window to a world unknown to Edwardian England.

Underlying the relationship was the extent of J.C. Williams' investment. Forrest's third expedition of 1912-1915 cost JC £3,108.13s 6d, and JC went on to help fund the 4th, 5th, 6th and last expeditions to take the total to about £11,000. This was about a third of the cost of all Forrest's expeditions and life from 1904-1932. Although, therefore, it has been suggested that this is £400,000 in today's money, it should be more fairly compared with the buying power of money at a time when you could build a house for £400.00. The total of JC's investment in the expeditions might, therefore, be similar to the cost of 22 houses, or about £2,000,000.

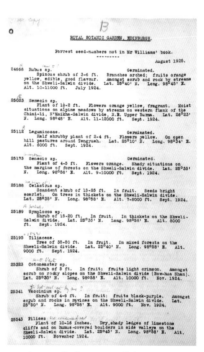

A sample from one of the many pages and schedules of Forrest's seed selections

However it was not just money that JC provided for Forrest. The two appear to have been genuine friends. JC provided a balance to the less equable Forrest and helped as a trusted intermediary for Forrest's business relationships in England.

This friendship and business partnership is attested to by the records, plant schedules, books and correspondence stored at Caerhays. The correspondence is voluminous; one box alone has 340 pages of letters from Forrest. Central to this correspondence was the mutual and genuine interest and knowledge of botany and plant breeding.

The correspondence is not however just about plants, but refers to other matters such as the competition among plant collectors, or the difficulties that Forrest encountered with societies and gardens in England. JC loved his visits to Scotland and the two seem to have shared a liking for wild country and a dislike of towns. Forrest wrote

*'I smiled when I read your opinion of London, for you have boiled it down quite to mine. Not for gold untold would I live in such a city. Even Edinburgh stinks in my nostrils. Humans when herded together in such small compass become impossible...'*

Their friendship, disguised by letters starting 'Dear Sir', survived formality and rigid protocols. Forrest would write of visits to missions, his concern about his own home, would tell of four men stripped, robbed and beaten and of a carrier murdered, while making acid comments on other botanists. He seems to have appreciated JC's support, writing *'It is indeed kind of you to send those cables for they give me much relief and encouragement'*, and on another occasion *'this is all one big growl, I know, but I must blow off to someone.'* At one time Forrest endured appendicitis, delaying an operation until the end of a trip in the countryside and during another illness wrote to JC *'during my illness [these] letters] gave me heart as little else could'.* This correspondence might refer to brigands or whether mail would get to England, to appalling roads, the weather, the rain, of difficulties in collection and of the organisation and numbering of species but would also tell of JC's holidays in Straithvaick.

JC was also helpful in the diplomacy required to organise expeditions for a prickly adventurer who found such discussions irritating, but who felt that he could write *'Please do not mention my plans to anyone'* and trust JC. The correspondence was never just about business. At the start of the First World War, J.C. Williams wrote to Forrest that *"It is hard to get away from the one subject for so long but it is certainly better to try... my sister's son went down in the Mauritius... all our four boys are in it somewhere".* Two of J.C. Williams' sons died in the war and it is possible that Williams sought relief from worries of the First World War and his family in the garden.

The correspondence was voluminous and masked a genuine friendship, but it remained formal. It takes two to correspond and although the letters are those of professional equals and friends, they are also reminders of a more formal age.

Forrest appears to have appreciated his connection with JC. In 1916, Forrest wrote *'The number of novelties [new species] will be well over 100, I feel sure, but in my opinion the credit is mostly yours for without you nothing would have been done. I do not mean the financing alone of the expedition, [but] your kindly encouragement and assistance given so freely to me was a far greater asset and helped me over very rough spots'.* For his part, JC Williams was happy with the connection with George Forrest and wrote in 1919 to Balfour, the director of the Royal Botanical Gardens in Edinburgh,

Western Szechuan: Popular Tree 60 x 10ft. West of Romi-Chango. 8,400ft. July 3 1908

Lao Chao, Forrest's headman, 5th from right, and 9 collectors with stacks of drying papers, ready roped to wooden mule saddles around 1920.
*(Courtesy George Forrest Photo Library)*

Packing cases of seeds and specimens for JC Williams of Caerhays ready for dispatch from China in 1914

'*Where Forrest serves us so well is in the iron way in which he battles to get the seed when most men would abandon the task as hopeless...*' J.C. Williams genuinely admired him, as he said, '*Forrest has his faults like the rest of us, but as far as the work he undertakes to do, his capacity, his energy and his knowledge are what we shall hardly see again in anyone*'.

Among the plants found in South West China were new varieties of rhododendrons and it was they that seemed to have been of particular interest to J.C. Williams. At a meeting of the Rhododendron Society on 6th May 1925, J.C. said: 'Perhaps we are not all quite sane on the subject of rhododendrons'.

The gardens of Caerhays now share a flora with the valleys of South West China. Forrest described this as an area of

'*Roads of no kind, deep jungle choked and panther haunted gorges, bounded by break neck precipices and dense forests of the lower altitudes... boulder strewn marshy moor lands with snow drifts and eternal mists... a chaos of screes, ragged peaks and glaciers with however flowers dominant everywhere*'. This was a country where for George Forrest, '*the sun, as it touches the tops of Mekong Divides, sends shards of turquoise light down the side gullies to the river which seems to be transformed to silver*'.

It is only some eighty years since the last extraordinary adventures of Forrest, who must be seen not just as a botanist but as an explorer, adventurer and risk taker. The connection of Forrest and other plant hunters with Caerhays reminds us that behind this great garden there has been a world of effort and discovery.

Tiger-leaping Gorge, SW China, in a view typical of the area travelled by plant hunters.

Francis Julian Williams
*Portrait by Rodger McPhail*

Francis Julian Williams
in his garden

# Chapter 15
# Charles Williams and his successors

## Charles Williams (1886-1955)

John Charles Williams' eldest son, Charles, married Mary Bolitho in 1915 and thereafter lived at Greenway in Devon. Greenway was subsequently owned by Agatha Christie and has recently been given to the National Trust. Charles and Mary had no children. Charles did not move to Caerhays until JC died in 1939.

Much of his time was spent in the House of Commons, where he was Deputy Speaker and a Privy Councillor. Charles was MP for Tavistock 1918-1922 and Torquay 1923-1955. His achievement in the House of Commons and the respect in which he was held were honoured by the offer of a baronetcy in 1934 and a peerage in 1945, both of which he turned down.

His other great interest was Scotland and stalking. He bought Glen Quoich in 1920 as a stalking lodge and forest and also rented Cluanie forest which was next door to it. He purchased a third forest, Barrisdale in 1950 which was only accessible by boat from Kinloch Hourn. In his life he stalked and killed 3,111 stags, a remarkable feat which is unlikely to be equalled by any individual even with modern transport.

Charles and Mary Williams in Coronation dress

Charles was also a keen hybridiser of rhododendrons and a determined competitor at RHS shows. During the Second World War, he kept the brambles in the garden at bay, and without those personal efforts with a scythe the garden might well have become overrun when the estate was denuded of its staff.

During the war Caerhays was home and school to 24 evacuee children from the East End of London. For these evacuees, the war must have been always present. It is often forgotten that Plymouth is only just over the horizon. News from London was not good and the war never seemed far away. One evacuee collected the mail from the Portholland post office and brought it to the governess at the castle to read. In it was a letter from the War Office saying that his family had all died in the Blitz.

Other evacuees had happier memories. The most famous of these was Harold Pinter, the playwright, but several of these Caerhays evacuees made successful careers overseas and have remained in contact.

This was the second war through which Charles had lived, a fact that emphasises the changes he saw during his lifetime.

A reminder of Charles Williams' work at Westminster shows him striding behind Churchill's right shoulder on a formal occasion.

At the start of the First World War, Charles had enjoyed nearly thirty years of the life associated with the wealth and property responsibilities of an earlier era. He was cousin to countless competent Williamses, many with great houses, great gardens or estates. He was at the centre of a network of businessmen, travellers, soldiers, and administrators and of a family with a long history of public service. Although Charles and Mary sadly had no children, this was not typical of his relations, who had large families. In the period at the end of the 19thC, several Williams families had ten or more children, ensuring a quantity of Williamses survived the generations. A younger child of one branch of the family that was, in 1906, 'sent to the colonies', was just one of a network of enterprising family members spread around the world. Colonel G.T.G. (Toots) Williams has recorded much about this extended family, with stories of travel, foreign investments, and Williams activities, hobbies, houses and by-ways. En masse, the Williams family are a formidable bunch. In Charles' time they may no longer have owned banks, but they were still at the centre of the country's political government. During the Second World War, Williamses fought with distinction on a number of different fronts; some were taken prisoner of war, some did not survive. Colonel Williams' extensive research records not only many adventures but also the businesses, hobbies and life interests of the family, which nearly always seem to have included gardens as well as country sports. Hunting and horses were once a common interest of the family, but the principal feature that has remained supreme throughout the last century has been a devotion to shooting. Meticulous shooting diaries have recorded a century of shooting not only in Cornwall, but around the world. Caerhays has continued the family tradition and now arranges shooting, although today, this inevitably includes a commercial approach.

Charles Williams lived through a great period of change. He inherited Caerhays at the beginning of the Second World War, and had to deal not only with death duties, taxes and great changes in business fortune, but also with the scattering of his close family, the diminution of the Williams estates, wealth and influence and great uncertainty about the future.

## Julian Williams

When Charles died in 1955, Julian Williams had not expected to inherit Caerhays. Julian, who had been President of the Cambridge Union in 1947, had begun a career as a politician and had already been adopted for a safe Conservative seat in Plymouth. In 1956, he married Delia Ferne Marshall, one of the formidable daughters of Captain Campbell Marshall from St Mawes.

However, with inheritance of Caerhays came the second mammoth bill for Death Duties in 15 years. This took the estate's available cash, and required capital sales. Even then it was only with the help of a Williams uncle, Peter Michael Williams of Burncoose, that the bill could be met.

Sales to help pay the tax included the whole Glen Quoich estate, part of which, with the lodge, had been submerged under 100 feet of water for Scotland's first hydro electric dam. The stalking and the estate were ruined and, although Charles had fought the plans all the way to the House of Lords, the compensation was derisory.

Evacuees to Caerhays 1939-1945
The group includes the playwright
Harold Pinter

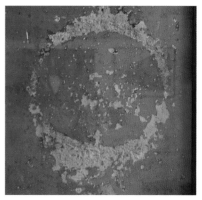

The marks left by the evacuees'
dartboard have been retained as a
memento of their stay.

Delia Williams and her son,
Charles Williams

Delia and Julian with their sons
Charles and David

The difficulties faced by Julian Williams when he inherited the Caerhays Estate in 1955 were not only the massive 'death duties', but also the costs necessary to modernise an estate which, although updated before the First World War, now needed complete renovation. The early 1960s also saw the demise of the outdoor privy and the arrival of bathrooms in estate cottages. These works have been a necessary but continual drain on the resources of the family.

Julian had no practical training in gardening or horticulture. He had been brought up at Werrington Park which has a fine Chinese garden but, as the youngest of three children in a family where male entail was the norm, he had not paid much attention to either plants or shooting. Nevertheless he quickly took up the challenge of the garden at Caerhays and, with the help and support of Philip Tregunna, the head gardener, he taught himself all that he needed to know from textbooks and garden archives.

Julian Williams leading the judges procession, as High Sheriff

He passed on this knowledge to his son Charles Williams who, as a small boy, was often forced to observe endless rhododendron leaves under the microscope. Charles has never since been able to forget how to tell an ellipidote (hairy) variety from a lepidote (scaly) one. However, life was not all botany lessons, since the children were always encouraged to escape to the garden which could nearly always involve a little more action.

Although Julian had no involvement with placing out or planting in the garden, he inherited the family's enduring ability to absorb and enjoy large numbers of detailed facts very quickly. His ideas about new hybridisation possibilities and his knowledge of the historical facts surrounding the discovery of Chinese plants were immense. Woe betide the visitor who attempted to catch him out on a plant name or the parentage of a rhododendron hybrid.

This sheriff's uniform was used by both Rt Hon. Charles Williams and by his nephew, Julian. Although other members of the family have since also been sheriff, the uniform would not fit any current member of the family.

As with previous generations Julian soon became involved in local politics and community affairs. He stood first as an independent for Cornwall County Council in 1964, retiring 22 years later, having been chairman for the last nine years. During that time the opposition never required him to fight an election either for his seat or as chairman. This is a truly remarkable record and a tribute to Julian Williams, who was later granted the CBE.

His other duties included 19 years' service on the Prince's Council, a position of particular relevance and interest to Cornwall.

However it is not just for public service that the Williams' of the 20thC should be remembered. They retained their commitment to the public enjoyment of the landscape of Cornwall, the most notable and often forgotten example being their purchase of the land and cliffs of the Dodman and the Nare, specifically and only so that they could then be given to the National Trust. Many have given land to such institutions, few have gone to the extreme of buying outstanding landscape in order to immediately give it away.

## Charles Williams and a new century

Julian Williams' son, Charles, was happily ensconced in London and working as a merchant banker when the opportunity arose to move back to Cornwall and live at Burncoose. This may not have seemed a difficult choice when comparing Clapham and Cornwall as places to bring up children, but it was still a huge decision for Charles and his family.

Delia and Julian Williams

From the early '70s, Charles had taken over the decisions on planting and setting out in the garden. Then, as Julian became more deeply involved with the affairs of the County Council, the Prince's Council, the Prince's Trust, the Young Farmers and numerous other local interests, Charles took over more and more of the day to day running of the estate, particularly with a decline in Julian's health as he neared retirement. It also seemed essential to try to diversify the estate's business away from being simply a traditional landed estate, particularly at a time when agriculture was becoming more unprofitable. The new management was not concerned just with the operation of the existing estate, but with trying to develop and improve its business base for the future.

Despite Julian's attempts to keep his mind active in retirement, ill health has prevented him completing the sorting and recording of all the personal family archives on which he had started work, and much therefore remains to be done. Life for Julian and his wife Delia became much more difficult when, from 2003, Delia was confined to a wheelchair. Julian's interest in the management of the estate declined.

The battle to keep the roof intact and the bank manager at bay has therefore been shared between two generations for much of the last 30 years. Although the continuing business of Caerhays will no doubt remain just as much a problem for future generations, it is hoped that current management and diversification will provide a base on which the next generation can build.

Charles Williams' coming of age party for staff, tenants and friends of the estate, 1st September 1978

A family celebration of John Williams' 21st birthday, shows three generations of the Williams family of Caerhays on 1st September 2008. *Photo Jaimie Parsons*

Julian Williams

Charles, Lizzie, John & Serena Williams

Serena Williams and John Williams, the next generation

# Chapter 16
## The Williams Mineral Collection

Cornwall became a leader in mining and the extraction of metals from rock by the end of the 18thC. Mine owners and amateur scientists therefore assembled great collections of minerals, the best known being that early Rashleigh collection which is now in the Royal Institution of Cornwall. The Williams family ranked alongside the greatest of those collectors and established a collection which not only represented Cornwall, but contained specimens from many parts of the world.

Minerals are found in the rocks of which our earth is made. Rocks themselves are natural aggregates or combinations, usually of one or more minerals. Minerals are therefore component parts, which have been divided for classification and study into a number of different groups.

A visitor to Cornwall is familiar with the rugged granite hills and granite buildings of the county. Granite is an igneous rock where the three biggest components are minerals which can be seen with the naked eye. The grey areas are quartz, the pink and white pieces are feldspars and the brown/black is mica. The variation in combination and the addition of other components is what gives granite that variety of texture and colour so well known in Cornwall. About 450 mineral species have been found in Cornwall and West Devon, which is more than in any other region of the British Isles.

The study of minerals arose first for tin mining and then for the more important copper. Both could be found as mineral lodes in rock formations and strata, and the mining engineers' understanding of the strata and minerals was important to mining business. For tin, there are only about forty minerals, most of which are rare, and of which only a few exist in Cornwall. *Cassiterite*, an oxide of tin with 78% tin is the most important. In contrast to tin there are several hundred copper bearing minerals, although not all of them exist in Cornwall. A study of minerals helps the geologist understand rock formations and the processing of useable content.

The amateur can understand that minerals are often the interesting elements of any rock formation, although few may have seen or appreciated the glory and variety, the splendour or the bright colours, the crystals and formation, the shapes of the multitude of different mineral samples. Minerals were extracted not only for their importance to mining businesses, but also for the delight that their colour and variety could give. A collection can reflect almost

Courtenay Smale, curator, holding a superb Azurite from Chessy-les-Mines, France

Liroconite - Wheal Gorland, Gwennap

Clinoclase - Wheal Gorland, Gwennap
A globular mass of curved blue-black crystals

all the materials of which the Earth is made and their range can be astonishing.

## The Origin of the Collection.

The Mineral Collection at Caerhays was assembled between 1780 & 1890 by generations of the Williams family.

The first important specimens were probably gathered by John Williams (1753-1841). John Williams was a mine agent, adventurer, copper and tin smelter and banker, and by 1783 was managing a number of copper mines in Gwennap. In 1799 he was not only the agent for about twenty two copper mines in Cornwall but also an adventurer in Wheal Gorland, Wheal Jewel, Wheal Hope, Tresavean and other mines in the area. He bought the Manor of Calstock in 1806 and the Old Gunnislake Mine, Calstock in 1825, from which many of the finest uranium-bearing Torbernite specimens were recovered. After his move from Burncoose to Scorrier House (built in 1778), this part of the family mineral collections was housed at Scorrier. In 1828 John Williams retired from business and settled at Sandhill, Calstock, until his death.

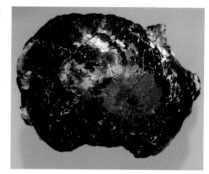

Clinoclase from Wheal Gorland, Gwennap. Believed to be the largest composite crystal of Clinoclase worldwide.

His eldest son, also called John, (1777-1849) F.R.S., Fellow of the Linnean Society, added considerably to the collection. John Williams Senior and his three sons, John, Michael, and William Williams, were all members of the Royal Geological Society of Cornwall, formed in 1814. John Williams Junior contributed many fine copper specimens to the Rashleigh Collection from the 1790s to the early 1800s. He had much more than a passing interest in minerals and geology and was elected an honorary member of the Geological Society in 1807, contributing to the transactions of that Society in 1817 through a paper entitled, "Account of some remarkable Disturbances in the Veins of the Mine called Huel Peevor, in Cornwall". In 1828 he was elected a fellow of the Royal Society.

Chalcophyllite - Wheal Gorland, Gwennap
Brilliant hexagonal plates

The early connection of the Williams family with the Gwennap area was perhaps fortuitous, but it helped them become the most important family in the area, and eventually, to mining interests and connections world wide. The introduction of high-pressure steam engines to facilitate the dewatering of mines opened up Cornwall's metalliferous mining areas, particularly the "copperbelt" of Gwennap. Amazing as it may seem, the mines in the parish of Gwennap were claimed, in the early 19thC, to be 'the richest square mile in the world'. Copper was widely distributed throughout Cornwall, but nowhere in the County has the variety and quality of secondary minerals matched those from the parish of Gwennap. By the very nature of their occurrence, these rare copper minerals, many in the form of copper arsenates, remain unmatched worldwide to this day and are top of many a collector's wish list.

The Williams collection benefited not only from the interest of the family in collecting specimens, but also from their business connections, ability to obtain specimens at home and overseas, and from their unique position in the mining activities of Cornwall. Although a collection provided a talking point for visitors to the house, it was also true that such a display of minerals allowed the owner of the country house to make a statement about the family wealth.

Connellite, Wheal Gorland, Gwennap;
close up showing azure-blue needles.

## Classification

However, the collection was assembled before the establishment of the broader science of mineralogy. The collections were not therefore systematic, but instead the minerals were classified by their physical appearance rather than by analysis or content.

A fierce debate on the origins of the earth had gathered pace in the eighteenth century, the two combatant theories being Plutonism and Neptunism. The former considered that the Earth originated from volcanoes whilst the latter favoured the oceans as the provider of the earth's rocks and minerals. Eventually the Plutonists won the argument.

The descriptions of minerals in the Williams Collection therefore relied on the limited knowledge of the day. Most present-day mineral names were unknown and mineralogists used the physical and chemical properties to record their specimens. The physical properties of colour, lustre, hardness, specific gravity and crystal form coupled with limited wet chemistry analyses were the means by which specimens were categorised. Chemical analyses were often qualitative rather than quantitative. *Lustre*, for example, is a measure of a mineral's reflecting properties, depending on its refraction, transparency and structure. Lustre might therefore have been further described as Adamantine (like diamond), Dull, Metallic, Pearly, Resinous, Silky, Vitreous (like glass), or Waxy.

A classic example of the transition in identifying and naming minerals is that of the mineral known today as Chalcophyllite. In 1801 the French mineralogist, Count de Bournon, described the mineral from Huel Gorland as an Arseniate of Copper in hexahedral laminae, with inclined sides. It was also formerly known as Tamarite, in recognition of its early discovery in the mines of the Tamar Valley.

## Later History

The mineral collection at Scorrier grew to be very large, and ranked alongside those of Philip Rashleigh (1729-1811) of Menabilly, and Joseph Carne (1782-1858) as one of the three finest in Cornwall, receiving frequent mention in the journals of the time. Dr John Ayrton Paris, the physician/author, referred to the Scorrier House collection in 1816, remarking on the magnificence of the Cuprite, Arseniates of Copper, and the Torbernite from Old Gunnislake Mine.

In 1817 Charles Sandoe Gilbert went so far as to comment in his "An Historical Survey of the County of Cornwall"

*"Scorrier contained the most valuable variety of mineral specimens of any house in Europe".*

Robert Allan wrote in his journal of a tour through Cornwall in 1824. *"We went to see Mr. Williams' Collection at Scorrier. He gives good prices and gets the best minerals. The old collection is a family one, extensive, and rich in red Coppers - a pity that John Williams Senior is living at Sandhill, and John Williams Junior at Burncoose as the minerals are in no sort of order and are much destroyed for want of some person to take care of them".*

In his 1828 version of "A Guide to the Mount's Bay and the Land's End" Allan made the following observation under the heading 'The Cabinet of John Williams Esq.'

*"...Scorrier House, about two miles east of Redruth, ... may therefore be visited by the mineralogist in the present excursion. This collection*

Connellite - Wheal Gorland, Gwennap
A superb specimen portraying brilliant azure-blue needles

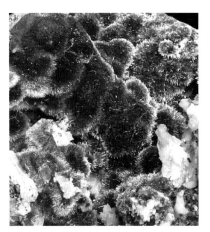

Olivenite - Wheal Gorland or Wheal Unity, Gwennap

Pharmacosiderite - Wheal Gorland or Wheal Unity, Gwennap
Bottle-green cubes

Scorodite - Wheal Gorland or Wheal Unity, Gwennap

*stands unrivalled in the magnificence of its specimens of Red Oxide of Copper, in octahedrons, cubes, and capillary crystals; it also contains the finest specimens of Arseniate of Copper in very perfect obtuse octahedrons; a mass of Uranite, which in size and beauty is superior to any specimens ever discovered; Blende, in octahedrons and cubes; Native and Ruby Silver; and a specimen of the Muriate of that metal (Horn Silver) so well known for its value that it may be said to constitute one of the most interesting objects in the collection. The Arseniate of Lead, in six-sided prisms, a most beautiful mineral, which was first analysed by Mr. Gregor, and has been found only in Huel Unity, may be seen in this cabinet in its most perfect forms".*

Chalcotrichite - Gwennap
A variety of Cuprite in fine capillary crystals

The collection was particularly rich in Cuprite, Liroconite, Clinoclase, Chalcophyllite, and Pharmacosiderite, all from Wheal Gorland - a veritable treasure chest of rare minerals.

There is also a fine series of Cassiterite from mines all over Cornwall, and Cerussite from the Pentire Glaze Mine, St. Minver. The latter was found in abundance in 1818 and the finest examples were hand-carried to Scorrier to avoid damage, the crystals being up to ten inches in length and extremely delicate.

Pyromorphite - Wheal Alfred, Phillack
Yellowish-green hexagonal crystals

John Williams Junior added many fine specimens from other parts of the British Isles and some foreign minerals, including a fine series of Azurite from Chessy-les-Mines, France. Later additions were made by John Michael Williams (1813-1880). These included the collection of John Taylor, mining engineer, in 1863.

The Wills of some members of the Williams family specifically refer to the minerals. The Will of John Williams, died 11th August 1849, late of Burncoose, states:

*"I give to my beloved Wife all plate furniture wine minerals in the house and stock on the farm..." In the event of his wife's death he states: "I give and bequeath to my Brother Michael Williams... the minerals at Scorrier during his life and after his decease to his son, John Michael Williams and his heirs for ever".*

The Will of John Michael Williams, died 16th February 1880, late of Caerhays Castle, Burncoose and Pengreep, states:

*"I give and bequeath to such one of my sons as shall attain the age of twenty one years and under the limitation hereinbefore contained shall become tenant for life of my said mansion houses at Burncoose and Caerhays Castle to which son I also give and bequeath all my minerals".*

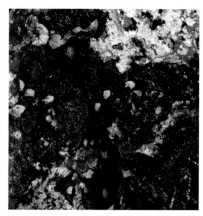

Turquoise, variety 'Henwoodite'
West Phoenix Mine, Linkinhorne

## Donations from the collection.

In 1863, the collections were moved from Scorrier House to Caerhays Castle. Then, in 1891 John Michael Williams' son, John Charles Williams, donated several thousand specimens from the Caerhays Collection to the Mining School at Camborne. They were placed in special cases presented by Mr. Williams, in the Basset Memorial Museum attached to the Mining School.

Two years later, in 1893, J. C. Williams decided to disperse the main collection, which still contained some 10,000 specimens, planning to retain only 300 items for himself. He invited the British Museum (Natural History), the Royal Institution of Cornwall, and the Robert Hunt Memorial Museum, Redruth, to visit him to select minerals for their collections.

J. C. Williams first wrote to Lazarus Fletcher, Keeper of Minerals

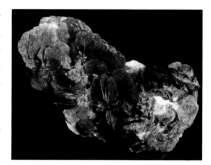

Torbernite -
Old Gunnislake Mine, Calstock
Composite rosettes of platy crystals,
formerly known as Chalcolite

in the Mineralogy Department of the British Museum (Natural History), on 26 May 1893:

*"I have here certain minerals which I am prepared to present each a portion of as you may select to the South Kensington Museum. I am taking out certain representative bits for retention in the family, and the remainder, (a very considerable amount) you could select from for your museum."*

This out of the blue windfall offer was acknowledged by Fletcher the following day. He thanked Mr. Williams and set out in detail the professional care the minerals would receive once accessioned into the Mineral Department. J. C. Williams was obviously impressed by Fletcher's detailed comments and replied on 30 May 1893:

*"I fear that you will find things in a sad mess here, but I have no doubt that amongst a lot of rubbish you will find some things which will repay the journey. It is my intention to give what you may not consider worth your moving to the Redruth Museum."*

Lazarus Fletcher and Henry Miers arrived at Caerhays on 8 June 1893 and proceeded to select and pack the minerals over the next few days. 510 specimens were packed in eight boxes and dispatched via the Great Western Railway's goods train on 13 June. Following confirmation from Fletcher that the specimens had arrived safely at South Kensington, J. C. Williams wrote on June 23 to *"ask however that my name is not placed on the things but if it is necessary to put something it should be a statement that they are from the collection of the late J M Williams."*

The national collection at the Natural History Museum, South Kensington, would be much the poorer were it not for John Charles Williams' benevolence in 1893.

Minerals were then given to both the Royal Institution of Cornwall's Museum and to the Robert Hunt Memorial Museum's Collection. Sadly, many of those items are no longer identifiable as from the Williams Collection, since they are without labels and the recipients lacked professional accessioning procedures.

The Robert Hunt Collection was transferred to the Camborne School of Mines in 1950, and to quote Sir Arthur Russell, the most important mineral collector of British Minerals in the 20th Century, the minerals were *"mixed with a jumble of other specimens in a sea of confusion"*.

## The Collection Today.

The present collection at Caerhays includes a number of specimens and labels acquired from dealers, based both in England and in mainland Europe. The style of the labels places them in the period between 1860 and the 1880s. The English suppliers include Samuel Henson of the Strand, London, Bryce-Wright of Great Russell Street, London, Thomas J Downing of London, and William Peters of Redruth, Cornwall. European suppliers of specimens include Emile Bertrand of Paris, Felix Pisani of Paris, and Dr. L Eger of Vienna.

In 2008, Charles Williams decided to reinstate a display of the Caerhays minerals. The post-1893 remnants of the former collection had been dispersed to a number of locations within Caerhays Castle. There appear to have been no printed 'Williams Collection' specimen labels at either Scorrier House or Caerhays Castle and, despite a comprehensive search, no mineral catalogue of any description has

Cerussite- Pentire Glaze Mine, St. Minver. White prisms known by miners as 'Jack Straw' crystals

Cassiterite - Wheal Coates, St Agnes Pseudomorphs of Cassiterite after Orthoclase.

Cassiterite - Dolcoath Mine, Camborne 'Sparable Tin' crystals

Buornonite, Herodsfoot Mine, Lanreath. Classic 'cogwheel' crystals on white quartz.

been located at Caerhays to date (2010). The challenge to assess the collection was a daunting one. However, examining the minerals has been a revelation.

Drawer after drawer of small cabinet size specimens gave rise to mixed emotions of excitement and disappointment - excitement in seeing many fine specimens in sound condition, tempered by disappointment in the condition of many other items which had suffered inadequate curatorship for decades. The sulphides appear to have suffered most, with many trays exhibiting nothing more than the powder of decomposed minerals. These were isolated from the collection and disposed of post-haste. Unfortunately, the damage was not solely confined to the minerals.

Very few specimens have labels giving their locality. Original labels had been rendered brittle and decomposed by chemical action in such a hostile environment and were impossible to preserve. Other surviving labels had become separated from their minerals. On a positive note, many minerals were in card trays with accompanying labels and appeared to have suffered little damage.

A second collection of minerals is housed in 16-drawer specimen cabinets supplied by the renowned furniture manufacturers, Howard and Sons, of Berners Street, London. These contain a fine selection of miniature size metalliferous minerals, arranged in accordance with their metallic elements. Some 1400 samples are accommodated in drawers with 100 compartments per drawer. The specimens carry pink labels with printed numbers. That this part of the Williams Mineral Collection has been carefully numbered and arranged is testament to the likelihood of there having been a corresponding catalogue or list. The search continues to locate such a document in the archives at Caerhays.

A third, more important, cache of minerals was discovered in the wine cellar. Although this was an environment appropriate for the storage of Bacchus' nectar, it was potentially damaging to the survival of mineral specimens. The specimens were piled, unwrapped, five or six high in wooden and cardboard boxes. What at first appeared to be a 'lost cause' in retrieving the specimens became progressively rewarding. Cabinet size specimens have been found of secondary Cornish copper, lead, iron, and uranium in the form of Chalcophyllite, Clinoclase, Liroconite, Olivenite, Connellite, Pharmacosiderite, Scorodite, Cerussite, Pyromorphite, and Torbernite, together with the suite of fine Azurite specimens from Chessy-les-Mines, Rhône, France.

These were the very same minerals that learned visitors to Scorrier House wrote about in glowing terms almost two centuries ago. Specimen after specimen of museum quality rose out of the water-sodden boxes and, after careful cleaning and identifying, has created the nucleus of the current display in the Caerhays Museum. Although the Williams Collection was not a systematic one and had considerable duplication of items, that representation in depth has in many ways been a blessing. The rare suite of secondary copper minerals from Gwennap, with all its duplication, is what has made the collection both unique and of great importance in the annals of Cornish Mineral Collecting.

JC Williams was generous in his gifts to museums. In Cornwall it is fortunate that the Royal Institution of Cornwall has so large and well set out a display, much of which is in cabinets given by JC

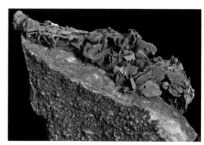

Chalcocite - Probably from Tincroft Mine, Illogan

Chalcedony - Trevascus Mine, Gwinear

Gold- 3 nuggets, probably from Cornwall, and an assay button

Fluorite - Bere Alston, Devon

Campylite from Dry Gill Mine,
Caldbeck Fells, Cumbria

Hematite - St. Gotthard,
Uri, Switzerland
Classic 'eisenrose' form.

Aquamarine, a variety of Beryl-
Nerchinsk, E. Siberia, Russia.

Mimetite from Dry Gill Mine,
Caldbeck Fells, Cumbria

Topaz on smoky quartz -
Siberia, Russia

Quartz showing parallel crystal growth
- from the collection at Caerhays.

Quartz, variety 'Amythest',
lining a geode

Epidote - Knappenwand,
Salzburg, Austria

Topaz - Nerchinsk, E. Siberia, Russia

Opal, a Boulder Opal -
Queensland, Australia.

Williams in 1905, JC having earlier been president of the Institution. That collection contributes to the achievement for which we should honour JC.

At Caerhays, the Williams mineral collection contains specimens which were probably the best from one that once contained over 14,000 items. This collection of outstanding specimens has not been seen in living memory, so that although it has long existed, it now provides all the excitement of a new discovery. The selection at Caerhays attempts to give some idea of the variety and scope of the samples.

However, it is of interest not just to the geologist or mineral specialist, but also to the more general visitor to Caerhays. The displays therefore include charming items such as the four water worn gold nuggets, probably from the Carnon Valley or the great ropey mass of native silver. Other curiosities include the coin embedded in volcanic lava, a selection of cut and polished agates or that diamond crystal, whose lack of glamour in its natural form often disappoints the visitor.

At Caerhays there are some 400 specimens in the main collection and something over 1600 miniature specimens. Although this may not be as extensive as it once was, the range and quality of items is astonishing. The Williams Mineral Collection is not only exceptional, but is also a reminder of the success of the family's mining concerns, of their interest in the collection and of the support the family gave to the mineralogical and geological societies of Cornwall and England.

A coin embedded in lava from Vesuvius
This 'tornesi dieci' coin is from the
reign of Ferdinand 11 (1830-1839)

A diamond crystal
in conglomerate

A selection of cut and polished agates

19thC Mineral Crystal Clasps
used for display

A mineral display cabinet at Caerhays

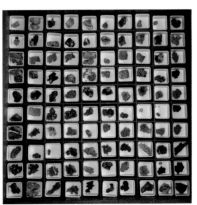

A drawer from the Howard & Sons
cabinets for smaller mineral samples

# Chapter 17
# Recipes from Caerhays

Until the end of the 18thC few recipes were written down. Methods of cooking were considered either common knowledge, or as the 'secret' trade and skill of the cook. Recipes were of no interest to the literate gentry and those who could read and write tended not to work in the trade of cook. We therefore have few records of what was eaten in the ordinary as opposed to grand households. Such recipes as survive are usually for meals of magnificence or the unusual. At Caerhays we are lucky to have recipes from several different eras.

## Young Sea Gulls: A Titbit from the 1580s

In his 1602 *Survey of Cornwall*, Richard Carew recorded foods that could be and were eaten in Cornwall. These included small and large birds, although he made the point that *'some carry a rank taste and require a former mortification, and some are good to be eaten when they are young, but nothing toothsome as they grow older.'* He explained that many gulls and sea birds, although incapable of breeding in captivity, nested on the grass of the sea shore *'without making any nests'*. Once hatched, the young were taken from their nests, fattened up and eaten.

A young Seagull: not to be eaten.
*Picture: Phoebe Herring*

*'The owner of the land causeth the young ones to be fetched about Whitsuntide for the first brood and some weeks after for the second. Some one, but not every such rock, may yield nearly thirty dozen of gulls. They are kept tame and fed fat......'*

Richard Carew goes on to describe how *'at Caryhayes, Mr Trevanion's house which bordereth on the cliff",* such gull chicks were kept housed in a 'court' or courtyard of his house as a source of summer food. This practice was presumably similar to that of many houses where young pigeon squabs were commonly farmed for food and for their down, fertilizer and pen quills.

We have tried to persuade someone to cook young gull chicks. However, not only is the species protected, but it seems likely that unless they have been fattened on grain, gull chicks are disgusting to eat. They continued to be eaten as a not uncommon food until a century ago, but only one person has been found who can remember this. They were not good memories.

Despite, therefore the rarity of this repast, and despite the close association with Caerhays, no recipe is included here.

## The Trevanion Cookbook

Early recipe books were not just for cooking, but also provided household care, medicines, furniture solutions and household repairs. Even the word *recipe* was not originally restricted to food, but meant a written note for providing any mixture, medical prescription or method of achieving some result.

The first so called cook books were therefore really manuals for a housekeeper, and it was in this tradition that Mrs Beeton published her first book, a book allegedly lifted from earlier books on housewifery.

One of the earliest of these household manuals was that called *'English Housewifry Exemplified'* by Mrs Elizabeth Moxon. Her book, published in 1764, has 450 recipes and among other things, notes on how to prepare *'various sorts of soops, made-dishes, pastes, pickles, cakes, creams, jellies, made-wines, etc....'*. This gives some idea of what were considered the important recipes.

The book was also described as *'a book necessary for mistresses of families, higher and lower women servants and confined to things useful, substantial and splendid and calculated for the preservation of health and upon the measures of frugality...'*

It is extremely fortunate that a similar and slightly earlier book exists at Caerhays. The Trevanion book has 394 recipes written out in beautiful copper plate.

Inscribed with the date 1759, it appears to have been written out for William Trevanion of Caerhays by 'JN'. A further inscription inside suggests it has been the property of E N T (for Trevanion). The book also has two other names from the 18thC, who might have been the housekeepers who used the recipes.

The pages of this book are delightful. They move from a recipe for soup, to a method of re-powdering a wig; from a linament to several cures for those bitten by a mad dog; from methods of making scents to methods of curing ham. Recipes for wine mixtures, biscuits, for 'a gangreen in any part'.. for 'the diet drink'

This is a fascinating mixture, and we hope that one day a facsimile will be produced. The book is amongst the earliest of this type of production and emphasises the interest of the householder in cures, ills, smells and practical housework. It also reminds us that the bite of a mad dog was a serious concern.

The spelling and grammar is eccentric, and the terms introduce us to a world of now forgotten foods and household products. This was a world where foods and spices now available to us were only then becoming practical.

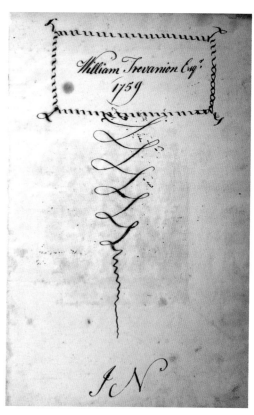

# Victorian, Edwardian and Country House Kitchens.

Some gentry houses have kept books or bundles of recipes, although not so many have survived as might be expected, because cooking recipes were considered the private information and secret of the cook. Surviving recipes do not provide as much information as might be expected on basic foods, on main courses, stews or every day cooking. Those that survive were often those kept by the Lady of the House, who did not of course cook for herself, but who wished to be able to offer specialities to guests or record some particular family favourite.

Since cooking was regarded as a specialist activity, it was the management of the cook that was seen as of importance. One has only to read the memoirs and records of the gentry through the last two centuries to realise how much of a mystery the work of the kitchen remained until after the Second World War. That war spelt the end of 'service' and of cooks. Where before the war, those employed 'in service' were a significant part of the working population, this had become almost insignificant by the time Queen Elizabeth came to the throne.

The recipes therefore tend to be the special or the extraordinary. Late Victorian recipes might include exotic starters (*take 12 cock lobsters*), soups for the invalid, recipes for many different scented waters, or for antimacasar mixtures, as well as for sweet puddings and sweet side dishes. Basic cooking for main courses was not listed unless you included the infinite ways for curing ham, or of dealing with offal.

One of the difficulties with choosing recipes for modern taste is that tastes have changed. The recipes that survive from the 19thC all tend to be too rich and too sweet for our taste.

More interesting at Caerhays is the evidence that an Edwardian approach to food and to everyday eating survived to just after the Second World War. The archives at Caerhays retain files on the applications and hiring of 'hall boys', that is, junior assistants to house staff, a job suitable for a 14, 15 or 16 year olds. None of those applications, with their references and assumptions about domestic work, could be understood today. Such employment and practices, although providing work and training for the young, would not be possible in our world of employment legislation and the dictates of the Health and Safety Czar. What is perhaps more extraordinary is to find that these advertisements for work at Caerhays date from just before, and from just after World War II, only some 70 years ago.

An Edwardian household refitted its great kitchen and provided the staff with new inventions for kitchens and housework. The illustrations show one or two of the curious implements that were once more common.

The magnificent range installed c.1900

Modern improvements:
A knife sharpener. A pottery urn.

Another example of modernisation was the wonderful patent drying room in the laundry, with its own boiler.

## The Daily Record

Another survival at Caerhays is the book that recorded the different meals cooked and served each day. Food was prepared not only for the owner and his family, but also for the staff and servants and to a separate room for the children. The illustrations are an example from 1946, chosen for the legible handwriting. It seems that 1946 may have been the last year in which the old system of recording continued.

Although there are no records of the recipes, the daily lists show that family and staff ate well. The meals seem to have been what might be called old fashioned or 'school' food, rather than imaginative cuisine.

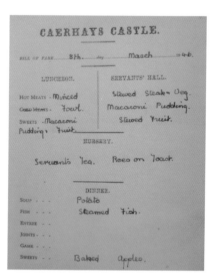

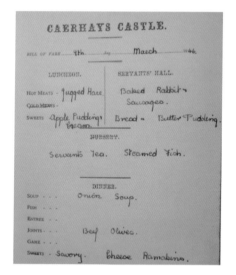

A week of eating at Caerhays in March 1946

## Two Recipes from the Trevanion Cookbook

The first, entitled 'My Grandmother's Cake' was written down in 1759, and so is probably a recipe of around 1710. Grammar and capitals have been rationalised. The mixture is very rich and the considerable quantities suggest it was intended either for a large household or for a feast day.

## My Grandmother's Cake

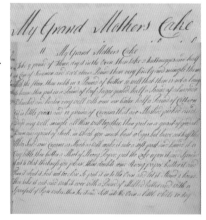

*Take a pound of flour, dry it in the oven, then take three nutt-megges and half a cane of sinamon and 5 or 6 cloves. Pound them very finely and mingle them with the flour. Then rubb in a pound of butter so well that there is not a lump to be seen; then put in a pound of loaf sugar grated, half a pound of almonds blanched and beaten very well with some rose water, half a pound of citron cut in little pieces and 12 pounds of currants that are mashed picked and dryd very well. Mingle all these well together then put in a quart of good ale barm and a pient of sack in which you must beat 10 eggs but leave out half the whites. Scald some creame as much as will make it into a soft paste and knead it a very little. Then butter a sheet of strong paper put the cake upon it and spread it out to what thickness you please. Then double some strong paper; butter it and pinn it about it but not too close So put it into the oven and let it stand 2 hours then take it out and wash it over with a pound of melted butter and with a spoonfull of rose water then Ice it and sett into the oven a little while to dry.*

Requirements:
1 lb of ordinary flour; 2 lb of full fat butter in two equal pieces
1 lb of castor sugar; 3 nutmegs; 1 stick of cinnamon; 6 cloves
½ lb by weight of blanched almonds
½ pint of rose water ½ lb of lemons or oranges
12 lbs of dried currants
2 pints of beer (the original ale would probably have had no hops)
A pint of sherry
10 eggs; Lightly heated full cream icing mixture as separate recipe.

My Grandmother's Cake

Susha Reynolds and Sian Thomas of Caerhays tried out the recipe but suggest amendments for modern taste and practice:

"We followed the recipe but halved the quantities. We guessed that 12lbs currants referred to the fresh weight, so we used 2 lbs of dried fruit (mostly currants). We also used ready ground almonds instead of the pounded blanched almonds. The rose water may have been important to help grind the almonds. After adding the sherry and a splash of rose water to wet the ground almonds, but adding only half of the beer, the mixture looked very wet. An extra ½ pound of flour was therefore added. We omitted the cream altogether. The mixture was still too liquid to bake on the suggested parchment paper, so we opted for a 9" square tin and baked in a moderate oven for 2 hours. Sian then "washed" the cake with a small amount of melted butter while it was still warm.

We were surprised to find that the end result was a perfectly acceptable, tasty cake!"

Susha Reynolds of Caerhays

A second recipe from the Trevanion Cookbook is for a 'sylla-bub'. These were exotic in the middle ages and a treat in the 18thC. This particular recipe is without fruit or base other than the wine and cream. Although simple to make, it may be strange to modern taste. It is one of many syllabubs in the book.

## To Make Whip Sillibubs

*Take a pint of white wine and sweeten it with a quarter of a pound of sugar. Strain it into a clean earthen pan then take a quart of cream and pour it high upon the wine, then take a piece of a swigg whiske and beat it up to a froth and as the froth comes let one take it with a spoon till your glasses be filled, keep them in a cool cellar till you use them.*

Requirements:
A pint of white wine;
Qtr pound of sugar;
A quart of Cream

Preparation:
There is no preparation needed, but you will need a strainer, and a hand whisk or egg beater. If you use an electrical mixer, take care not to over mix. Serve the mixture in flat wide wine glasses.
1. Mix a quarter lb of sugar with the wine
2. Strain the mixture so that there are no lumps. This may not be necessary if fine sugar is used.
3. Add a quarter of cream
4. Whisk the mixture until it starts to froth.
5. Immediately pour the mix into wine glasses.
6. Store in the refrigerator, or in a cool larder.
7. Remove from chilled storage to serve.
8. Since components are only cream and wine, decorate with one single grape.

This recipe is an easy way to make a very tasty, simple, good looking appetizer or sweet. The type and style of the wine, the 'secret' ingredient, can make quite a difference.
The end result is absolutely delicious.

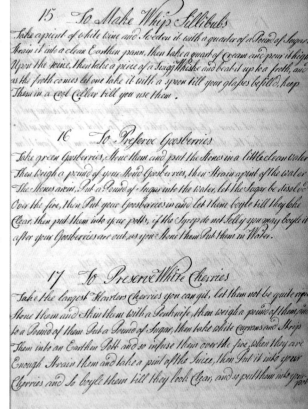

Sian Thomas of Caerhays who prepared the 'Whip Syllabubs'

# Chapter 18
# Caerhays Today

Modern Caerhays is not just a home but a complex of businesses which help maintain the estate. Despite the increased and varied activities, responsibilities to the estate do not change, although visitors to the estate are often unaware of much that is undertaken.

The first in any list of activities is probably maintenance. With responsibility for a great building goes the necessity to ensure it is kept in good order. This is work that is often unappreciated. At Caerhays, it is not just a matter of maintenance but of improvement or correction of long standing problems in old buildings. Repairs and renovation work never cease and we plan they should continue for the future.

Maintenance of the gardens and grounds are an obvious responsibility and cost. This includes guarding and maintaining the landscape and the historic features of the countryside. We have never tried to calculate how many miles of medieval stone hedge or of river bank we have to look after. We just know it is a lot and that they will always need and receive repair.

Scaffolding at Caerhays

In a modern world we are unlikely to attain the levels of manpower that were devoted to the gardens, to gardening and to the grounds before the First World War. However, the other business interests at Caerhays have been able to fund what is now a very considerable operation. This operation is only effective through the good will and interest of those who work and help at Caerhays.

Maintenance is not confined to buildings, to grounds, or even to furniture. Caerhays also has a great quantity of records, plans and information from previous centuries. Much of this, particularly the correspondence on plants and on the China expeditions, or the mineral collection, is of national importance. Papers and records cannot often be seen as money earning, but the records at Caerhays have also to be sorted and maintained. Fortunately, with the help of Mr and Mrs Edwards, who had worked in the County Archives, we have made a start on sorting, assessing and listing the quantities of paper at Caerhays. This is a process likely to continue for a good time yet, and is as important, in its way, as the repair of a roof.

Although there is therefore an essential level of activity at the modern Caerhays that cannot earn money or contribute to the cost of operation, we have, in the 20thC, added other businesses. It is these that fund maintenance, and it is these that will be developed to ensure the future for Caerhays.

Rolls of maps and quantities of books and boxes are in the archives.

## Tourism

Most landed estates, at least in Cornwall, no longer survive on traditional rental incomes from their land and estate cottages. A first stage has been to make houses, cottages and Caerhays itself, available to visitors and holiday makers. The Castle and gardens were first opened to the public in 1992, and much more has been added to interest visitors over the last 20 years. It has often been said that successive recent governments have seen the countryside as a tourist theme park. Like others, Caerhays has been fairly quick to react to this but has also added a variety of other facilities for visitors.

## Beaches

It is usually the Crown who owns the tidal foreshore. Private owners will normally own the land only to a mid point between high and low water. However in 1862, the Duchy of Cornwall sold some Cornish foreshore to raise money. Since then the estate has owned the coastal foreshore for a further six fathoms out to sea from low water. This is really quite exceptional and in theory means that Porthluney and Portholland Beaches could be kept private. In reality, Porthluney beach provides useful additional revenue through car parking charges and a beach café.

## The Vean

It was my wife, Lizzie Williams, who, receiving some money from the unexpected sale in 2004 of a family business, decided to restore the former rectory at Caerhays, known as The Vean. This large Georgian rectory had not been lived in by the parish rector since after the First World War but was not actually sold by the church to the estate until 1948.

Death Duties and more pressing maintenance meant that the renovation of The Vean had been a low priority. When the last tenants left in 1961, the roof fell in and the building gradually became a ruin. The first planning application to rebuild The Vean on the same footprint as before, reusing the granite frontage and stone from the ruin, was turned down by the planners on the grounds that the building was 'outside the curtilage of the hereditament'. Quite how a rectory on the historic rectory site, only about 180 yards from the church, could be outside the boundary of the village was rather beyond us. However, after many letters of local support, as well as some expensive legal assistance and the help of English Heritage, approval for rebuilding was granted.

Rebuilding took 61 weeks and the builders, Dean & Dybell, as well as many others, deserve great credit for a superb end result. The Vean is furnished with period Georgian furniture as a private country house but with the most modern comfort features.

From the outset, The Vean was never going to be a conventional summer holiday let. The building has eight en suite bedrooms and comfortably sleeps 16. It has a commercial kitchen, industrial laundry (which can service the whole estate) treatment room and a full-time staff of six including a manager. The building has a licence to serve alcohol and is, in effect, a private hotel which can be rented as a whole to a group, or to individuals. The Vean has proved a superb venue for visitors booked for country sports or shooting days on the estate, and

The view from The Watchtower

The beach at Porthluney in summer

The Vean, before the start of work by Lizzie Williams

The rebuilt front entrance of The Vean

is always well booked from October to January, each year.

Other bookings have been for weddings and special events. Since the Vean has a full licence to conduct weddings, some weddings are held there. Others are held in the church with the reception at The Vean, which has a specially designed marquee attached to the building which can seat 70 people for a meal. Receptions are also held in a marquee alongside the castle, overlooking the sea.

The Vean has become a venue for family reunions, family celebrations, garden tour holidays, private bridge parties and special corporate events. Out of season mid week and spring breaks are offered to family or business groups.

Future plans for the Vean include adding a covered swimming pool, although this will mean another lengthy discussion with the planners.

The Vean, rebuilt

Inside The Vean

## Holiday Cottages

Caerhays now has nine holiday houses, achieved through reuse of interesting buildings. Each is designed to be of higher quality than those available elsewhere.

Because agriculture was producing a torrent of losses for many estates, other farms and estates converted farm cottages to provide holiday accommodation. However, as competition increased, so occupancy rates tended to stagnate and many have now seen occupancy decline.

Caerhays therefore made two policy decisions from the outset.

Firstly, we would not convert existing houses on the estate into holiday accommodation. Conversion of existing houses would have meant that, in a small parish with only 74 electors, spread around the tiny villages of Caerhays, Portholland and the even tinier hamlets of Rescassa, Trevarrick, and Tregavarras there would have been no local community left, especially in winter. It was decided to convert only derelict old buildings into holiday accommodation.

Secondly we would try to ensure that the houses would be 5 star rated by The English Tourist Board.

The Engine House was the first opened, in 2002, and another eight houses have followed

Preparing food for guests at The Vean

Weddings at Caerhays

The Engine House

The Old Village Hall

since then. These are achieving occupancy levels rather higher than the norm, both because of the superb locations close to the sea, and because of high standards in internal decoration and furnishing.

The nine houses are:

> The Old Village Hall
> The Engine House
> The Boathouse
> Bottom Lodge
> The Fish Sheds
> Lime Kiln Cottage
> The Old Carthouse
> The Rabbit Warren
> Ventonveth Barn

As the names suggest, these are all interesting buildings; one is within the castle itself, with stunning views over the park and sea.

All this work has had to be financed. Although one conversion had some help from a European grant, the rest of the money has been borrowed from the bank. We hope that once the debt is repaid over the next decade, the estate will have both a new source of income and a valuable asset.

In addition, the estate has also helped tenants to fund and convert three other derelict properties as holiday lets. These lettings are linked to the main Caerhays holiday cottage website.

The Bottom Lodge

The Old Village Hall

The Boat House, East Portholland

The Fish Sheds, West Portholland

The Old Carthouse

The Engine House

## Corporate Events

The estate actively provides for a whole range of corporate events. These include board meetings, business planning away days, product film shoots, overseas tour groups, cruise ship visits and corporate hospitality. These events often involve utilising the whole range of the estate's facilities from The Vean and The Old Village Hall through to the gardens and main rooms of the castle itself. There is also a wide range of catering options.

Events may be linked directly or indirectly to garden tours, shooting parties, weddings or family reunions. Once visitors have an idea of what is available, we find that customers of one activity will often return to try something different on the estate.

Business meetings at Caerhays

'Rebecca' was filmed at Caerhays

## Country Sports and Shooting

The shoot employs a shoot manager, three full-time keepers and, during the season, several other catering and back up staff. Because Caerhays is large enough to allow shooting parties to take place every day of the week during the season without the need to go over the same ground, around 80 days of shooting are arranged each year. These are let to American and overseas parties, to household, City and industry names, and to roving syndicates and groups of friends from throughout the UK.

Caerhays has specialised in the breeding of Kansas pheasants, which are much more colourful than other breeds. They may also have some greater immunity to disease, and are certainly attractive to look at. The vast majority of the pheasants and partridges on the estate are bred and raised on the estate in our own incubators, brooder houses and release pens. This makes Caerhays somewhat different from many establishments which buy in day old chicks or seven week old pheasant poults from game farms. The hope is that by keeping a 'closed flock' the risk of disease being introduced from outside will be reduced.

The Caerhays Shoot is inspected annually and accredited as a member of The Shoot Assurance Scheme.

Clay pigeon shooting is also offered to visitors who can use the full set of electronic clay traps. There is also a qualified instructor for youngsters or beginners interested in taking up shooting.

## The Home Farm

The farm covers some 725 acres (293 hectares) and is a broad mix of traditional enterprises. 'Caerhays Farms' is run by a farm manager and one full-time member of staff with the support of outside contractors at harvest and lambing times.

Livestock includes both sheep and cattle. Around 600 Dorset ewes have their lambs in early November. These lambs are then sold from late February on through the spring under a Waitrose contract. In a normal winter the grass continues to grow and these premium lambs are also finished on root crops such as swedes and typhon.

The cattle include a pedigree herd of around 30 Saler cattle,

Formal dinners and lunches at Caerhays

Kansas Pheasants

Pheasant rearing pens

Preparing for a day's shooting

Enjoying a day out

John Trudgeon,
retired Estate Manager

Kansas Pheasant

Philip Tidball,
Head Gamekeeper

bred from the original seven imported from France in 1999. The attraction of Salers is that, as French mountain cattle, they are very hardy with good conformation. They calve outside without undue difficulty. The purpose of the Salers is therefore to introduce renewed hybrid vigour when crossed with Charolais or Hereford cattle in suckler cow herds.

Caerhays has a further 220 crossbred Saler cattle in a suckler cow herd together with a small number of purebred Highland cattle. The Highland cattle are largely ornamental in today's market, although they may be a deterrent to uninvited tourists.

Around 60 acres of wheat is grown for consumption by the pheasants on the shoot and, while the price remains reasonable, a similar acreage may be grown for sale. When the price drops, then potato, vegetable, bulb or maize growers rent some fields on a temporary basis.

A limitation on the productivity of the Home Farm is that over 250 acres are in some form of Stewardship agreement. In order to benefit wildlife and the environment, such an agreement prohibits the use of artificial fertilisers and incorporates other rules which restrict production. All the coastal fields on the estate are in Stewardship with full public access. In hot summers, they produce very little grass for livestock. The water meadows along the River Luney valley are flooded during the winter months and only available for grazing in the summer. Caerhays is not an organic farm but one third of it is farmed in a manner which could comply with the formal rules of organic farming if this was ever desirable.

Farming policy for the future is to continue to farm the land in hand, to add a spread of different niche enterprises, and to take full advantage of such grants or funding that may be available.

Farm grants make a substantial contribution to the gross income of the farm. Despite this, the Home Farm has made little real profit in the last 20 years. This lack of profit has worsened as a result of both government pricing and supermarket squeezing of farm gate prices for food products. It could easily be argued that the Estate would have been better off letting the Home Farm to a tenant, at a guaranteed return. However, that has never been an option as the estate needs to control and manage the land and to meet the requirements of the other non-farming activities at Caerhays, including the shoot.

Successful Saler Cattle at Caerhays

## Other Estate Property

Over the last 30 years both the number of tenanted farms and the number of dairy units have dropped dramatically. Survival in farming business has forced tenant and landlord alike to amalgamate farms and to increase their size to make them viable. Where once 150 acres and 100 milking cows could have generated a reasonable living for a family the figure today is probably three or four times that, together with a need for enough capital to support continued dairy farming.

The arrival of Nitrate Vulnerable Zones, which restrict the timing, level and usage of animal waste on the land, alongside strict new cross compliance rules, have added to the cost of routine farming operations at a time when prices have been falling for the end products. As a result farm rents have been static for at least two decades. The only increase in rental income for the landlord has come from reletting former farmhouses (with a pony paddock and no land) to outsiders and (at best) hobby farmers. Short term lettings of this sort can often generate more rent than a farmer might have paid for the whole farm with full security of tenure for his successors.

## Heritage Status

Much of the estate is within an Area of Outstanding Natural Beauty (AONB) and on the edge of the coast, a Site of Special Scientific Interest (SSSI). Since 1992, the estate has also been designated as of 'Outstanding Heritage Status'. This status was agreed with the Capital Taxes Office on the advice of English Heritage, the Historic Monuments & Buildings Commission, The Royal Botanic Gardens at Kew and English Nature. In return both for public access to designated areas and for compliance with a set of management rules for the estate, no Inheritance Tax is payable when the property descends through generations. This makes a considerable difference to the forward planning and management of the estate.

In addition to the areas designated as being of Heritage Status, the remaining land is incorporated into a Maintenance Trust. All income generated by the Maintenance Trust can only be used to support and maintain the defined 'heritage assets'.

The Caerhays Heritage and Maintenance scheme, which remains a fairly unusual and little known form of tax planning first introduced in the 1980s, therefore underwrites the continuity of the whole estate into future generations.

## Forestry

Unfortunately, Caerhays is isolated by narrow roads unsuitable for timber haulage and so, although there are around 320 acres (134 hectares) of woodland, it has proved impossible to establish a timber or even a firewood selling business on the estate. Much of the woodland was planted between 1880 and 1900 either to benefit shooting or to protect the new gardens. After World War 1, commercial management had vanished. By the 1960s, much of the beech and sycamore plantings were over mature or damaged by the frequent gales. The opportunity for timber sales had passed and the problem was one of felling and replanting old woodland after 80 years of neglect.

The one conifer wood, 'Parnall's Hill', planted after the Second World War in the Portholland Valley, was entirely out of keeping with the setting of the valley as a natural broad-leaved plantation and has been progressively thinned. In 1986 a five year Forestry Commission plan was agreed and has continued since then. Over the last 25 years some 8ha of new woodland has been planted on steeper slopes which were no longer viable for farming. Around 15ha of existing woodland has been felled and replaced to increase the age range and diversity of the woodland and to maintain its visual or amenity use for the public.

The 1990 hurricane acted as a catalyst for this replanting programme. Twelve acres of woodland in one area of Forty Acre Wood was flattened in one morning and many of the historic trees in the deer park overlooking Porthluney Cove disappeared. Prior to 1990, timber sales had been negligible. The hurricane ensured that paying contractors to clean up the mess became the norm, a situation that still con-

Forestry continues at Caerhays

tinues. Regrettably, the Forestry Commission grant aided replanting programmes have, instead of being of assistance, proved to be a large nett expense to the estate. These losses have been increased by the need to comply with the new UK Woodland Assurance Scheme Standards, which seems to represent another bureaucratic imposition of little value or use.

Nevertheless, the woodland is now managed and regenerated, as indeed originally planted, with country sports in mind. Rides are maintained, laurel thickets trimmed and new plantations established not just with an eye to their landscape value but also to the income potential from country pursuits.

## Management and Maintenance

As well as the castle, the grounds, the buildings and other structures of the estate, the large number of cottages and houses also need maintenance. This obligation continues to be relentless. Of the 100 or so cottages and farmhouses on the estate around a quarter are let rent free or on very reduced rents to current and former employees of the estate. There are still a few full-repairing leases and some farm tenants too have to maintain their farmhouses and buildings. However these exceptions leave a lot of property which requires looking after. The change of most tenancies to Assured Shorthold Tenancies with two to three year rent reviews gives the estate some flexibility but carries a large maintenance bill.

The Estate has a full-time maintenance team of three. In years gone by the estate might well have had its own carpenter, joiner, painter and electrician. Nowadays, so many trades can only be performed by approved specialists that many maintenance tasks have to be contracted out.

Maintenance seems to have its own rhythm and fashions. At the time of writing, the principal problems are chimney linings and cesspits. However, no matter what the activity, much attention and time must now be spent obeying the requirements of regulations, the Environment Agency and of course 'Elf and Safety'.

There is sometimes a great drama such as the hurricane of January 1990, after which many scantle slate roofs covering 80 buildings had to be replaced. We were fortunate to get help with this through 140 separate claims of insurers. More routine maintenance includes painting the external joinery of all cottages every four years in the long-standing cream colours which have been used for at least 50 years. In an area of high rainfall, close to the coast, window and joinery repairs continue all year round.

Replacement joinery

## Larger Projects and Renovations

The estate has a shareholding in KPK Builders & Developers Ltd which is based at Burncoose Nurseries, employs around 20-25 full-time staff, and has two external directors. KPK specialises in restoration and renovation work on listed buildings in particular.

KPK has completed five phases of a castle reroofing programme which started in the early 1990s. There is still one further phase to go. In each phase a section of lead roof is removed, re-smelted and re-laid to a modern and higher specification while the granite battlements are restored, replaced and underpinned. There are very few building

Scaffolding and roofworks at Caerhays

businesses in Cornwall with the skills necessary to complete specialist work of this sort at height. KPK also renovated the former staff accommodation in the castle known as the 'Rabbit Warren'. At times of crisis, such as after the hurricane or other storms, it has proved extremely useful to be able to call on a team of specialist staff capable of dealing properly with the problems of listed buildings.

## Burncoose Nurseries

No consideration of the modern activities at Caerhays can ignore the contribution and importance of the nurseries and plant businesses at Burncoose. Much business depends too on continuing to ensure that the international botanic reputation of Caerhays and Burncoose continues undimmed. It is important therefore that the lines of honours and medals received for botanic efforts should continue. As I write, in 2010, we are fortunate to have gained yet another gold medal for our stand at the Chelsea Flower Show. This is Burncoose's 21st Chelsea gold medal in the last 26 years. In the same period Burncoose has won more gold medals at RHS flower shows than any other UK nursery.

Burncoose is now a very considerable nursery, and has developed to become one of the biggest of UK plant mail order businesses. Its website receives 1.5 million visits a year and almost 70% of its orders come over the internet.

## Retail Sales

Based on the experience gained at Burncoose, internet shopping promises to be an important development which will allow the sale of branded Caerhays products alongside Burncoose plants. New ranges are already available through both the Caerhays and Burncoose websites. This is another way in which Caerhays can reach out to new customers at the same time as marketing and promoting Caerhays as a tourist destination.

Facilities at Caerhays include The Magnolia Tea Room and The Caerhays Gift Shop, both of which provide welcome relief and opportunity for visitors. There is also a separate plant sales unit at Caerhays.

Finally, amid all this talk of the importance of business, it is worth remembering that the estate continues to stage charitable events and, as it always has done, to help out local organisations. At least one major event each year is organised for charity.

Andrew Mills, Nursery Manager, among the phormiums

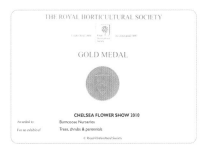

A gold medal from 2010

One of the many rows of certificates and medal records

Bluebells in Burncoose garden

The Magnolia Tea Rooms

Caerhays Gift Shop

The purpose of this chapter was to give some idea of the different business activities at Caerhays and of the way they may develop through the years ahead. All one can say with confidence is that ensuring the future of Caerhays will require considerable business development, rather less bureaucratic regulation, and a willingness to be flexible in the face of whatever is thrown our way.

However, no future would be possible without the support of the many staff who work at Caerhays. There is now a considerable establishment of varied specialists and responsibilities. Present survival or planning a future would not be possible without the help and dedication of those who play a part at Caerhays.

Staff at Caerhays in July 2010

| Back Row | Bob Eden, Sally Gammel, John Trudgeon |
|---|---|
| Middle Row | Jimmy Andrew, Jack Tidball, Philip Tidball, Magi Malin, Sheila Tidball, Mimi Brown, Cheryl Kufel, Mary Kemp, Mark Pheasey, Susha Reynolds, Jaimie Parsons, Mike Levett, Russell King, Kerry Burns, Ken Mills, Gillian Frazer, Randy Mooney, Graham Thomas, Jane Goddard, Robbie Andrew, Liz Miller, Arthur Broom. |
| Front Row | Jamie Snell, Sian Thomas, Pam Kitts, Kathy Vellanoweth, Terena Broom, Joss Newman, Viv Greenaway, Gemma Jones, Linda Mooney, Heather Tulip, Liz Tomas, Elaine Rowe, Sarah Rundle, Phil Tregunna, Monica Trudgeon, Alison Mays, Robin Rundle & Bimsey the dog. |

# Section Four
# The Gardens at Caerhays

19    The Gardens         177

20    Garden Walks     193

The appendices include:
1       40 of the best Magnolias in the Caerhays collection
2       A National Collection of Magnolias
3       Magnolia hybrids bred at Caerhays and Burncoose
4       Camellia x williamsii hybrids bred at Caerhays and Burncoose
5       Rhododendron hybrids bred and raised at Caerhays
6       Rare and evergreen Oaks at Caerhays- *Lithocarpus* and *Quercus*
7       The Podocarpus Collection at Caerhays
8       A selection of Champion Trees at Caerhays

Azalea 'Caerhays Lavender'

Rhododendron 'Golden Oriole' var 'Busaco'

Azalea 'Greenway'

Rhododendron davidsonianum Caerhays Pink Form

# Chapter 19
## The Gardens at Caerhays

"On reflection I was left with one clear thought about Caerhays. This was that there is now a real sense that the excitement and drive of JCW's original planting ambitions has been recaptured. The combination of new wild-source plants and new garden cultivars, particularly magnolias, have provided you with the same opportunities that the estate had in the early part of the 20th century. The key difference is, however, that the earlier plantings, now in stunning maturity, provide the framework and backdrop to your work.

"I was equally impressed that you have grasped the, always difficult, nettle of renewing the structural plantings - overstory trees, shelterbelts and windbreaks, accent and foil plants. You will know better than anyone how important these are in maintaining the vital microclimates that give every garden of worth the subtle nuances that provided its character and uniqueness. It is never easy to undertake clearance and felling programmes but it has to be done. A stout heart in the early stages is the only way forward."

Magnolia 'Caerhays Surprise'

Mark Flanagan, Keeper of the Gardens,
Crown Estate and Royal Landscape, Windsor

## The Gardens Today

Caerhays is a woodland garden covering the whole of Castle Wood and extending on into Kennel Close Wood, Forty Acre Wood and Old Park. With recent clearings and new plantings there are well over 120 acres of garden tended by a team of four or five gardeners led, since 1996, by Jaimie Parsons. The gardens are open to the public for over 100 days from mid February to the end of May and attract around 14,000 visitors a year. To some this may seem a very early spring start and rather a short period of time to be open. Caerhays is, however, very much a traditional Cornish spring flowering garden and, by June, the trash and vegetation which grows so quickly in our wet climate (55-60 inches of rain per year) has

A view along the main ride

less obvious appeal to visitors. Caerhays is not a manicured or planned garden in the conventional sense. It is, however, designated as being of outstanding importance by The Royal Botanic Gardens at Kew and Registered as a Grade II* Park and Garden by English Heritage under the old style designations.

As far as was known, and until Stephen Tyrrell's recent and remarkable discoveries about enduring elements of a Jacobean garden, it was thought no garden had survived at Caerhays from before the end of the 19thC. The first gardens on the site were underneath the present castle lawns and in an enclosed precinct towards the lake. They included terraces, a bowling green and a decorative water feature. Around 1700 a large terraced garden was added to the north of the precinct. This was walled, with turrets to the north corners, with two viewing mounts and with water features in the middle. There may also have been walk through shrubberies to each side of the walled section. When the castle was rebuilt, the Trevanions re-planned the landscape around the castle. This probably included landscaped shrubs and borders, with avenues and walkways.

The Williams family re-organised the landscape scheme again, and added large areas of manicured gardens to the west of the 1700 walled garden. However, the earlier 19thC plant introductions of Joseph Rock, Hooker and Abbe Delavay from China and the Lobb brothers in South America are largely absent. Caerhays only came into its own as a premier Cornish or British garden after 1900 when an ongoing family interest in plants combined with the opportunity and desire to link with the exciting plant exploration work taking place in China. Although gardeners disseminated new plants widely amongst neighbouring or family estates such as Heligan, Trewithen, Tregothnan and Stanage, much of the material at Caerhays (and Werrington Park) is unique. The first plants of many new species, formerly unknown in Western Europe, can still be seen today more than a hundred years on.

Julian Williams with The Garden Book

The garden at Caerhays has a unique microclimate. The prevailing and frequent westerly gales rage over the top of the sheltered garden. Sea mists bathe the woodland in moisture and humidity which is very suited to the Chinese mountain habitats from which so many magnolias and rhododendrons originate. In addition the rich acidic soil is ideal for growing ericaceous plants. Just as many might regard the castle as an ugly building without its setting in the Luney valley, so the gardens themselves would also be impossible to replicate if set in a less favourable environment.

To appreciate what the gardens are really about imagine you are halfway up a mountain in the Chinese province of Yunnan 100 years or so ago, and then enjoy the reality of Caerhays.

J. C. Williams

## The Chinese Plant Hunters

The gardens at Caerhays stem from the work of two great Chinese plant collectors, E.H. Wilson (1876 - 1930) and George Forrest (1873 - 1932). If they were the ones who risked their lives collecting plant seeds from new species unknown in Western Europe, visiting parts of China which were still, even at the start of the 20th Century, unknown lands which appeared to be from the Dark Ages, it was the sponsors and funders of their expeditions who then grew on the spoils in their new gardens.

J.C. Williams, who owned Caerhays, Burncoose and Werrington Estates, bought his first 25 Chinese rhododendrons from the Veitch Nursery in Exeter in 1903. In 1905, The Garden Book at Caerhays records the first of these new Chinese specimens, which had been collected by Wilson, being planted out on the hillside above the castle. By 1906 over 50 new species of rhododendrons were being planted out and the creation of the garden was well under way.

Part of what we look at today as the core of the woodland garden would have been coastal scrub. The remainder, at the top of the garden, was still fields. JCW and his garden staff, which numbered over 50 by 1910, made inroads into the scrub to create small sheltered planting coupes. They also wisely planted dense shelterbelts to protect the new introductions.

The excitement of the first new arrivals was tempered by the risks being taken by the plant collectors. In Szechwan and Yunnan, where disputes were still being settled with bows and arrows, and where Forrest was to narrowly escape the fate of many indigenous tribesmen who had their hearts cut out and eaten, there was a considerable risk that collectors would be unable to return. For this reason their plant introductions had to be protected at all costs with little thought of ultimate size or fancy colour schemes. Survival was all important.

Nestling plants together for protection to help create their own microclimates is how we would perhaps describe it today. Probably more likely was that JCW and his head gardeners were trying to replicate the densely wooded mountain slopes of Yunnan by planting thickly and in clumps.

In 1911 George Forrest switched allegiance to work for JCW. His third Chinese expedition, 1912 - 1915, was funded entirely by JCW on his own to the tune of £3,108.13s.6d. This would be over £400,000 in today's money. JCW was also to make major financial contributions to Forrest's next four expeditions, which were ended by his death in Tengyueh, China, in 1932.

Literally thousands of packets of seeds began to arrive at Caerhays

*See chapter 15 for pictures and more details of George Forrest*

and the onset of World War 1 in Europe appears to have made no difference to the collectors' continuing work. JCW, Wilson and Forrest were great correspondents. Forrest's letters to JCW meticulously record his discoveries while JCW's replies often go into great detail about the first flowerings of these new plants. Forrest's collecting was not limited to rhododendrons alone but encompassed a wide range of other genuses including acer, magnolia, michelia, manglietia, to mention but a few of his woody (as opposed to herbaceous) plant introductions.

A selection of original, and possibly the most important, of Wilson's and Forrest's introductions at Caerhays are listed below. It is interesting to note the longevity of some of these plants which continue to be record sized UK trees in their own right 80 or more years after planting. It would seem that Chinese magnolias will live to be a hundred but many rhododendron species peak at the age of 60 - 70.

One can only speculate on how many seeds failed to germinate and which were consequently never named. Some may have been rediscovered in more recent times by botanists but many more may well await rediscovery. Although JCW paid Forrest a bonus for each new species of rhododendron he brought back, and although this may have helped cause the same species to be given several different names, the sheer volume of discoveries made by Wilson and Forrest remains staggering to comprehend in this day and age.

J.C.Williams (right) & Rothschild in the new rockery

## Examples of Plants Originally Introduced by Forrest

| Collectors No. | Some original Forrest Introductions |
| --- | --- |
| 25184 | Acer taronense |
|  | Acer forrestii |
| 25156 | Camellia saluenensis |
|  | Castanopsis concolor |
| 27393 | Camellia reticulata |
| 24190 | Cinnamomum glanduliferum |
| 25197 | Camellia sinensis |
| 24030 | Lindera communis |
| 26509 | Magnolia nitada |
| 24214 | Magnolia campbellii subsp. mollicomata |
| 26506 | Manglieta insignis |
| 26580 | Michelia doltsopa |
|  | Michelia floribunda |
| 24183 | Quercus lamellosa |
|  | Rhododendron griersonianum |
|  | Rhododendron russatum |
|  | Rhododendron martinianum |
|  | Symplocos glomerata |

Michelia doltsopa

Rhododendron griersonianum

Camellia reticulata

Magnolia nitada

Rhododendron russatum

# Examples of Plants Originally Introduced by Wilson

| Collectors No. | Some Wilson introductions surviving at Caerhays |
|---|---|
| 4506 | Acer giraldi |
| 498 | Aesculus wilsonii |
| 304 | Catalpa duclouxii |
| 4116 | Magnolia dawsoniana |
| 914 | Magnolia sargentiana |
| 923 | Magnolia sargentiana var. robusta |
| 204 | Prunus pilosiuscula |
| 4239 | Rhodo. davidsonianum - Caerhays Pink Form |
| 4257 | Rhodo. decorum |
| 1250 | Rhodo. fargesii |
| 4255 | Rhodo. hanceanum |
| 10955 | Rhodo. morii |
| 887 | Rhodo. stamineum |
| 1810 | Rhodo. orbiculare |
| 1350 | Rhodo. williamsianum (original plants have died - but one remains at Burncoose) |
| 886 | Rhodo. wilsonii |
| 479 | Sorbus hupehensis |
| 291 | Styrax hemsleyanus |
| 290 | Styrax wilsonii (original died but seedlings survive) |
| 313 | Trochodendron arallioides (Old Park) |

Rhodo. davidsonianum -
Caerhays Pink Form

Rhodo. hanceanum

# Hybridisation at Caerhays over Three Generations

### Rhododendrons

The 1918 Volume of the Botanical Magazine is dedicated to John Charles Williams "whose careful study and skilful tilth of this genus rhododendron and only equalled by the liberality with which his knowledge and material have been made available to benefit and to enrich the Botanical Magazine".

The source material for an entirely new hybridisation programme had arrived at Caerhays and JCW, his head gardeners and family successors, have all continued this work. This is perhaps what makes Caerhays so interesting a garden today.

JCW shunned publicity and sought anonymity for his plant breeding work except perhaps among the other great gardens which were also emerging and developing through the work of the Chinese plant hunters. These gardens included Bodnant, Borde Hill, Dyffryn and Exbury as well as The Royal Botanic Gardens in Edinburgh, the RHS garden at Wisley and the Arnold Arboretum in Massachusetts.

In E.H. Wilson's 'Plantae Wilsonae' Volume 1 he writes "this species is named (Rh. williamsianum) for Mr. J.C. Williams of Caerhays Castle, Cornwall, England. The first amateur to appreciate the value of the rhododendrons of Western China. In his garden the best collection of these new varieties is now to be found". Throughout JCW's voluminous garden notes and records he always refers to this plant only by its collector's number: 1350.

It is no surprise therefore to discover that of the 268 rhododendron crosses which he made between 1897 and 1929 only a very few were ever named.

By the 1920s some 400 new species of rhododendron had arrived in the UK. The possibilities for hybridisation were enormous and varied.

Rhodo. orbiculare

Styrax wilsonii

Trochodendron arallioides

Crossing two species generally creates hybrid vigour and JCW used this knowledge to the full in trying to improve hardiness, colour, size of flower and conformation in his rhododendron hybrids.

It was only in 1933 that Lionel de Rothschild visited Caerhays to intercede with JCW to name some of his new hybrids and register them with the RHS. This is how 'Blue Tit', 'Yellow Hammer' and 'Humming Bird' first came to public notice after registration with the RHS.

In 1942, and three years after JCW's death, a further five of his very best hybrids were recognised, including 'Crossbill' and 'Red Admiral'. These hybrids are still for sale at Burncoose Nurseries today, proving that they have stood the test of time.

In the appendices of this book is a full list of the Caerhays rhododendron hybrids which have been registered with the RHS and received awards of one sort or another. As can be seen, the programme has been and is ongoing, particularly with the arrival of some tender new species collected by Tom Hudson in Northern Vietnam.

There have only been four head gardeners at Caerhays since 1897:-

| | |
|---|---|
| John Martin | 1897 - 1922 |
| Charles Michael | 1922 - 1956 |
| Philip Tregunna | 1956 - 1996 |
| Jaimie Parsons | 1996 - |

Only they will ever know where the credit should really be given for this ongoing hybridisation work which can take up to 15 years from the cross to the first flowering of its progeny.

## The Origin of the x williamsii camellias

In the 19th Century the camellia had been thought of as a tender greenhouse plant fit only to grace the vast conservatories of places like Chatsworth. The first japonica camellias came to Caerhays in 1902 and were planted out as foliage plants in distant woods. The first named camellia japonica variety arrived in 1902. 'Lady Clare' still resides fairly comfortably alongside the front door of the castle.

Camellias were, however, very much a sideline for JCW until, in March 1918, George Forrest discovered what has come to be known as Camellia saluenensis. His field notes state:- "17686 Thea speciosa Pitard Form A1331-A1847 - Volcanic mountains of NW of Tengyoch. Lat 25° 10 N. Altitude 8000 feet. Evergreen shrub of 6-12 feet. Flowers single, rose pink. Open stony hillsides". In January 1922 JCW wrote "some camellias are nice, speciosa probably".

JCW's records show he only made one batch of camellia hybrids, (number 181), in 1923 which were then sown in 1924. The cross was between two pink forms of the then new Camellia saluenensis which still struggle into flower in their old age on the external walls of the castle and the single red Camellia japonica first planted at Caerhays in 1902.

From this cross emerged what we now know today as the worldwide range of x williamsii camellias. JCW's first hybrids were named after his wife (Mary Christian) and himself.

The new generation camellia plants were much more floriferous and vigorous than their parents. The flowers were much larger and they dropped to the ground when finished rather than browning on the bush. The plants had an enormously long flowering period with some starting in November ('November Pink') and December ('St Ewe') and ending in April. Most importantly of all, they were fully hardy

Phillip Tregunna (left), Frank Knight (former Wisley Curator) and Roy Lancaster in April 1984

The same three again, 25 years later, holding an earlier photograph.

Camellia 'Lady Clare'

Camellia saluensis (light form)

throughout the UK, although it took two generations for the public to fully catch on to this.

The camellia had come out of the glasshouse for good and it is perhaps ironic that the person who went to such great lengths to avoid publicity should now have his name attached to the literally thousands of camellia hybrids bred subsequently from this genetic line all round the world.

At Caerhays, Camellia saluenensis was then crossed with 'Lady Clare' to produce Camellia 'Caerhays' and Camellia 'George Blandford'. These were the first double flowered forms of Camellia x williamsii.

Perhaps the most widely grown of all the Camellia x williamsii is 'Donation'. This was however bred at Borde Hill by Colonel Stephenson Clarke.

A full list of those x williamsii camellias bred at Caerhays and Burncoose can be found in appendix 4 of this guide. Sadly 'would be' British camellia hybridisers have little to work with today because most popular double flowering camellias do not set seed in our climate and, in many instances, camellias are so inbred that the blowsy flowers no longer contain the anthers and stamens necessary for seed production. Often all we can call 'new' are chance 'sports' which appear irregularly on certain camellias from time to time.

With the current prohibition of camellia imports into the UK from America we are missing out on the next generation of exciting new US hybrids. In the 1960s Caerhays received many scores of new varieties from Milo Rowell and Maynard Munter in California and visitors can appreciate these all over the garden.

Unless the recent discovery of new tender yellow flowering species of camellia in China and Vietnam opens up opportunities for new hybridisation work, JCW's achievement is unlikely ever to be matched.

## Magnolias

The first of the new Chinese magnolias to flower at Caerhays in 1919 was what we now know to be M. sprengeri 'Diva'. This was collected by E.H. Wilson and the plant was bought in 1912 from the Veitch nursery at Coombe Wood, North Devon. Magnolia wilsonii first flowered in 1920 but it was not until the early 1930s that other tree magnolias such as M. x veitchii, M. campbellii and M. sargentiana began to perform. Magnolia dawsoniana and M. sargentiana var. robusta, which are amongst the most spectacular of all the early spring displays today at Caerhays, came via the Chenault Nurseries in France in the 1930s.

It was soon discovered that many of these Chinese tree magnolias provided copious amounts of seed and that the seedlings germinated easily. In the 1950s and 1960s many seedlings were widely distributed across Cornish gardens and much further afield. Since it takes at least 15 years, and sometimes up to 40 years, for tree magnolias (whose parentage includes campbellii or mollicomata) to flower, it was a long time before people realised the depressing reality that few of these seedlings produced flowers which were anything like as good as their parents.

This did not stop lots of people naming (but seldom properly registering) their own seedling as a "new" hybrid. A good many of the named varieties in prominent gardens throughout the UK may indeed

Camellia japonica

Camellia saluenensis (dark form)

Magnolia sprengeri 'Diva'

Magnolia 'Caerhays Surprise'

be plants of great beauty but they are not sufficiently distinct to be worthy of a name.

At Caerhays we have been consistently ruthless in not naming our own hybrids even where they are very probably the product of specific and deliberate crossing. For that reason and also, of course, because of the enormously long lead-in times which are involved in crossing magnolias, we have only named a few in the last 50 years.

These are listed in appendix 3 together with details of their parentage. In their own way they are all unique in colour, flowering time or habit and they have all received awards from the RHS. There are other new crosses which will only be named if we can exhibit them at one of the monthly RHS spring shows. This is easier said than done, with spring gales and frosts often spoiling the flowers at the crucial time.

Mention should, however, be made of Magnolia 'Caerhays Surprise' which remains one of the best magnolias for a small garden and which flowers in only three to five years. Philip Tregunna had the foresight to find viable pollen on an exceptionally late flower of M. mollicomata and crossed it with M. liliiflora 'Nigra' which would normally be flowering some two months later in May. The offspring have the habits of both parents as well as hybrid vigour and an exceptional dark purplish-red flower.

The introduction of a range of new yellow flowered magnolias in the last 15 years opens up a whole new range of opportunities for magnolia hybridisation work at Caerhays. However, if you cross an American yellow with a Chinese pink the likely end result may well be a Cornish brown!

## A National Collection of Magnolias

The purpose of a national collection is to establish in one place as many species and cultivars of a particular genus as possible to enable the public to see them and assess them together. The holder of a national collection is responsible for ensuring the survival of the genetic store of such plants so that they are available for future hybridisation, research or reintroduction into the wild.

Caerhays has many original magnolia species which came direct from China and still thrive today. Much of the forest area from which Wilson and Forrest collected seed has now been burnt for firewood, ring barked by goats or cleared for agriculture, so the potential importance of these plants in genetic terms is obvious.

The old rule was that if you had 75% of the species and cultivars of a particular genus listed in Hilliers Manual you were eligible to apply to the National Council for the Conservation of Plants and Gardens (now renamed Plant Heritage) to become a collection holder. In 2001 our application was accepted and the collection covers all Magnoliaceae. In other words it includes not just magnolias but also what, until very recently, the botanists referred to as michelias and manglietias. These have now all been renamed as magnolias which certainly confuses things for all concerned, not least in the labelling of all 650 or so plants in the Caerhays collection. Labelling is a precondition of being a National Collection holder.

The Caerhays collection now includes at least one (and often

Magnolia 'Serene'

Magnolia 'Genie'

Magnolia 'Darjeeling'

Magnolia 'Star Wars'

Magnolia 'Heaven Scent'

several) specimens of plants from 72 species of magnolia, 222 separate named cultivars and around 205 unnamed seedlings or cultivars. There are four other national collections in the UK. These are at Windsor Great Park, Bodnant, Wentworth Castle and Newton St Cyres, Devon. The idea is that if a climatic disaster or disease affects one collection in one part of the country the others may hopefully survive.

A full listing of the entire Caerhays collection together with details of location, planting dates, parentage and other pertinent notes, is contained on the Caerhays website at www.caerhays.co.uk and in the appendices.

The collection now contains a number of the new and exciting worldwide developments in magnolia breeding:-

Magnolia 'Goldstar'

i)      The collection has many of the best new magnolia hybrids bred in New Zealand. These are now well established and well known plants include 'Star Wars', 'Heaven Scent', 'Serene', 'Apollo', 'Atlas', 'Darjeeling' and 'Iolanthe'.

ii)      In more recent times Ian Baldick and Vance Hooper have treated us to the best of their own breeding work. 'Ian's Red' and 'Red as Red' will grow in popularity as enthusiasts see them in flower but Vance Hooper's 'Genie' will soon face down 'Black Tulip' as the darkest coloured magnolia flower.

iii)      The Chinese collectors such as Tom Hudson from Tregrehan have been reintroducing species of michelia and manglietia, which were perhaps unknown to Wilson and Forrest, and these too can be seen at Caerhays today. The reality may well be that Forrest and Wilson did collect these species but that the seeds failed to germinate or were killed by an early cold winter before the plants could be properly named.

Magnolia 'Yellow Bird'

iv)      All the American bred Gresham hybrid magnolias and the liliiflora x stellata hybrids known as 'The Girls' can be seen in one place, thus again demonstrating the futility of naming too many seedlings from one cross which all turn out to be too similar.

v)      Yellow magnolias started at Caerhays with 'Elizabeth' and 'Butterflies' which were a present to my father during a visit of the International Magnolia Society in 1987. Since that time we have gathered together a further 28 named hybrids whose parentage can be traced back to M. acuminata. 'Yellow Bird', 'Yellow Fever', 'Miss Honeybee' and 'Goldstar' were the best of the second generation of yellows which arrived in the 1990s. Today we are starting to assess the third generation of yellows both from the US and from Philippe de Spoelberg at Herkenrode in Belgium. 'Daphne' may prove to be the best but 'Lois' and 'Green Bee' are good runners up, to mention just a few. The great excitement of the magnolia world in the next 20 years will be to produce a TRUE yellow magnolia which flowers in March well before the leaves appear. We are still some way off this objective.

Magnolia 'Elizabeth'

The first cross between Magnolia and Michelia at Caerhays was a sensation when it first flowered at Caerhays in 2007. Magnolia 'Yuchelia' is a hybrid between M. acuminata 'Miss Honeybee' and Michelia figo. This too opens up exciting new avenues for future hybridisation work in which Caerhays will continue to try to play a leading role.

Magnolia 'Yuchelia'

## The Tree Register and Champion Trees at Caerhays

Way back in 1964 Alan Mitchell first visited Caerhays to measure those trees in the garden which were original Chinese introductions and/or very rare in their own right. Those dendrological records were subsequently updated several times over the years so that they record large parts of the life-span and longevity of important tree specimens at Caerhays.

A clinometer, used for measuring trees

Following Alan's death The Tree Register was established as a charity to collate a database of notable and record trees throughout the UK and Ireland. This unique register contains over 150,000 trees (as well as all Alan's data) and is the only comprehensive source of information on the size and location of trees.

Trees are measured in two ways. Once you have struggled with the concept, a clinometer provides dendrologists with a quick way of measuring tree height. Trees are also measured by their girth roughly 1.5 metres from ground level.

After some lengthy measuring sessions in 2006 Owen Johnson from The Tree Register concluded that Caerhays had over 80 Champion Trees.

This compares to 311 at Kew Gardens, 120 at Westonbirt and 82 at Windsor. Within Cornwall Tregrehan have 35, Trewithen 27 and Lanhydrock 10. At the risk of starting a bout of gardening one-upmanship or tree snobbery, this does help to demonstrate the botanic importance of the garden at Caerhays. Nevertheless, old trees pass out quickly, so all records remain under threat.

Many of the champion trees at Caerhays are indeed elderly species magnolias and michelias which came direct from China. Many are also more unusual Wilson and Forrest introductions, such as Aesculus wilsonii, Trochodendron arallioides, Meliosma beaniana or Acer forrestii.

More importantly for the future of the garden overall, quite a number of these record trees are less than 50 years old and nothing at all to do with the Wilson/Forrest era. Crabiodendron yunnanense, Persea thunbergii and Ilex perado subsp. perado tell the story of more recent generous gifts from other gardens and, in particular, from the late John Bond of the Savill and Valley Gardens at Windsor who showered Caerhays with plants which were too tender for Berkshire.

Some of these champion trees are extremely dull and this of course accounts for their continuing rarity. Others fail to set seed (Prunus pilosiuscula) or even flower (Emmenopterys henryi) in our climate so propagation by conventional means is largely impossible. This too accounts for their continuing rarity.

Others, in contrast, are much more widely grown and would even be considered common in cultivation. Magnolia delavayi, Ilex platyphylla, Ligustrum confusum and Acer palmatum 'Senkaki' ('Sango-Kaku') would certainly come into this category.

Those of our record trees which are readily accessible in the main Castle Wood are marked on a map in the appendices to allow visitors to explore the trees at their leisure. The full list of Champion Trees can be found on the Caerhays website.

Acer palmatum 'Senkaki' (Sango-Kau')

## Podocarpus

The Podocarpus is an evergreen shrub or tree. There are 105 species of Podocarpus, of very different appearance. They can vary from 1 to 25 metres high and have spirally arranged leaves and cones.

My interest in Podocarpus stemmed from a visit to Caerhays by Chris Page who was then the principal conifer expert at The Royal Botanic Garden, Edinburgh. Chris said that the stand of Podocarpus salignus, which contains over a dozen mature male and female trees of 50 feet or more in height, was larger and more mature than anything still left in Chile. This particular species is much sought after for furniture making and, in consequence, is under serious threat. Since the trees at Caerhays grow readily from cuttings and self-seed themselves abundantly it did seem that we might be able to contribute to reforestation projects in the future.

Podocarpus salignus

The P. salignus are at the top of the garden and would appear to have been planted in the late 1930s. In JCW's planting records he was given a plant of P. andinus (also Chilean) by Giles Loder in 1920. A P. nubigenus (also Chilean) arrived in 1916 and these two species survive today near the castle but there is no record of where the P. salignus came from that can be found.

I then became interested in the hybridisation work of Graham Hutchins at County Park nursery with New Zealand podocarpus and began to collect the genus more seriously from 1995.

The great attraction of these New Zealand Podocarpus for Caerhays is that they will tolerate strong winds and salt sprays while also excluding the under-draught from new plantings in exposed positions as they are mainly dense, low growing shrubs. The New Zealand species P. nivalis and P. lawrencei together with P. hallii and P. acutifolius have spawned a plethora of interesting hybrids. Some have excellent colours in their spring new growth while others colour up better in the summer or autumn. As well as being wind resistant, they are attractive plants in their own right and highly collectable.

Other South African Podocarpus species may prove to be more dubious when we next get a really cold winter but, for the moment, they add further diversity to the collection.

This now numbers 11 species and 40 hybrids. At a time when Defra are forcing us to remove large swathes of Rhododendron ponticum shelterbelt to prevent the spread of Phytophthera ramorum, then the podocarpus may yet have their day. Whether we go on to apply for National Collection status largely depends on the energy and determination of Jaimie Parsons to maintain the planting records of these confusing but attractive plants which can look so very different at different times of the year.

A list of the growing collection can be found in the appendices.


## Other Collections

It would be all too easy for visitors to miss out on the full diversity of the gardens at Caerhays if they were to think that rhododendrons, camellias and magnolias are all that is on offer.

### Evergreen Oaks

There are at least 25 species of Quercus and the closely related Lithocarpus at Caerhays (see appendix). Quercus oxyodon is a one-off in that no other mature plant exists in cultivation in the UK. The plant produces flowers but, as yet, no acorns, although it was already 27 feet tall in 1966. More recently, Nigel Holman of Chyverton and Tom Hudson of Tregrehan have reintroduced this species from the wild. However, in immaturity, the young plants do not much resemble the original. Lithocarpus pachyphyllus, with its extraordinary seed clusters, is another key feature of the garden at Caerhays. Lithocarpus hanseii is so rare that no formal description exists and the extraordinary Quercus uvarifolius from Japan has defied identification by almost all the experts. More recently we have been planting out a range of new evergreen oaks from Mexico kindly given to us by the Hillier Arboretum. These look borderline but time will tell.

Pseudopanax laetus

## Unusual maples

The Acer griseum at the top of the garden was once a record tree but the 1990 hurricane reduced its size considerably. The plant also suffers from lead poisoning where the tree took the full blast of shotgun pellets instead of a hare. The two Acer henryi on the main ride were also record trees before the 1990 hurricane but may yet recover their position, despite being planted in 1903. The snake bark maples are well represented in the collection with a number of recent plantings of the outstanding Acer x conspicuum and Acer tegmentosum varieties

## Japanese plants

These are also well represented at Caerhays. Most of the grafted cherries which JCW imported from Japan lived no more than 30 or 40 years and these have been replaced. If we think of japonicas we quickly get into Mahonia, Acer, Camellia, Chaenomeles, Cleyera, Euonymus, Ligustrum, Kerria and Skimmia, all of which are represented at Caerhays. More importantly the so called Wilson 50, the 50 evergreen azalea varieties collected by Wilson on Mount Kurume, all used to exist at Caerhays. Some have died out due to disasters with fallen trees, others have not found favour with the public in garden centres, but well over half still exist at Caerhays today. The best are 'Hinomayo', 'Kirin', 'Shin sekai' and 'Hinodegiri'.

Hoheria sextylosa 'Pendula'

## Australasian plants

Until completion of a new clearing and the widening of some existing paths in 2008 most visitors to Caerhays would have been unaware of the two quarries filled with tree ferns. Many are now in fact self-sown but the old and new trunks fit well together in damp microclimates which resemble their natural habitat. Caerhays also has a growing collection of pseudopanax whose foliage makes a striking and unusual contrast to many of the surrounding Chinese plants. P. laetus, with its huge green leaves and large spiny purplish-red seeds, is a good case in point.

Caerhays used to boast a fine collection of seven record sized Nothofagus species. These were all uprooted in the 1990 hurricane but replacements are now well established and growing on quietly in the background.

Hoherias and Eucryphias often get forgotten at Caerhays because they flower in mid to late summer but, again, Caerhays has a large collection including Eucryphia moorei which was once a record tree but, having fallen over, is up to 20 feet again shooting from the base.

Eucryphia moorei

## Enkianthus, Staphylea and Stewartia

If one looks in the specialist reference books there are relatively few species of enkianthus, staphylea or stewartia which cannot be found at Caerhays. A new enkianthus collection has now achieved flowering size in the new planting on Hovel Cart Road. Although E. cernuus rubens may still be many people's favourite the relatively new E. campanulatus varieties named 'Venus', 'Victoria' and 'Hollandia' are quite something. The evergreen Stewartia pteropetiolata has long been a record tree at Caerhays but S. rostrata is a very attractive early summer flowering tree. Bladder Nuts (Staphylea) or 'Chinese Lantern Trees' as we used to call them as children, may have relatively insignificant flowers, but wait for the pinkish nuts!

Enkianthus campanulatus 'Venus'

## Deciduous Azaleas

There are a great many deciduous azaleas on the drive at Caerhays. The later flowering varieties are clearly species and hybrids of US origin. Although others look more like the better known Knaphill or Exbury strains none quite match the most popular varieties grown by today's nurserymen. There is a huge naming task here but, this aside, there is a marvellous show in late May for those who are strong enough to walk that far. The adjacent, but more modern, hydrangea collection on the drive comes into its own in July.

## Ferns

The moist climate and weather conditions at Caerhays have always encouraged ferns. Ferns include an enormous range of plants and the species include tree ferns, rarities such as Royal Ferns and the common Bracken. Some ferns can be eaten, or used for herbal remedies and many can be found in inaccessible and unexpected places. They are important in the plant and animal economies of uncultivated areas. Nowadays they are much used as decorative plants and in displays for and with more colourful plants. There are also some species which are a real pest; these too need further research.

Initial studies, carried out for the estate in 2010, suggest that ferns and their associated genera are worthy of further investigation. There is an astonishing variety of ferns at Caerhays which must not only be recorded but made available for further study, display and to visitors.

Tree ferns near the Auklandii Garden

## Replanting Programmes

In the 1960s and 1970s the normal plan was to remove one smallish area of over mature planting to make room for a new start with new hybrids or new plants. Often nature intervened to fell trees into areas that did not need clearing but the programme continued regardless. Climate disasters also altered the course of change in the gardens. The winter of 1963 dealt a severe blow to many of the more tender michelias. The 1976 drought brought death to the mature big leaf Rhododendron sinogrande and macabeanum as well as weakening the mature beech shelterbelts.

Nothing could compare, however with the hurricane of 25th/26th January 1990 (the October 1987 storm missed Cornwall). The estate had over 130 separate insurance claims on dwellings and farm buildings, 30 acres of woodland was flattened and about 20% of the garden was lost.

My father left immediately for a lecture tour of Australia in deep depression. By the time he returned, and considerably to his surprise,

Clearing up after the January 1990 hurricane Flash (left), Charles Williams, Philip Tregunna and Kerry Burns

the destruction in the garden had almost been cleared up. This was largely the result of a quick and efficient grant scheme implemented by English Heritage.

By the spring of 1991 around twelve acres were ready for replanting and brand new shelterbelts were in place in fields all around the garden edge. Visitors now question whether the hurricane ever happened as, nearly 20 years on, with our phenomenal Cornish growth rates, there are few gaps left.

The National Magnolia collection caused the next great impetus to expand the garden. If you work on three or four tree magnolias per acre in maturity then a lot of new space was going to be needed for the 200 or so new hybrids acquired between 1995 and 2003. In preparation for this clearings were made at:-

**Penvergate in Forty Acres Wood**. Now the home of the best yellow flowered magnolias and the best M. officinalis var biloba.

**Forty Acres Wood**. A huge new ten acre clearing here now houses the collection of Gresham hybrid magnolias from the USA. This area makes a wonderful vista when viewed from the drive.

**Giddle Orchard**. This four acre clearing can be viewed from the main drive. One day we hope it will be the gateway to new public access to Old Park Wood.

*New planting at The Hovel Cart Road*

**Hovel Cart Road**. A cold and north facing clearing of five acres in what was once just trees. When the shelterbelts get established this will, however, be one of the best areas of the garden for looking down on plants from the top of a steep bank. It is proposed to extend this area in the next few years.

**Kennel Close Field**. This 10 acre field at the top of the garden has been taken out of agricultural production. Progressive shelterbelts of ilex oak, pinus insignis, beech and laurel have now been established for three years and the paths hardcored. It will be five to seven years before one can plant any really choice plants here but already some tougher aesculus species, which will become feature trees, are in place. This will mean that the whole visitor route around the garden will need to be altered.

So, by 2003, the pace of change and the speed of growth in the size of the garden were already beginning to rival the period before The First World War.

Then came another natural disaster in the form of Sudden Oak Death (SOD). In the summer of 2003, SOD was first discovered at Caerhays and Heligan. It probably occurred in most other Cornish gardens as well, although many kept quiet about it. What we had thought was a bad outbreak of honey fungus in our Rhododendron ponticum shelterbelts in a humid summer (nothing new here) turned out to be Phytophthera ramorum, a similar but not identical phytopthera to the one killing Lithocarpus trees in California.

Defra reacted boldly, appearing to have acquired an instinct for compulsory destructive measures. Although they came to the conclusion that SOD was endemic in the ponticum shelterbelts at Caerhays, as elsewhere on the south coast of England, they still demanded immediate destruction without compensation.

A painful learning curve then ensued while Defra discovered the fact that P. ramorum had been endemic in Dutch nursery stock for over a decade and that it was impossible to infect an English oak with SOD even in laboratory conditions. In a democracy, compulsory destruction,

*Caerhays in autumn*

in the public interest, is normally paid for from the public purse.

English Heritage were able to explain to Defra the importance of shelterbelts in historic gardens, and after many years of meetings and debate Defra eventually agreed to fund some ponticum removal at Caerhays on a planned basis over six years. This would allow time for the new shelterbelts of laurel and aucuba to replace Rhododendron ponticum.

However, the destruction of so much had freed up large areas of the garden for replanting with something other than Rhododendron ponticum. The new clearings at Slip Rail, in the Rookery, on Sinogrande Walk and at Red Linney on the drive are the result.

Without SOD the replanting of shelterbelts and the recent expansion of the garden would have been much more limited. The law of unintended consequences has benefited Caerhays again!

Grafted specimen magnolias
at Burncoose

## The Role of Burncoose Nurseries

The 30 acres of garden at Burncoose were owned and managed by the Williams family throughout the last century. Prior to 1983, and before garden centres and plant sales were fashionable in gardens, country estates relied on local nurserymen to market the plants produced by their head gardeners. In the 1960s Treseders Nurseries in Truro performed this role. In the 1970s it was South Down Nurseries in Redruth. In 1983 David Knuckey and his son Philip agreed to move their nursery to Burncoose. Today Burncoose is one of the largest and most successful plant mail order businesses in the country. This has huge implications for Caerhays.

As Caerhays is so far off the beaten track there was never much point in establishing a retail business there. This is the role which Burncoose now performs for the estate. Caerhays supplies Burncoose Nurseries with the majority of its camellia, rhododendron and azalea cuttings. These are then grown on to be sold through the Burncoose Nurseries website and mail order catalogue as well as in the nursery itself. In this way Caerhays gardens and Caerhays bred plants can become much more widely known. However, the principal benefit of Burncoose Nurseries for Caerhays is that Burncoose has access to the best new plants from around the world. These can be identified and procured for Caerhays on trade terms to fill the large number of new planting places which have been created in the garden.

JCW paid for and obtained the very best from China. Today Burncoose can locate and procure the very best new magnolias from Stepping Stones Nursery in New Zealand, Eisenhut's nursery in Switzerland, Magnoliastore in The Netherlands or McCrackens Nursery in the USA. Licences can be obtained to bring plants in from China and contacts are maintained with botanists and growers bringing new species from expeditions to little known parts of the world.

In the past, Caerhays, in its self-contained and somewhat insular way, relied on the generosity of its friends for gifts of new plants. Little was ever paid for and much of the best that was new passed us by. With the resources available to Caerhays at Burncoose, this is no longer the case.

## The Future

For Caerhays to remain an important garden into this 21st Century it has to stop relying on its history and turn instead to new challenges.

With hindsight my father, Julian Williams, probably enjoyed the heyday of JCW's plantings in the 1960s. He remembers that much more of the garden was then in its prime than is the case today. Ornamental trees and shrubs appear to live between 60 and 80 years. Allowing time for plants to establish themselves, one generation of gardeners therefore tends to plant for the benefit of the next two. Although parts of the over mature parts of the garden were replanted after the hurricane, much remains to do.

If we were to sit back and do nothing the gardens at Caerhays would decline into the overgrown bramble patch which so nearly overwhelmed it during the Second World War. A handful of Cornish gardens have experienced this sort of decline. They are fortunately the exception and not the rule.

For Caerhays to remain a potentially "great" garden (whatever that means) it must continue to provide spectacular spring displays to wow the public. It must also continue to preserve, nurture and propagate scientifically rare and unusual plants. Above all, it must expand and develop the range and diversity of plants which it grows. No true collector ever completes his collection.

All this is, after all, the fun of gardening through nature's disasters.

# Chapter 20
# A Tour of the Garden

Caerhays has a large garden covering some 120 acres. In practice a tour of the whole garden would be quite a walk. Four clear routes around the garden have therefore been laid out, offering options for different days, and different ambitions. They are graded to allow for walks of different lengths to be planned. Advice is available for those with disabilities or in wheel chairs as to the best route. Some clearly marked parts of the garden are unsuitable and some wheel chairs can be more versatile than others.

The **Red route** takes visitors through the Auklandii Garden and onto the terraces above the house. If, on arrival at the front door of the Castle, visitors feel that they have gone far enough then they can sit and enjoy the views of Porthluney Cove from the lawn. If they want to venture further then, by turning up the front tarmac drive, they can proceed as far as they wish up the **Green route**.

The energetic should retrace their steps on the **Red route** and rejoin the **Blue route**. This is the way to the best parts of the garden and keeps the sun out of visitors' eyes as they go round. The **Blue route** is reasonably flat for most of the way and keeps to the main paths in the garden. About half way along the **Blue route** visitors have the choice of turning up into the top of the garden on the **Yellow route**. It was here that the 1990 hurricane caused the worst damage, although this is no longer obvious as the new plantings take shape and mature. Those taking the **Yellow route** pass George's hut and rejoin the **Blue route** at the Donkey Shoe and, from there on, it is all downhill.

Half way down the slope, visitors should veer left into a large new clearing overlooking the River Luney valley and the rest of the Caerhays Estate. The water tower in the distance is only a mile or so from Heligan Gardens. The wood to the left is Old Park and was part of the garden until before the First World War. To the right is Forty Acre Wood where two large new clearings have been replanted with magnolias in the last fifteen years. Hopefully both these outlying parts of the garden will be open to visitors before long.

Retracing their steps, and proceeding further down the slope, visitors on the **Blue route** have a choice. They can either carry on down past the quarry, and so on to the Castle, or they can turn left down Hovel Cart Road on the **Green route** and so to the main front drive. This is at its best in March for the magnolias, but deciduous azalea time in May should not be missed.

The view from the 'Four in Hand' across the lake.

Magnolia 'F. J. Williams' in the Auklandii Garden

The slopes on the **Blue route** are steep and there are steps to negotiate beside the site of the Old Playhouse. This path is impassable for wheel chair users and unsuitable for the very elderly or infirm who should proceed to the Castle along the drive on the **Green route**.

It is difficult to see more than a fraction of the garden in just one visit. The camellias are at their best in February and March, the tree magnolias usually peak in mid March and the best of the rhododendrons are in April. In May come the azaleas.

Royal Horticultural Society Awards:

The letters AM, FCC, or AGM on plant labels indicate that awards have been given to those plants by the Royal Horticultural Society.

    **AM** - Award of Merit
    **FCC** - First Class Certificate
    **AGM** - Award of Garden Merit

Camellia 'Caerhays'

Rhododendron impeditum 'J.C. Williams'

Magnolia 'Caerhays Belle'

Azalea 'Caerhays Lavender'

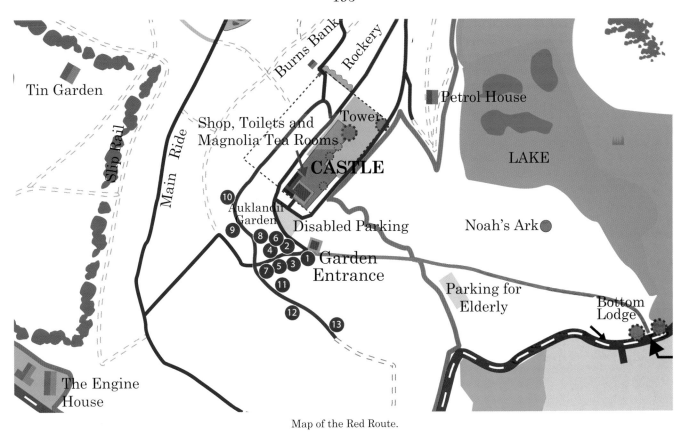

Map of the Red Route.

## The Red Route

**Red 1** - The first magnolia you will see across from the garden entrance is M.x veitchii. It possesses the biggest girth of any magnolia in the garden (12 feet). It is also a Champion Tree (i.e. the largest example of its kind in Britain.). AM 1912.

**Red 2** - Azalea 'Hinomayo'. As you can see these were planted in large groups in order to make more of an impact. AM 1921. FCC 1945.

**Red 3** - Drimys winteri. Introduced from Chile in 1827. They say that the sailors would take the bark with them on long trips to chew on, as it is high in vitamin C, which would prevent scurvy. AM 1971. AGM 2002.

**Red 4** - Rhododendron 'Cornish Red'. A cross between Rhododendron griffithianum and a Rhododendron williamsianum planted in 1921.

**Red 5** - Lithocarpus pachyphyllus which has enormous clusters of nobbly greenish fruits. Hillier's 'Manual of Trees and Shrubs' states that the fruits appear to be infertile but this tree has matured and produces many fertile acorns which we have regularly germinated.

**Red 6** - Magnolia campbellii Alba seedling which has very pale pink flowers. This tree features in Thomas Packenham's book "Meetings with Unusual Trees" where the author refers to it as appearing to be covered with pink flamingos.

**Red 7** - Dicksonia antarctica. The Australian tree fern which arrived in Cornwall by accident when the trunks were used as ballast in large ships. Once in port they were thrown to one side but revived

Magnolia campbellii Alba seedling

## The Red Route

and began to shoot. These were then planted using stones to encircle them (perhaps also to support their fat trunks). They have grown on happily for over 100 years and now self sow themselves all over the gardens.

The Auklandii Garden was named after the Rhododendron auklandii (now renamed griffthianum) which was destroyed by a freak whirlwind and replanted with donations from tenants, staff and friends to celebrate Mr Charles Williams' 21st birthday in 1978. You will see the plaque beside the path.

**Red 8** - Rhododendron 'Saffron Queen' - a fantastic yellow. You need to look closely to avoid missing the peeling bark on the main trunk. AM 1948. A Caerhays hybrid.

**Red 9** - Magnolia sargentiana robusta x M. mollicomata 'Lanarth'. After many years we have now named this Caerhays hybrid 'F.J. Williams'. AM 2010

**Red 10** - Magnolia 'Caerhays Surprise' was bred by Philip Tregunna (retired Head Gardener) in 1959. It first flowered in 1967. Awarded the Reginald Cory Cup in 1973 for the best new plant introduction. AM 1973.

If you carry on along the path you will arrive on the primrose, cyclamen and daffodil covered banks above the front door. There are various seats where you can view the house and take in the panorama of the bay. However, if you return to the entrance of the Auklandii Garden, and go straight on past the tree ferns you will see:-

**Red 11** - Rhododendron falconeri. An impressive Himalayan rhododendron introduced by Sir Joseph Hooker in 1850. It flowers very late in the season in May or June. AM 1922. AGM 2002.

**Red 12** - Above the path, the long line of magnolia seedlings planted in the early 1960s shows just how varied the results can be in terms of size, shape and colour. None have turned out to be anything special or worthy of naming.

**Red 13** - Below the path there is a group of yew trees overshadowing some remains associated with earlier buildings at Caerhays.

To extend your walk you can now return to the crossroads and head up the **Blue route**.

Rhododendron 'Saffron Queen'

Magnolia 'F.J. Williams'

Rhododendron falconeri

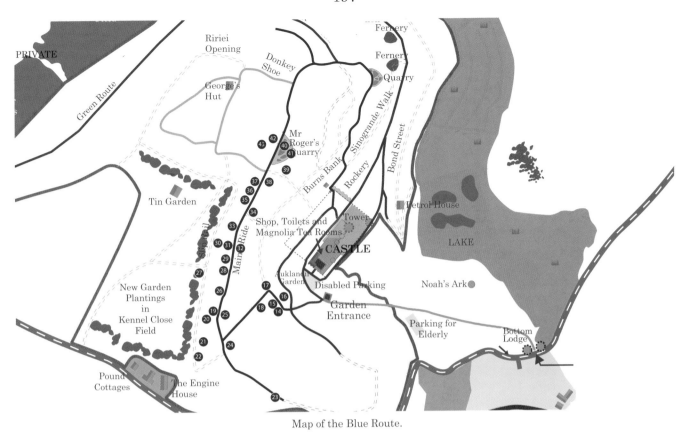

Map of the Blue Route.

## The Blue Route

**Blue 14** - Magnolia sargentiana robusta x M. sprengeri 'Diva'. Bred by Charles Michael (former Head Gardener) and from the same batch of seeds as Magnolia 'Caerhays Belle'. Perhaps this will be formally registered and named one day, as it is well worth it.

**Blue 15** - The original Magnolia campbellii collected in China and planted in 1910 took 40 years to flower and is one of the first magnolias to flower. This is normally in the middle of February as the seasons seem to be getting warmer and earlier.

**Blue 16** - Below the path is another Magnolia x veitchii which was 72 feet tall with a 7 foot 3 inch girth in 1966; it is probably rather bigger today. FCC 1921. Champion Tree.

**Blue 17** - A large clump of one of the earliest x williamsii camellias bred at Caerhays and named after the founder of the garden. These are the original plants of Camellia x williamsii 'J C Williams'. FCC 1942. AGM 2002.

**Blue 18** - Prior to the 1990 hurricane, when they lost their tops, both these Magnolia x veitchii were over 120 feet tall. One of them is again approaching this sort of height.

The area beyond the two Magnolia x veitchii had around 20 mature beech trees.

Magnolia campbellii

Camellia x williamsii 'J.C. Williams'

Magnolia x veitchii

# The Blue Route

After one stormy night, a beech tree was blown down onto one of the two veitchii magnolias. Further investigation showed the remaining beech trees to be in poor health, so in 2000 we made the decision to remove them, as they were threatening many other choice plants. The area has been replanted with several yellow magnolias and future replacements for some of the best home grown Caerhays hybrids.

By now you will have reached the top path; please do turn around and look back, as the view is fantastic.

**Blue 19** - Turning left at the top of the path brings you to two ancient Camellia reticulata 'Captain Rawes' above the path. This was the first reticulata to dazzle the eyes of Western European gardens. The plant is named after Captain Rawes of the East India Company who brought it from Canton in 1820. FCC 1963.

**Blue 20** - The tall upright tree with purplish new growth which you see above the reticulatas was described by E H Wilson as one of the most beautiful trees of the Chinese forest. Despite being a mature tree which is over 90 years old, Emmenopterys henryi has yet to flower at Caerhays.

**Blue 21** - Magnolia dawsoniana was originally introduced by E H Wilson in 1908. This plant arrived from France circa. 1921. AM 1939. Champion Tree.

**Blue 22** - Well up above the path is an interesting cluster of mature evergreen Chinese oaks, including Quercus phillyreoides, Q. acuta and Q. glauca.

**Blue 23** - You are now only one field away from the sea so our windbreaks here are absolutely vital. In 1991 we planted a double row of Pinus insignis in the field on the other side of the road as, in time, the mature trees within the garden windbreak will need removing and replanting underneath with laurel.

**Blue 24** - On your return, hidden away below the path, is a yellow Magnolia 'Butterflies' which quickly fades to cream and off-white after the flowers have opened.

**Blue 25** - It is easy to miss rarities because they appear at first glance to be dull or because they flower later in the year. Stewartia pteropetiolata was introduced by George Forrest in 1912 and is thriving here 90 years on. Champion Tree.

**Blue 26** - This is the first small area of the 1990 hurricane damage which visitors will see. Magnolia 'Star Wars' seems to be the longest flowering of all magnolias (about 6 - 8 weeks in total) and can have a second flush of flowers later in the season. It has even been known to produce a few flowers around Christmas. AM 1991. AGM 2002. Champion Tree.

**Blue 27** - This area is known as The Slip Rail. The slip rails are in fact the entrance to a new expansion of the garden into Kennel Close field where we have planted new windbreaks and here, when they have grown, we will start to expand the National Magnolia Collection. This area will also provide better access for disabled visitors in the future when we create a new second car park at the top of the field.

**Blue 28** - Rhododendron 'Crossbill' (Rh. spinuliferum x Rh. lutescens). A Caerhays hybrid raised by J.C Williams and named in 1933.

**Blue 29** - Camellia 'Adelina Patti' is prone to what is called

Quercus acuta

Stewartia pteropetiolata

Rhododendron 'Crossbill'

"sporting". If you look closely you will find pure red and pure white flowers on odd branches alongside the conventional pink flowers with a white edge. AM 1996. AGM 2002.

**Blue 30** - This is the second, rather larger open area of 1990 hurricane damage. There are some specimen plants which will hopefully dominate in 50 years' time and a great many other plants with shorter life spans which will eventually be completely overshadowed by the specimen trees.

**Blue 31** - Acer henryi had its top ripped out in the hurricane of 1990 but still remains a Champion Tree.

**Blue 32** - As you walk beside the laurel hedge there are several paths through the hedge. Down the first path just before the tree fern, you will see some clumps of Caerhays bred rhododendrons, some of which are early and some of late flowering. They will be assessed over several years on the basis of their flower colour and growth rate. Any that are deemed good enough will then be exhibited to the RHS to see if they are worthy of registration and naming.

Rhododendron 'Red Admiral'

**Blue 33** - Back on the main path you pass under Quercus lamellosa, another Champion Tree. According to the 18th edition of W.J. Bean's 'Trees and Shrubs' this Quercus lamellosa is the only recorded example of this species growing outside in the British Isles. It came here from the Burma/ Yunnan border and only just survives our climate as you can see. We have two in the garden. Above you, there is another area of new planting. A huge chestnut once stood here which survived a bolt of lightening but

Quercus lamellosa

Magnolia 'Philip Tregunna'

eventually became too old and could not withstand the winter gales. Sometimes new areas for replanting are created 'naturally'.

**Blue 34** - Below the laurel hedge to the left is Magnolia 'Philip Tregunna', a hybrid between M. sargentiana var robusta x M. campbellii. Bred and raised by Philip Tregunna, the head gardener at Caerhays who retired in 1996 after over 40 years of service, although he still helps out in his retirement. FCC 1992.

**Blue 35** - Back on the main path you come to Camellia 'George Blandford' which is a Caerhays hybrid and takes its name from a former gardener and gamekeeper who worked at Caerhays for over 70 years. George's ashes were scattered underneath this plant. His son, Maurice, also worked in the house as the butler for nearly 40 years. AM 1965. AGM 2002.

**Blue 36** - 20 years ago and prior to the damage caused by Dutch Elm disease, this area used to house a stand of elms. Woodland gardens evolve and develop just as quickly as any other type of garden and here you will find perhaps the best known yellow flowering magnolia, Magnolia 'Elizabeth'. AGM 2002.

Camellia 'George Blandford'

**Blue 37** - Forms of Fagus sylvatica 'Purpurea' or 'Purple Beech' can be seen here in different shades of red or purple. Perhaps these were planted too closely so one or two will have to be felled in time.

**Blue 38** - Turn now below the laurel hedge and look to the right. The present Curator of Wisley believes that this clump of Acer 'Senkaki' (now renamed 'Sango - Kaku') with spectacular colour in both spring and autumn, may well be one of the largest in the country. They are doing remarkably well considering they are growing on an old stone pile. AM 1950. AGM 2002.

**Blue 39** - Look now to the left. Easily overlooked is a stand of huge Michelias which have varying leaf forms and probably include more than one as yet unidentified species. These are now a little exposed due to the opening up of another area of over mature beech trees below but they still all produce flowers.

If you now return to the main path you can carry on along the **Blue route** or you can take the longer **Yellow route** which will bring you back onto the Blue Route at the Donkey Shoe.

**Blue 40** - Magnolia 'Lanarth' planted in the quarry is a most dazzling colour. FCC 1947.

Magnolia 'Lanarth'

**Blue 41** - Behind it in the quarry is one of the two original M. campbellii Alba. FCC 1951. There are several small quarries in the gardens and woodland. The stone was used for the construction of the castle itself. The sheltered conditions and dramatic landforms of such quarries have attracted gardeners in several Cornish gardens. Other notable examples are found at Port Eliot, Catchfrench and Trewidden.

**Blue 42** - Above, and through the laurel hedge, you will find Quercus oxyodon; another rare evergreen oak which is believed to be one of the few existing in the UK. Champion Tree. AM 1998 for foliage.

**Blue 43** - Hidden away here is a rare Mexican Magnolia macrophylla subsp. dealbata which flowers in the summer. This tender plant came from the Temperate House at The Savill Garden, Windsor, when it was refurbished.

Magnolia campbellii Alba

To continue your walk you can now return to the start of the **Yellow route**.

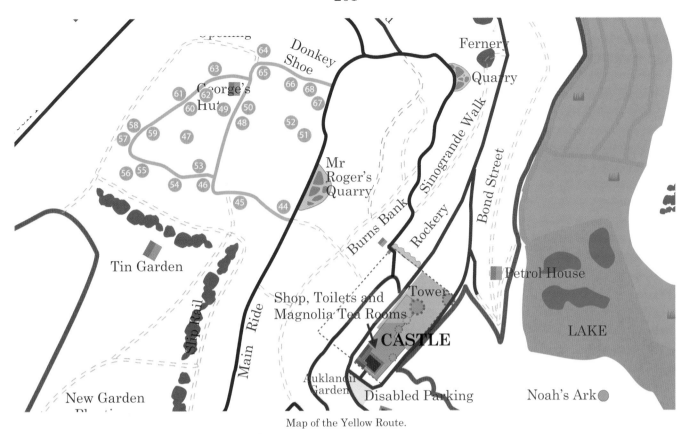

Map of the Yellow Route.

## The Yellow Route

**Yellow 44** - This clump of Camellia saluenensis hybrids may only show a few tail end flowers in spring but, by late autumn, they are already full of colour.

**Yellow 45** - You now walk under a fantastic red Rhododendron called 'Mrs Butler'. Beside the path here is also a scented Rhododendron 'Lady Alice Fitzwilliam'. FCC 1881. AGM 2002. These can be short-lived but are well worth their place in anyone's garden. In a colder climate they would need to be grown in pots and brought in during the colder winter months.

**Yellow 46** - Shielded within a protective coating of camellias is the tender Rhododendron stenaulum with its delightful peeling bark and unusual dark purple new growth. The flowers have a slight scent. AM 1937.

Further on the path splits to the left but, if you carry on you will see:

**Yellow 47** - The large area on the left was a mature part of the garden with many record specimens until the hurricane of 1990 flattened the whole lot. Many people said "great, more room for new planting", but there were some fine record sized Nothofagus lost here. After replanting, this area has filled up quite quickly with some rarities and other more common plants. As time has gone on we have started to take out the more common plants to give the rarities more room.

**Yellow 48** - Tucked away on the right is an interesting foliage plant, Gevuina avellana, the 'Chilean Hazel' with its huge pinnate leaves. It has panicles of white flowers followed by bright red berries. AM 1983.

Rhododendron 'Lady Alice Fitzwilliam'

Rhododendron stenaulum

## The Yellow Route

**Yellow 49** - Her Royal Highness Queen Elizabeth the Queen Mother planted this Magnolia sargentiana var robusta seedling during one of her visits to the garden in 1981. Initially the flowers were small and pale but they have improved considerably with age, as is so often the case with seedling magnolias.

The Queen Mother planting a Magnolia sargentiana var robusta seedling

Michelia doltsopa

**Yellow 50** - This Michelia doltsopa may not be the tallest in the garden but it is certainly the most accessible. If you have never smelt the fragrance before, you may well be overwhelmed. Better smelt at a distance, some may say! AM 1961.

**Yellow 51** - Tucked away behind the Michelia doltsopa is a huge clump of about 12 Podocarpus salignus. This clump is said to be larger than anything left surviving in the wild in Chile today. Hence it may one day be of use to anyone seeking to reintroduce the plant back into the wild. AGM 2002. Champion Tree.

**Yellow 52** - Further in you can find Rhododendron 'Caerhays Rebecca', a Caerhays hybrid named following the BBC's filming of Daphne du Maurier's 'Rebecca' at Caerhays in 1985.

You will by now have come across a tin-sided hut called 'George's Hut'. This was named after Mr George Blandford who worked as a gamekeeper. This area was where pheasants were once reared with bantams in coops in the open rides.

Rhododendron 'Caerhays Rebecca'

For the purposes of this guide we will now return to the left turning on the Yellow route.

**Yellow 53** - You now pass under a massive Magnolia delavayi; an evergreen magnolia of Chinese origin which can flower from July to November but seldom if ever sets seed in our climate. FCC 1913.

**Yellow 54** - You then pass a plant which looks three parts dead for most of the year, although it is not. Hoheria angustifolia has bark which looks as if it has been gnawed by rats. AM 1967.

**Yellow 55** - The large clumps of Rhododendron 'Mrs Butler' hybrids which then surround you, are one of the most floriferous and gaudy displays in the garden during April.

Magnolia delavayi

**Yellow 56** - Another Chinese introduction by E H Wilson from 1900, tucked away behind the Mrs Butler hybrids, is Lindera megaphylla with its handsome trailing evergreen leaves. Champion Tree.

**Yellow 57** - A Rhododendron macabeanum is to the left of the path. In its prime in early April when in full flower, this can be one of the most stunning plants in the garden. However some of these large leaf Rhododendrons take a year off and then produce very few flowers. FCC 1938. AM 1937. AGM 2002.

**Yellow 58** - Kalopanax pictus is startling for its thorny stems and well worth its place for its acer like leaves and autumn colour. It is commonly known as 'The Devil's Walking Stick'. Touch it at your peril.

**Yellow 59** - Just to muddle things up a bit is a plant which some

Rhododendron macabeanum

might consider better suited to the herbaceous border. Two examples of Rosa roxburghii touching the path earn their place as Wilson introductions from 1908, although only planted here in 1991.

**Yellow 60** - Prior to the 1990 hurricane this Acer griseum was believed to be the largest in the country. The tree still shows a wound incurred from shotgun pellets aimed at a hare at its base (Hares and rabbits are no friends of magnolias or woodland gardens). AM 1922. AGM 2002.

Rosa roxburghii

Berberis wilsoniae

**Yellow 61** - Berberis wilsoniae was discovered by Wilson in 1904 and named after his wife. It appears an insignificant plant in spring but has coral berries and brilliant red autumn colour. FCC 1907.

**Yellow 62** - Magnolia 'Goldstar' (M. acuminata var subcordata 'Miss Honeybee' x M. stellata) has flowers much like stellata in shape. They open as a primrose yellow but fade back to creamy white as the flowers age.

**Yellow 63** - Another massive evergreen oak, Lithocarpus cleistocarpa, with draping silvery new growth, can be seen on the left. Occasionally it produces just a few acorns. Champion Tree.

At this point both Yellow routes rejoin and you should again be beside George's Hut. Continue towards the **Blue route**.

**Yellow 64** - Within the Rhododendron ririei opening in March you can usually see Magnolia sargentiana robusta, Magnolia mollicomata, a Magnolia campbellii seedling and a Magnolia 'Lanarth' seedling all flowering at the same time. This enables you to identify clearly which shape and flower forms represent each species.

**Yellow 65** - On the corner as you veer right is an elderly Styrax japonicus with its nearly grey bark and masses of pendulous white flowers in June. These attract insects by the thousand. FCC 1885. AGM 2002.

**Yellow 66** - Just off the path is Rhododendron macrocarpum which was discovered in China in 1931 and has the most odd huge red pendulous fruits. These we sow in open loam seed beds for germination but you have to protect them well from mice. AM 1947.

**Yellow 67** - Moving off the path you come to Magnolia nitida. An evergreen magnolia with leathery dark shining green leaves and rich dark red new growth which fades slowly to green. The flowers are creamy white and have a scent a little like that of a sliced lemon. AM 1966. Champion Tree.

**Yellow 68** - To the left of Magnolia nitida is the original Magnolia 'Caerhays Surprise'. About 15 years ago this plant died to ground level but has since reshot as a multi-stemmed tree.

You can now return to the **Blue route.**

Lithocarpus cleistocarpa

Styrax japonicus

Rehderodendron macrocarpum

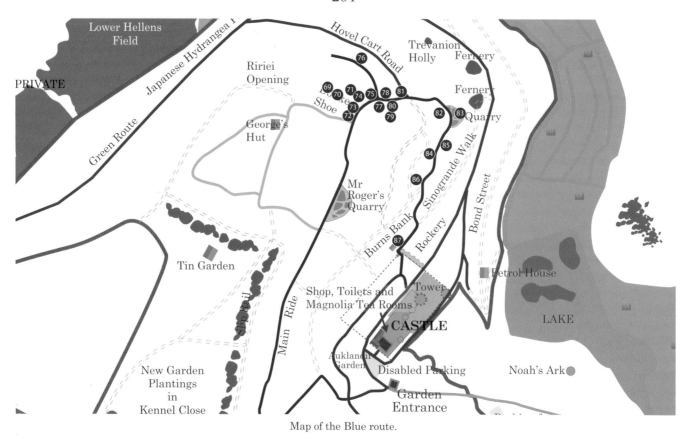

Map of the Blue route.

## The Blue Route (continued)

**Blue 69** - Behind the largest Michelia doltsopa in the garden and also in the UK, lurks a large clump of Rhododendron wilsoniae. Despite its name the species is not exactly eye-catching. AM 1971.

**Blue 70** - In front of the Michelia doltsopa sits a hybrid: Michelia doltsopa 'Silver Cloud'. Its scent is superb but very different from M. doltsopa. Cinnamon scented is the most common comment and it is therefore no accident that Cinnamomum camphora and Cinnamomum glanduliferum are located right alongside.

**Blue 71** - Just below Michelia doltsopa is a large clump of Rhododendron loderi 'King George'. Due to its height, it can only be seen in full flower with difficulty, but the peeling bark is well worth a look on its own. AM 1968. FCC 1970. AGM 2002. Champion Tree.

**Blue 72** - Back on the path you may smell an Azara microphylla 'Variegata' which is vanilla scented. This is the hardiest of the Azaras which come from Chile.

**Blue 73** - Magnolia mollicomata 'Lanarth'. On first flowering the flowers were muddy pink all over but, by the third year, the colour came true albeit only on one branch. Today this is undoubtedly one of the best plants in the garden for colour. This is the New Zealand form of M. 'Lanarth' and has much larger flowers with a different shape from the original introductions seen elsewhere in the garden.

**Blue 74** - Camellia reticulata 'Mary Williams'. AM 1942. FCC 1964. is close enough to touch Camellia 'Cornish Snow' AM 1948. AGM 2002. Both were raised at Caerhays but have very contrasting habits.

Magnolia 'Lanarth'

**Blue 75** - Before the laurel hedge is Pieris 'Charles Williams'; a striking form raised here from George Forrest's seed and named after the Rt. Hon. Charles Williams who lived at Caerhays from 1939 to 1955. The adjacent Camellia 'Mary Williams' was named after his wife. AM 1965.

**Blue 76** - Turn left under the laurel hedge to view another of the recent (2000) new clearings and a panorama of the Luney Valley. This can be a cold spot which will take time to warm up and colonise as the shelterbelts grow and develop. The clearing houses some new and exciting Podocarpus varieties. We also hope to clear the area to the left, thus joining up with the planting on the main drive.

**Blue 77** - On leaving this area you see, ahead of you, Hoheria glabrata which flowers in late summer. AM 1911. FCC 1946.

**Blue 78** - J C Williams was in close contact with the Rothschilds of Exbury and it is no surprise to discover one of their earlier hybrids, Rhododendron 'Mrs Lionel de Rothschild', growing as a large clump at Caerhays. AM 1931. FCC 2001. AGM 2002.

**Blue 79** - Another Magnolia, 'Caerhays Surprise', found here grows in far more shade and is in a colder spot than the others. In consequence it flowers a couple of weeks later, usually in May.

**Blue 80** - Camellia 'Mrs D W Davis' - the flowers are enormous in size and off white. AM 1960. FCC 1968.

**Blue 81** - Rhododendron desquamatum has aromatic oblong leaves which are dark brown and scaly beneath. The flowers are dark mauve and the colour really hits you as you walk down the path. Certainly not one to be missed. AM 1938.

At this point you can carry on the **Blue route** to the castle or follow the **Green route** down onto the main drive. If you choose to follow the **Green route** then go to Green 100. Wheel chair users must follow the **Green route.**

**Blue 82** - As you go down the path you will now be overlooking the main quarry. As you walk down the path, the plants on the right hand side are Rhododendron orbiculare AM 1922. AGM 2002. Rhododendron davidisonianum AM 1935. FCC 1955. AGM 2002. Rhododendron lutescens and Rhododendron argyrophyllum AM 1934. These all arrived in Wilson's second seed lot in 1906.

**Blue 83** - Below the path on the left is Rhododendron staminium, Rhododendron fortunei (now called Rhododendron discolour). AM 1922. FCC 1922. AGM 2002. Rhododendron ovatum and Rhododendron fargesii AM 1926. AGM 2002. These species were also among the very first batches to arrive at Caerhays in 1905, so you are now at the place from which the garden that you have walked around has developed. If these plants had failed then there might well not have been a garden for you to see today.

**Blue 84** - Touching the path and each other are two more Caerhays plants: Camellia 'Caerhays' and Rhododendron impeditum 'J C Williams'. The latter is supposed to be a dwarf rockery plant but grows far taller than that in our climate here. AM 1969.

**Blue 85** - Below the path you can see an area of Rhododendron ponticum cleared in 2008 which is known as Sinogrande Walk, but is now far too exposed an area for us to grow big leaved rhododendrons.

Pieris 'Charles Williams'

Rhododendron desquamatum

Once our choice conifer and liquidambar trees have grown up we shall again be able to plant more tender rhododendrons here.

**Blue 86** - This bank is edged by a superb example of 'Jack and Jill' Cornish hedging made in the 1920s. Hardly a stone is out of its original place. A Mr Burns built it and his grandson, Kerry Burns, has been a key figure in the garden here for the past 38 years.

**Blue 87** - At the end of the path you walk past the site of the Old Playhouse, which has now rotted away, and down some steps into a square tower. This tower, one of the corner towers of the walled c1700 garden once had an internal stair to a rooftop viewing platform. You go through the tower to find yourself overlooking the castle.

Overlooking the castle

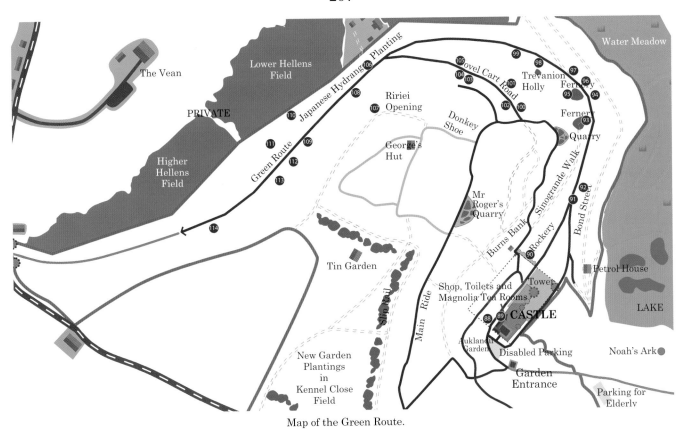

Map of the Green Route.

## The Green Route

You join the **Green route** on the gravel by the castle.

**Green 88** - Magnolia 'Caerhays Belle', on your left, was planted above the battlements in 1951. It took 14 years to flower for the first time and was named after George Blandford's wife, Belle, who lived in the adjacent stable flat. FCC 2009. Champion Tree.

**Green 89** - On your right, outside the former ladies toilets (now marked private), are Camellia saluenensis and Camellia japonica. It was from these two now decrepit plants that the original x williamsii camellias were hybridised at Caerhays. They are now found all around the world.

**Green 90** - As you pass under the arch onto the drive you will find the rockery on your left. Despite a considerable amount of new planting it still contains some of the original rhododendrons which were thought (sometimes wrongly) to be of dwarf habit. They include Rhododendron valentiniaum AM 1933. Rhododendron weyrichii, Rhododendron russatum AM 1927. FCC 1933. AGM 2002. Rhododendron spinuliferum and Rhododendron sanguineum subsp. didymum. There are also two small plants of Rhododendron martinianum named after John Martin, the first head gardener at Caerhays.

**Green 91** - You will now have moved on to the 'Four in Hand', which is the turning point for horse drawn carriages. You will also have the very best view over the newly restored lake and can enjoy the large clumps of Azalea 'Amoena' in the foreground which were

## The Green Route

planted in 1897. You can also see a planting of Erica arborea 'Albert's Gold' carried out in 2002 in honour of Her Majesty Queen Elizabeth's Golden Jubilee. By no means all of the plants have survived!

**Green 92** - Below the drive, along Bond Street, there are large plantings of Camellias 'J C Williams' FCC 1942. AGM 2002. 'Saint Ewe' and 'November Pink' AM 1950. These can now be seen because we have cleared the top area and replanted with a rich mix of camellias. This camellia bank will also stop some of the under-draft affecting the new planting along Sinogrande Walk.

**Green 93** - The fernery comes next and is now rather more visible due to clearing away the Rhododendron ponticum. Many of these tree ferns are self sown seedlings and, as you can see, some are growing down the side of solid rock. You will also see that when trunks get blown over the growing point starts to turn upwards and continues on growing upright again.

**Green 94** - Looking across the valley into Forty Acre Wood opposite you will glimpse another clearing where around forty new American magnolias were planted in 2002. When these are more mature we will open up a new vista across the drive.

**Green 95** - The second small quarry also contains a group of Dicksonia antarctica. These samples came from the Blue Mountains in New South Wales, Australia, and were brought back, it is believed, by a member of the Treseder family. The Treseders were nurserymen in Truro for many years.

**Green 96** - Touching the drive opposite the fernery is the rare Cornus walteri that was introduced by Wilson in 1907. It is a dull plant which may well account for its rarity.

**Green 97** - The recent removal of a dead English Oak has made room for a yellow variegated Tulip tree, Liriodendron tulipifera 'Aureomarginatum' AM 1974. AGM 2002.

**Green 98** - Above the drive is the Trevanion Holly which was hit by a falling fir tree in January 2008. One of the few relics of the Trevanion family who lived at Caerhays from around 1370 until 1840.

**Green 99** - In early spring, the sweet scent which you catch here on the drive emanates from the shrubby honeysuckle, aptly named Lonicera fragrantissima.

**Green 100** - Sometimes genuinely dwarf plants prosper in a woodland setting. After nearly thirty years of struggling, Acer japonicum 'Aureum' now just about merits its position. FCC 1884. AGM 2002.

If you had turned from the **Blue route** onto the **Green route** at the top of the Hovel Cart Road this is what you would see next.

**Green 101** - There are relatively few deciduous rhododendrons and only one pure white one, Rhododendron quinquefolium. This flowers before its leaves emerge. It is getting rather old now. AM 1931.

**Green 102** - The more established new planting above the Hovel Cart Road features mainly late spring flowering plants and is designed to entice visitors down to the main drive where the best azaleas can be found. The area was cleared in 1999.

Acer japonicum 'Aureum'

**Green 103** - Rhododendron 'Ostara'. An early flowering mucronulatum hybrid with striking reddish-purple flowers on bare stems.

**Green 104** - In the new planting itself but, sheltered by the large Rhododendron 'Cornish Reds' below, is a new collection of Rhododendron williamsianum hybrids, most of which were bred in Germany.

**Green 105** - On from the 'Cornish Reds' below the path are two original plants of Acer forrestii planted in 1906 which are now showing their age.

By now you should be back on the main front drive.

**Green 106** - There was always quite a range of hydrangeas dotted along the main drive. A new planting of some of the more exotic Japanese species and cultivars was started here in 2002, which brightens up the drive in summer.

**Green 107** - Right at the very top of the clearing furthest from the drive is Magnolia 'J C Williams' which won a First Class Certificate when exhibited at the RHS in London in 2002.

**Green 108** - Closer to the drive is Acer negundo var violaceum with its long reddish-pink flower tassels in March. AM 1975.

**Green 109** - There are several plants of Rhododendron nobleanum in the area including the Caerhays raised hybrid, 'Winter Intruder', registered with the RHS in 2007. They provide a colourful display between December and February if not prematurely frosted, as is often the case.

**Green 110** - Below the drive just above the laurel hedge are two plants of Magnolia sieboldii, another late flowering and scented species. FCC 1894. AGM 2002.

Rhododendron 'Ostara'

Rhododendron 'Cornish Red'

Acer forrestii

The Main Drive

Acer negundo var violaceum

Magnolia sieboldii

**Green 111** - The Magnolia 'Iolanthe' growing below the drive has a peculiar drooping habit which may be caused by young pheasant poults roosting in its branches.

**Green 112** - Tucked in behind Acer palmatum 'Osakazuki' AGM 2002 is a collection of nearly all the x williamsii camellias raised at Caerhays. One is able to compare them all in one place.

**Green 113** - Above the drive, and just below a plantation of fairly nondescript seedling Camellia reticulatas, is a clump of Rhododendron mucronulatum. This is another winter flowering species with superb rose-purple flowers from December through to February.

**Green 114** - Carrying on up the drive you will now find a huge clearance. The area has been planted back as woodland but with a wide strip of ornamental tree and shrub planting adjacent to the drive. The garden will therefore soon extend, for the first time, right up to the Top Lodge. Below the drive you can see that we have planted a fine new avenue of evergreen Ilex oaks. Once grown up these should protect the new planting right the way down the drive.

Across the valley you can see the early nineteenth century Caerhays Rectory, called 'The Vean'. This was restored in 2006 by my wife, Lizzie Williams, and opened in 2007 as a venue for weddings, corporate entertainment, family gatherings and shooting parties. The earlier rectory stood in the rectangular block of trees downhill to the left of The Vean.

Magnolia 'Iolanthe'

The Vean

# Section Five
# Appendices

## Plant Schedules

| | | |
|---|---|---|
| Appendix 1 | 40 of the best Magnolias in the Caerhays collection | 213 |
| Appendix 2 | A National Collection of Magnolias | 217 |
| Appendix 3 | Magnolia hybrids bred at Caerhays and Burncoose | 223 |
| Appendix 4 | Camellia x williamsii hybrids bred at Caerhays and Burncoose | 225 |
| Appendix 5 | Rhododendron hybrids bred and raised at Caerhays | 229 |
| Appendix 6 | Rare and evergreen Oaks at Caerhays- *Lithocarpus* and *Quercus* | 235 |
| Appendix 7 | The Podocarpus Collection at Caerhays | 237 |
| Appendix 8 | A selection of Champion Trees at Caerhays | 241 |

## Historic Schedules

| | | |
|---|---|---|
| Appendix 9 | Domesday Manors at Caerhays | 243 |
| Appendix 10 | Later Manorial History and Historic Settlements | 245 |

## Sources and References

| | | |
|---|---|---|
| Appendix 11 | Principal Sources; Further Reading; Acknowledgements. | 251 |

## Activities and Contacts at Caerhays

| | | |
|---|---|---|
| Appendix 12 | Activities at Caerhays; web addresses and telephone numbers. | 255 |

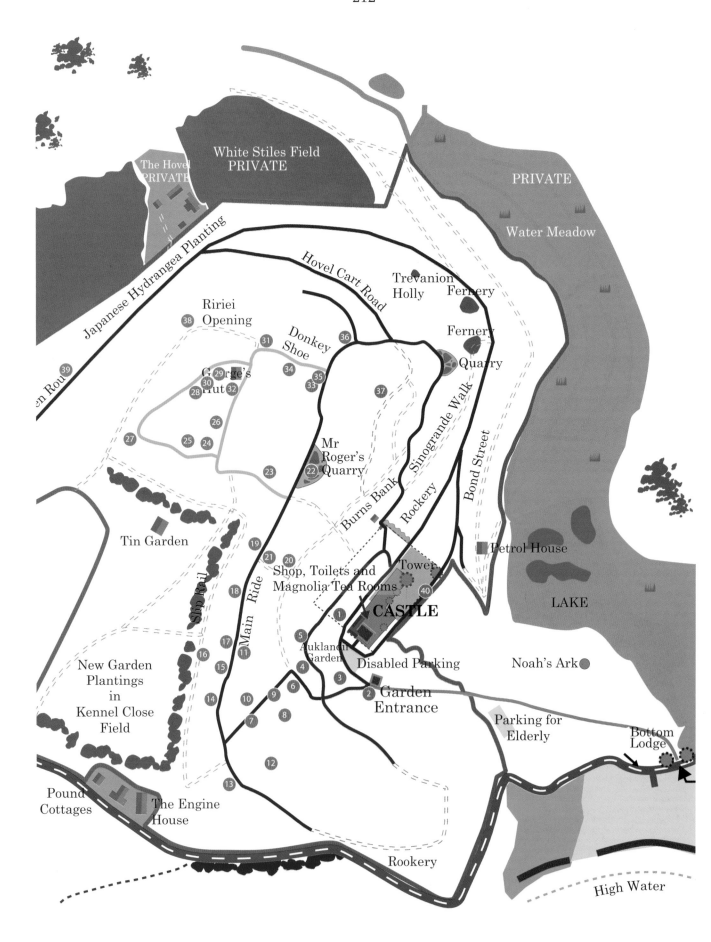

# Appendix 1
# 40 of the best Magnolias at Caerhays

1. (sargentiana var robusta x sprengeri 'Diva')
'Caerhays Belle'

2. x veitchii 'Peter Veitch'

3. campbellii Alba seedling

4. (sargentiana var robusta x mollicomata 'Lanarth')
'F.J. Williams'

5. (campbelli var mollicomata x liliiflora 'Nigra') 'Caerhays Surprise'

6. campbellii

7. (acuminata 'Miss Honeybee' x Michelia figo) 'Yuchelia'

8. (acuminata x denudata) 'Sundance'

9. (x brooklynensis 'Woodsman' x 'Elizabeth') 'Hot Flush'

10. sprengeri 'Diva' 'Burncoose'

11.  ('Miss Honeybee' x M. 'Gold Crown')
     'Daphne'

12.  campbellii 'Kew's Surprise'

13.  dawsoniana

14.  sargentiana

15.  (campbellii x liliiflora )'Star Wars'

16.  x brooklynensis 'Evamaria'

17.  delavayi

18.  (liliiflora x x veitchii) 'Heaven Scent'

19.  (acuminata x denudata) 'Elizabeth'

20.  sargentiana var robusta

21.  (sargentiana var robusta x campbellii)

22. campbellii Alba

23. macrophylla subsp. dealbata

24. (denudata x 'Vulcan') 'Shiraz'

25. (liliiflora x 'Mark Jury') 'Serene'

26. ('Mark Jury' x soulangeana 'Lennei') 'Atlas'

27. sieboldii

28. campbelli 'Darjeeling'

29. (acuminata var subcordata 'Miss Honeybee' x stellata 'Rosea') 'Gold Star'

30. (soulangeana x liliiflora 'Nigra') 'Genie'

31. campbellii 'Betty Jessel'

32. sargentiana var robusta seedling (Planted by H.R.H. The Queen Mother)

33. nitida

22.

23.

24.

25.

26.

27.

28.

29.

30.

31.

32.

33.

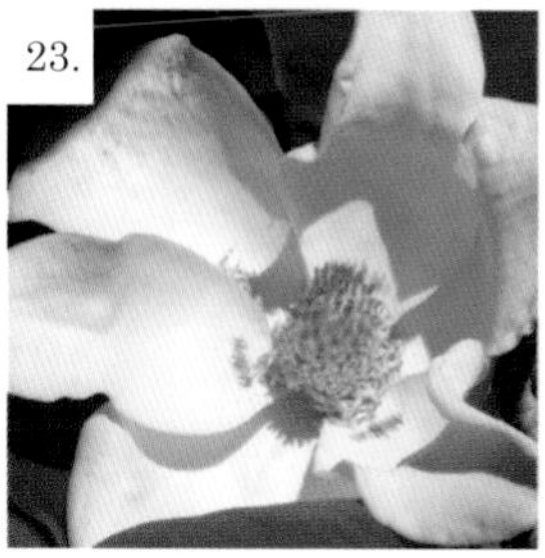

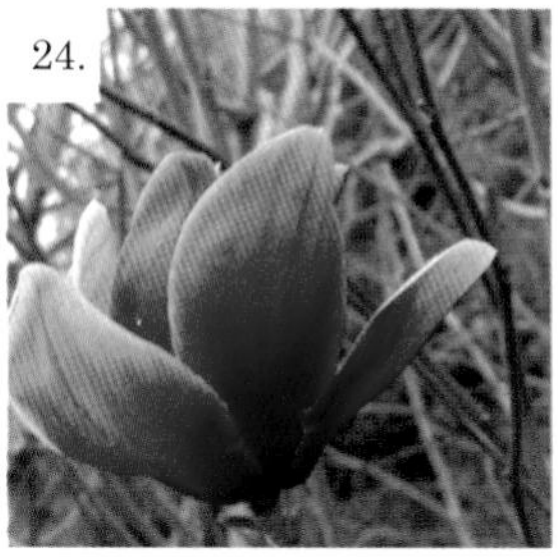

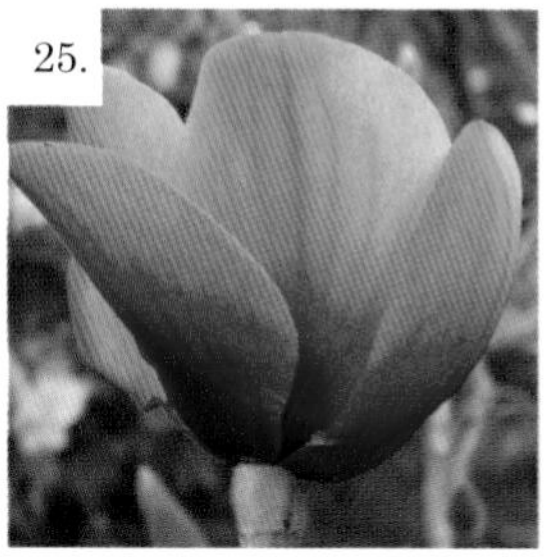

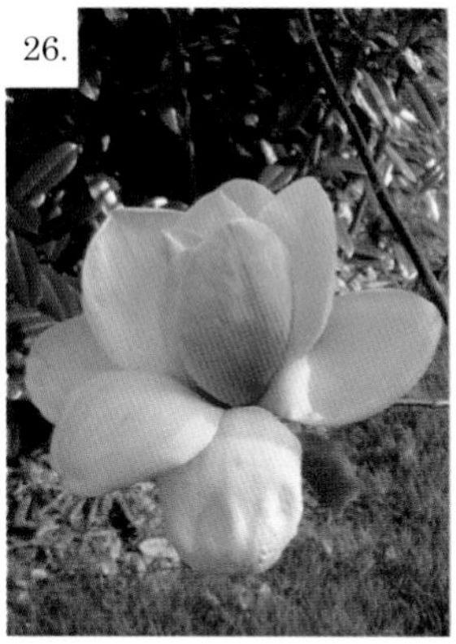

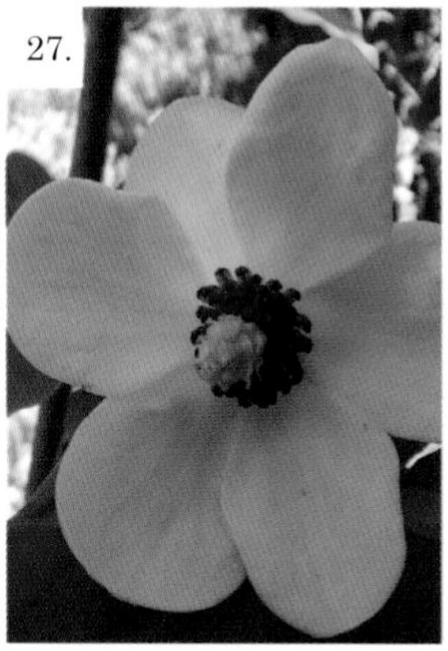

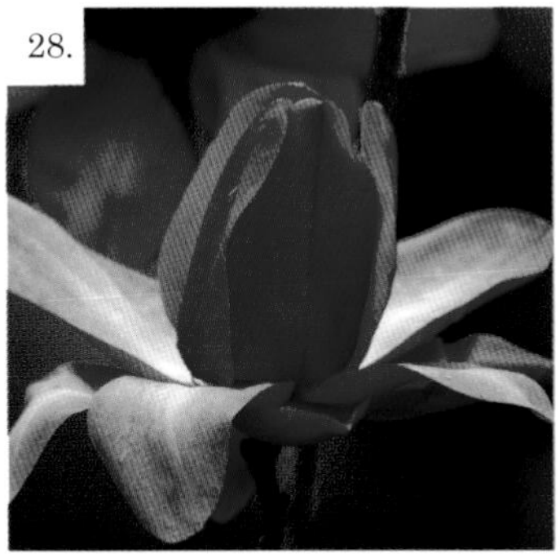

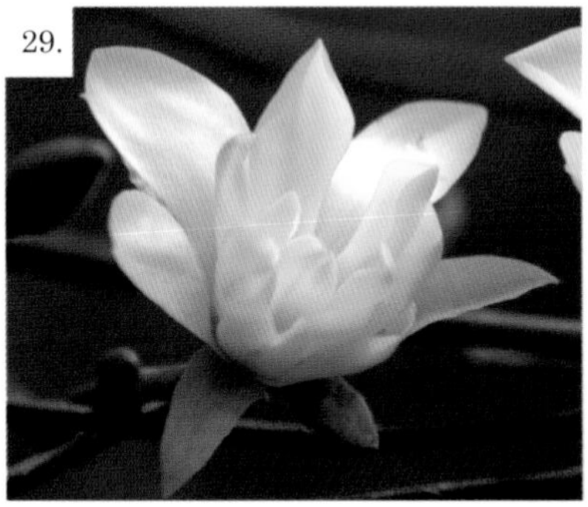

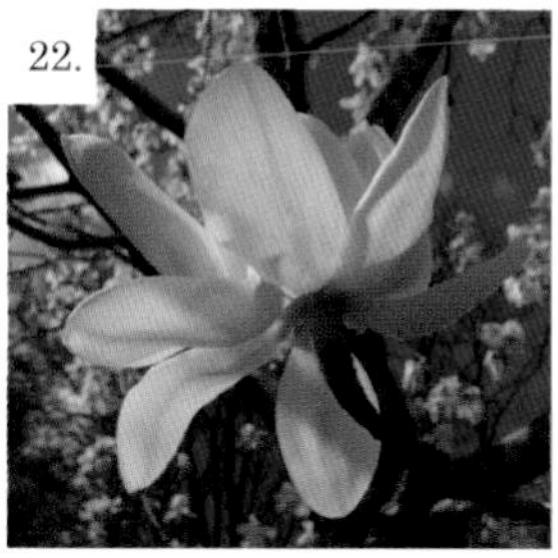

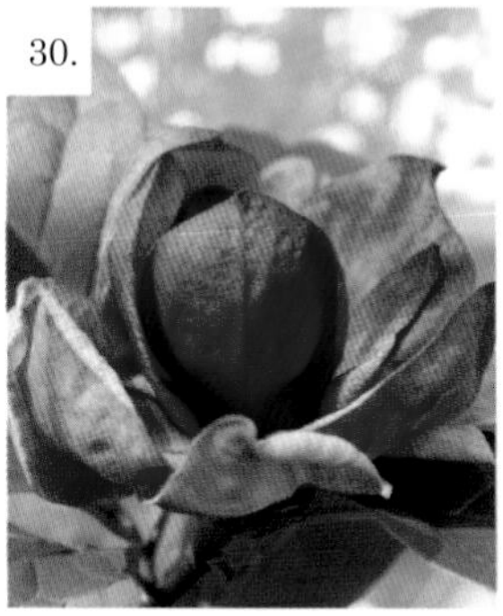

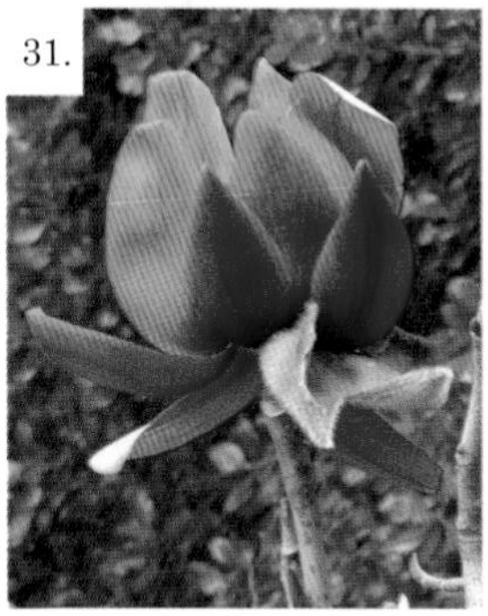

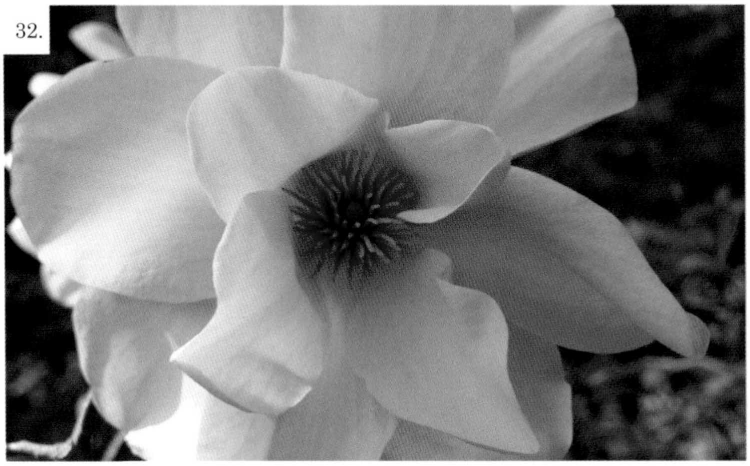

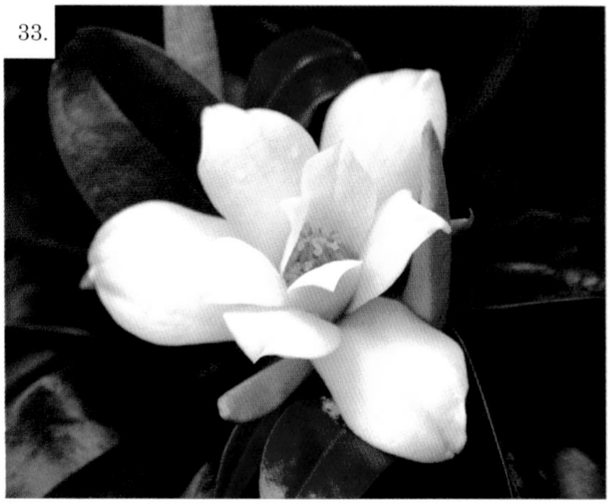

34. (campbellii var mollicomata 'Lanarth' x sargentiana var robusta) 'Mark Jury'

35. (globosa x hypoleuca) 'Summer Solstice'

36. campbellii var mollicomata 'Lanarth'

37. (soulangeana 'Picture' x unknown) 'Pickard's Schmetterling'

38. (sargentiana robusta x sprengeri 'Diva') 'J.C. Williams'

39. ('Mark Jury' x soulangeana 'Lennei') 'Iolanthe'

40. grandiflora

# Appendix 2
# A National Collection of Magnolias

Magnolia 'Sunsation'

## A. Magnolia Species

*i    Magnolia*

amoena

acuminata

acuminata var. subcordata

biondii

campbellii

campbellii Alba Group

campbellii subsp. mollicomata

campbellii (form) 'Lanarth' (Caerhays) (4 forms)

campbellii (form) 'Lanarth' (New Zealand)

cylindrica

cylindrica NA60704 SAS S SC China

dawsoniana

dealbata (macrophylla subsp. dealbata)

delavayi

denudata

fraseri

globosa 5391

grandiflora

kobus

kobus var. borealis

liliiflora

macrophylla

macrophylla subsp. ashei

nitida

obovata (hypoleuca)

officinalis

officinalis var. biloba

rostrata

salicifolia

salicifolia var. concolor

sargentiana (pure)

sargentiana var. robusta

sieboldii

sieboldii subsp. sinensis holsoniana)

soulangeana

sprengeri var. 'Diva'

sprengeri double form

sprengeri var. elongata

stellata

'Magnolia x loebneri
'Mag's Pirouette'

stellata forma keiskei

tripetala

virginiana

wilsonii

zenii

*ii.    Manglietia (now Magnolia)*

conifera var. chingii

hookeri

insignis

kwangtungensis (moto)

tamaulipana

yuynanensis

*iii.    Michelia (now Magnolia)*

carthcartii

chapensis

chevalieri

doltsopa

figo

figo var. crassipes

fulva tregata (sapa-vietnam TH2005)

floribunda

foveolata

laevifolia (yunnanensis)

macclurei

martini

maudiae

pachycarpa

platypetala

*iv.    Hybrids between 2 species with a collective name*

x kewensis (salicifolia x ?)

x proctoriana (salicifolia x ?)

x thompsoniana (tripetala x virginiana)

x veitchii (campbellii x denudata)

x wieseneri (obovata x sieboldii)

## B. Named Magnolia Hybrids and Clonal forms

acuminata x denudata 'Legend'

acuminata x denudata 'Golden Pond'

acuminata x denudata 'Golden Goblet'

acuminata x denudata 'Elizabeth'

acuminata x denudata 'Moonspire'

acuminata x denudata 'Petit Chicon'

acuminata x denudata 'Purple Platter'

acuminata x denudata 'Lois'

acuminata x denudata 'Sundance'

acuminata x denudata 'Yellow Fever'

acuminata x denudata 'Yellow Sea'

acuminata var. subcordata 'Ellen'

'Limelight' (acuminata var. subcordata x 'Big Pink')

acuminata var. subcordata 'Miss Honeybee'

'Yellow Bird' (acuminata x brooklynensis 'Eva Maria')

'Albatross' (cylindrica x veitchii 'Peter Veitch')

'Ambrosia' (x brooklynensis 'Eva Maria' x x brooklynensis)

'Ann' (stellata x liliiflora 'Nigra')

'Apollo' (campbellii subsp. mollicomata 'Lanarth' x liliiflora 'Nigra')

'Athene' ('Mark Jury' x soulangeana 'Lennei alba')

'Asian Artistry' (denudata x sprengeri 'Diva')

'Atlas' (denudata x sprengeri 'Diva')

'Aurora' (sargentiana var. robusta x 'Star Wars')

'Banana Split' (x brooklynensis 'Woodsman' x soulangeana 'Lennei' x 'Elizabeth')

'Brixton Belle' ('Sweet Simplicity' x 'Black Tulip' x 'Sir Harold Hillier')

x brooklynensis 'Black Beauty'

x brooklynensis 'Eva Maria'

x brooklynensis 'Hattie Carthan'

x brooklynensis'Moonspire'

x brooklynensis'Woodsman'

'Burncoose White' (campbellii subsp. mollicomata) - (Burncoose Tennis Court)

'Butterbowl' ('Yellow Bird' x 'Sundance' x 'Yellow Dance')

'Caerhays Belle' (sargentiana var. robusta. x sprengeri 'Diva')

'Caerhays Surprise' (campbellii subsp. mollicomata x liliiflora 'Nigra')

'Cameo' (soulangeana x ?)

campbellii 'Betty Jessel'

campbellii 'Darjeeling'

campbellii 'Lamellen Pink'

campbellii var. alba 'Chyverton'

campbellii var. alba 'Ethel Hillier'

campbellii var. alba 'Sir Harold Hillier'

campbellii var. alba 'Strybing White'

campbellii var. alba 'Trelissick Alba'

campbellii subsp. mollicomata 'Maharanee'

campbellii subsp. mollicomata 'Mary Williams'

campbellii subsp. mollicomata 'Werrington'

'Candy'

'Carloa'

'Cecil Nice' (denudata x sargentiana var. robusta)

'Charles Coates' (sieboldii x tripetala)

'Charles Raffill' (campbellii x campbellii subsp. mollicomata)

'Cleopatra' (sargentiana x ?)

'Chyverton Red' (dawsoniana x sprengeri 'Diva')

'Coral' ('Legend' x 'Butterflies')

'Daphne' ('Miss Honeybee' x 'Gold Crown')

'Daybreak' (x brooklynensis 'Woodsman' x 'Tina Durio')

'Delia Williams' (sargentiana var. robusta x mollicomata)

denudata 'Forrest's Pink'

denudata 'Fragrant Cloud' ('Dan Zin')

denudata 'Gere'

denudata 'Yellow River' ('Fei Huang')

'Eleanor May' (campbellii subsp. mollicomata 'Lanarth' x x soulangeana)

'Elizabeth Holman'

'Eskimo' (kobus 'Norman Gould' x soulangeana 'Lennei')

'Fireglow' (cylindrica x denudata 'Sawada's Pink')

'F J Williams' (sargentiana var. robusta x mollicomata 'Lanarth')

'Frank's Masterpiece' (soulangeana 'Deep Purple Dream' x 'Paul Cook')

'Galaxy' (liliiflora 'Nigra' x sprengeri 'Diva')

'Genie' (soulangeana x liliiflora 'Nigra')

'George Henry Kern' (stellata x liliiflora)

'Gold Cup' (soulangeana 'Lennei' x 'Elizabeth')

'Golden Endeavour' (subcordata 'Miss Honeybee' x 'Sundance')

'Goldstar' (acuminata 'Miss Honeybee' x stellata 'Rubra')

grandiflora 'D. D. Blanchard'

grandiflora 'Edith Bogue'

grandiflora 'Exmouth'

grandiflora 'Gallissonniere'

grandiflora 'Goliath'

grandiflora 'Harold Poole'

grandiflora 'Little Gem'

grandiflora 'Mainstreet'

grandiflora 'Overton'

grandiflora 'Russet'

grandiflora 'Symmes Select'

'Greenbee' (acuminata 'Miss Honeybee' x 'Gold Crown')

'Hawk' (sargentiana var. robusta x ?) Chyverton hybrid

'Hot Flash' ('Woodsman' x 'Elizabeth')

'Ian's Red' ('Vulcan' x soulangeana 'Burgundy')

'Iolanthe' ('Mark Jury' x soulangeana 'Lennei')

'J.C. Williams (sargentiana var robusta x sprengeri 'Diva')

'Kew's Surprise' (campbellii x campbellii subsp. mollicomata)

'Legacy' (denudata x sprengeri 'Diva')

liliiflora 'Holland Red'

liliiflora 'Nigra'

x loebneri 'Ballerina'

x loebneri 'Donna'

x loebneri 'Green Mist'

x loebneri 'Leonard Messel'

x loebneri 'Mag's Pirouette'

x loebneri 'Merrill'

x loebneri 'Powder Puff'

'Lotus' (x soulangeana 'Lennei Alba'
x 'Mark Jury')

'March till Frost'
(liliiflora x cylindrica x 'Ruby')

'Mark Jury' (campbellii var. mollicomata 'Lanarth' x sargentiana var. robusta)

'Margaret Helen' (campbellii var. mollicomata x liliiflora 'Nigra')

'Maryland' (grandiflora x virginiana)

'Millie Carlyon'
(soulangeana 'Lennei' x 'Paul Cook')

'Milky Way' ('Mark Jury' x soulangeana 'Lennei Alba')

'Mossman's Giant' (campbellii subsp. mollicomata x sargentiana var. robusta)

'Old Port' (soulangeana x ?)

'Olivia' ('Miss Honeybee' x 'Gold Crown')

'Peachy' (acuminata 'Fertile Myrtle' x sprengeri 'Diva')

'Pegasus' (Chyverton hybrid)

'Philip Tregunna'
(campbellii x sargentiana var. robusta)

'Plum Pudding' (? x ?)

'Pinkie' (stellata 'Rosea' x liliiflora 'Reflorescens')

'Porcelain Dove' (globosa x virginiana)

'Princess Margaret' (campbelli Alba Group x sargentiana var. robusta)

'Pristine' (denudata x stellata 'Waterlily')

Pseudokobus 'Kubushi-modoki'

'Purple Sensation' (mollicomata 'Lanarth' x liliiflora 'Nigra')

'Randy' (liliiflora 'Nigra' x stellata)

'Red Lion' (liliiflora x campbellii)

'Ricki' (stellata x liliiflora 'Nigra')

'Ruth' (mollicomata 'Lanarth' x soulangeana)

'Serene' (liliiflora x 'Mark Jury')

'Shiraz' ('Vulcan' x denudata)

'Sidbury' (campbellii x campbellii subsp. mollicomata)

'Sleeping Beauty' ('Miss Honeybee x denudata 'Sundance')

'Solar Flair' ('Woodsman' x 'Gold Star')

soulangeana 'Alba'

soulangeana 'Alba Superba'

soulangeana 'Alexandrina'

soulangeana 'Brozzoni'

soulangeana 'Dr Callies'

soulangeana 'Lennei'

soulangeana 'Lennei Alba'

soulangeana 'Rubra'

soulangeana 'Rustica Rubra'

soulangeana 'Satisfaction'

soulangeana 'Speciosa'

soulangeana 'Sundew'

'Spectrum' (liliiflora 'Nigra' x sprengeri 'Diva')

sprengeri var sprengari 'Burncoose'

sprengeri 'Copeland Court'

sprengeri 'Eric Savill'

sprengeri 'Lamellen Surprise'

sprengeri 'Marwood Spring'

'Star Wars' (campbelli x liliiflora)

'Stellar Acclaim' ('Woodsman' x 'Gold Star')

stellata 'Alixeed'

stellata 'Centennial'

stellata 'Keiskei'

stellata 'Jane Platt'

stellata 'Royal Star'

'Summer Solstice' (globosa x obovata)

'Sunspire' ('Woodsman' x 'Elizabeth')

'Susan' (liliiflora 'Nigra' x stellata 'Rosea')

'Susanna Van Veen' (sargentiana var. robusta x sprengeri 'Diva')

'Sunburst' ('Woodsman' x 'Gold Star')

'Sunrise'

'Sunsation' ('Woodsman x 'Elizabeth')

'Sweet Heart' (sprengeri 'Diva' x sargentiana var. robusta)

'Sweet Valentine'
('Sweet Simplicity' x 'Black Tulip')

'Theodora'

'Tranquility' ('Woodsman' x 'Gold Star')

'Ultimate Yellow'
(acuminata x x brooklynensis)

x veitchii 'Isca'

x veitchii 'Peter Veitch'

virginiana 'Havener'

virginiana 'Henry Hicks'

virginiana 'Satellite'

'Vulcan' (mollicomata 'Lanarth' x liliiflora hybrid)

'Wada's Snow White' (denudata x salicifolia)

x wieseneri 'Aashild Kalleberg'

wilsonii x goteborgensis (Clone 2)

'Yakeo' ('Anne Rosse' x liliiflora)

'Yuchelia'
(acuminata 'Miss Honeybee' x Michelia figo)

zenii 'Pink Parchment'

## Gresham Hybrids

'Darrell Dean' (soulangeana 'Rustica Rubra' x x veitchii)

'David Clulow' (x veitchii x soulangeana 'Lennei Alba')

'Delicatissima'
(soulangeana 'Lennei Alba' x x veitchii)

'Candy Cane' (Unknown )

'Crimson Stipple'
(soulangeana 'Lennei Alba' x x veitchii)

'Frank Gladney'
(campbellii x pink Gresham hybrid)

'Heaven Scent' (liliiflora x x veitchii)

'Joe McDaniel'
(soulangeana 'Rustica Rubra' x x veitchii)

'Manchu Fan'
(soulangeana 'Lennei Alba x x veitchii)

'Mary Nell' (soulangeana 'Lennei Alba' x x veitchii 'Peter Veitch')

'Peppermint Stick' (liliiflora x x veitchii)

'Peter Smithers'
(soulangeana 'Rustica Rubra' x x veitchii)

'Raspberry Ice' (liliiflora x x veitchii)

'Rouged Alabaster (soulangeana 'Lennei Alba' x x veitchii)

'Royal Crown' (liliiflora x x veitchii)

'Sayonara' (liliiflora x x veitchii)

'Sweet Sixteen' (soulangeana 'Lennei Alba' x x veitchii)

'Tina Durio' (soulangeana 'Lennei Alba' x x veitchii)

*Pickard's Hybrids*

'Pickard's Crystal'

'Pickard's Firefly'

'Pickard's Garnet'

'Pickard's Opal'

'Pickard's Ruby'

'Pickard's Schmetterling'

'Pickard's Snow Queen'

'Pickard's Stardust'

## C. Named Michelia Hybrids

Michelia doltsopa 'Silver Cloud'
Michelia x foggii 'Allspice'
Michelia x foggii 'Jack Fogg'
Michelia maudiae 'Touch of Pink'

Magnolia 'Vulcan'

## D. As yet Unnamed Hybrids

| | |
|---|---|
| 1 | acuminata 'Golden Girl' x 'Miss Honeybee' |
| 1 | acuminata var. subcordata x heptapeta (denudata) |
| 1 | acuminata 'Fertile Myrtle' x sprengeri 'Diva' |
| 1 | acuminata 'Golden Glow' x 'Miss Honeybee' |
| 1 | acuminata 'Variegata' |
| 1 | 'Alexandrina' x 'Yellow Lantern' (acuminata var. subcordata x soulangeana) |
| 1 | campbelli Yellow form (ex Mt Congreve) |
| 1 | campbelli subsp. mollicomata x sargentiana var. robusta 'Mrs FJ Williams' (not registered) |
| 2 | campbelli subsp. mollicomata x campbellii |
| 1 | campbelli subsp. mollicomata 'Variegata' |
| 1 | 'David Clulow' x sprengeri var. elongata |
| 4 | JP Hybrid |
| 1 | 'Pink Royalty' x 'Daybreak' |
| 2 | 'Lennei' x 'Daybreak' |
| 3 | sargentiana var. robusta x mollicomata |

| | |
|---|---|
| 2 | sargentiana var. robusta x mollicomata 'Lanarth' (New Zealand) |
| 3 | sargentiana var. robusta x 'Lanarth' x campbellii 'Darjeeling' |
| 4 | sargentiana var. robusta x campbellii |
| 2 | sargentiana var. robusta x sprengeri 'Diva' |
| 1 | sargentiana var. robusta x campbellii Alba Group |
| 1 | sprengeri 'Diva' x sargentiana var. robusta |
| 1 | stellata x loebneri |
| 2 | sinensis x wilsonii x highdownensis x wieseneri |
| 1 | virginiana x tripelata x thompsoniana |
| 1 | 'Woodsman' x 'Patriot' |
| 1 | 'Yellow Bird' x 'Patriot' |

## E. Seedlings Raised at Caerhays but Unnamed

| | |
|---|---|
| 4 | 'Atlas' |
| 5 | 'Caerhays Belle' |
| 20 | campbellii Alba |
| 1 | campbellii |

| | |
|---|---|
| 7 | campbellii var. mollicomata 'Lanarth' |
| 13 | campbellii var. mollicomata |
| 5 | dawsoniana |
| 2 | delavayi (Tom Hudson collected) |
| 3 | 'David Clulow' |
| 16 | 'F J Williams' |
| 3 | 'Kew's Surprise' |
| 3 | 'Lotus' |
| 1 | 'Philip Tregunna' |
| 3 | 'Rouged Alabaster' |
| 31 | sargentiana var. robusta |
| 1 | sargentiana var. robusta x 'White Form' |
| 10 | sprengeri 'Diva' |
| 3 | 'J.C. Williams' |
| 25 | Unknown |
| 3 | x veitchii |
| 2 | virginiana |
| 2 | 'Wada's Snow White' (denudata x salicifolia) |

Magnolias by Michelle Bennett Oates

# Appendix 3
# Magnolia hybrids bred at
# Caerhays & Burncoose

'Caerhays Surpise'
(M. campbellii x mollicomata x
M. liliiflora 'Nigra')

Bred by Philip Tregunna , Head Gardener, in 1959.
First flowered in 1967. AM and Cory Cup in 1973.

Magnolia 'Delia Williams'    Magnolia sprengeri 'Diva' 'Burncoose'

'Caerhays Belle'
(M.sargentiana var robusta x
M. sprengeri 'Diva')

Bred by Head Gardener, Charles Michael, in 1951.
It took 14 years to flower.

M. campbellii 'Kew's Surprise'

A seedling of  M.'Charles Raffill' (M. campbellii x M.campbellii var mollicomata)  raised at Caerhays. FCC and Cory Cup 1967. First flowered in 1967.

Magnolia 'Philip Tregunna'    Magnolia 'Kew Surprise'

'J C Williams'
(M. sargentiana var  robusta x
M. sprengeri 'Diva')

Registered with the International Magnolia Society
in 1997. Measured 45ft tall with a girth of 5ft in 2001. FCC March 2002.

'Delia Williams'
(M. sargentiana var robusta x
campbellii var mollicomata)

First flowered in 1972 seven years after being
planted out. Registered 2009.

'F.J. Williams'
(M. sargentiana var robusta x
M. mollicomata 'Lanarth')

Planted in 1987, registered and named 2009.

M. sprengeri var 'Diva'
'Burncoose'

A seedling of sprengeri 'Diva' raised by Arnold Dance, Head Gardener, at Burncoose . It first flowered in 1972 and was awarded  an AM in 2000.

'Philip Tregunna'
(M. sargentiana var robusta x
M. campbellii)

First flowered in 1968. Awarded FCC in 1992.
Named after Philip Tregunna, Head Gardener
at Caerhays from 1956 to 1996.

Key to the illustration:
1. Magnolia 'Caerhays Surprise'
2. Magnolia 'J.C. Williams'
3. Magnolia 'Philip Tregunna'
4. Magnolia 'Caerhays Belle'

One of a series of paintings by commissioned by the Williams family to record the range of x williamsii Camellias bred and raised at Caerhays since the 1930's. The artist, Victoria Gordon, was formerly a botanic artist working at Kew. The series is now available as limited edition prints at the Gift Shop or online at: www.caerhays.co.uk

# Appendix 4
# Camelia x Williamsii hybrids
# bred at Caerhays & Burncoose

1. 'Beatrice Michael' (japonica x saluenensis)

AM 1980
Named after the wife of the head gardener at Caerhays in the 1940's and 1950's.

2. 'Burncoose'

Introduced in 1985 very dense and compact habit.

3. 'Burncoose Apple Blossom'

Introduced in 1986 Bred by Arnold Dance, head gardener at Burncoose.

4. 'Caerhays' (saluenensis x 'Lady Clare')

AM 1969

5. 'Carolyn Williams'

Chance seedling.

6. 'Charles Michael' (japonica x saluenensis)

AM 1987
Named after the head gardener at Caerhays in the 1940's and 1950's.

7.    'George Blandford' (saluenensis x 'Lady Clare')

AM 1965 & 1974. AGM 2002
Nearly always out in December. Named after a gamekeeper and gardener at Caerhays who worked on the estate for over 70 years.

8.    'J.C. Williams' (japonica x saluenensis)

FCC 1942. AGM 2002
The first clone of x williamsii.

9.    'John Pickthorn'

Introduced in 1962. Chance seedling.

10.    'Mary Christian' (japonica x saluenensis)

AM 1942. FCC 1977. AGM 2002
Named after J.C.Williams' wife. The variegated leafed form originating from Hillier's Nurseries is known as 'Golden Spangles'.

11.    'Mary Jobson' (japonica x saluenensis)

Introduced in 1962 as a chance seedling.
One of the very few scented varieties of camellia.

12.    'Mary Larcom'

Chance seedling.

13.    'Monica Dance'

Curious striped petalling. Bred by Arnold Dance, head gardener at Burncoose and named after his wife.

14.    'Muskoka'

AGM 2002
Chance seedling. Named after a place in Canada.

15.    'New Venture' (japonica x 'Gauntlettii')

Bred by Philip Tregunna, head gardener at Caerhays until 1996.

16. 'November Pink'
(japonica x
saluenensis)

AM 1950
Nearly always out by the
first week of November.
Trailing habit.

17. 'Philipa Forward'

Introduced in 1962.

18. 'Rosemary
Williams'

Introduced in 1961.

19. 'Saint Ewe'
(japonica x
saluenensis)

AM 1947. FCC 1974. AGM
2002
Named after a nearby
village to Caerhays.

20. 'Saint Michael'
(japonica x
saluenensis)

AM 1987.
Named after the parish
church of St Michael
Caerhays.

21. 'Mary Williams'
(reticulata hybrid)

AM 1942. FCC 1964
Named after The Rt. Hon.
Charles Williams wife.

22. 'Cornish Snow'
(cuspidata x
saluenensis)

AM 1948
The reverse cross made
by Hillier Nurseries is
identical but pink and
called 'Winton'. Usually
flowers from December
until April.

One of a series of paintings by commissioned by the Williams family to record rhododendron hybrids bred and raised at Caerhays since the 1930's. The artist, Victoria Gordon, was formerly a botanic artist working at Kew. The series is now available as limited edition prints at the Gift Shop or online at: www.caerhays.co.uk

# Appendix 5
# Rhododendron hybrids
# bred and raised at Caerhays

| | | |
|---|---|---|
| campylocarpum(s) x williamsianum<br>Moonstone Group | R:  J C Williams<br>REG: J C Williams (pre 1933)<br>N: J C Williams<br>INC: ICRA(1958)<br>I: J C Williams (1933) | Key to Breeding and<br>registration details<br><br>R = raised by<br>H = hybridised by<br>G = grown to first flower by<br>S = selected by<br>N = named by<br>I = introduced by<br>INC = incorporated into<br>    records at the time<br>    of publication of the<br>    first Register (1958)<br>REG = registered by |
| campylocarpum(s) x williamsianum<br>'Moonstone Pink' | R: J C Williams (pre 1933) | |
| campylocarpum(s) x williamsianum<br>'Moonstone Yellow' | R: J C Williams (pre 1933) | |
| griffithianum x fortunei subsp<br>discolor<br>Cornish loderi group | REG: J C Williams (1933)<br>R: J C Williams (pre 1933)<br>INC: ICRA (1958)<br>I: J C Williams | |
| spinuliferum(s) x lutescens<br>Crossbill Group<br>(pink form) | REG: J C Williams (1933)<br>N: J C Williams (1933)<br>I: J C Williams<br>INC: ICRA (1958)<br>R: J C Williams (1933) | |
| spinuliferum(s) x lutescens<br>'Caerhays Crossbill' | REG: C H Williams & J Parsons<br>(2009)<br>N: C H Williams (2009)<br>I: J C Williams<br>INC: ICRA (1958)<br>R: J C Williams (1933) |  |
| moupinense x sulfureum<br>(Golden Oriole Group)<br>'Busaco' | REG: F J Williams (1964)<br>N: F J Williams<br>I: F J Williams | Rhododendron 'Busaco' |

moupinense (white form) x
sulfureum
(Golden Oriole)
'Talavera' FCC 1963. AM 1947

R: C Williams (pre 1947)
I: C Williams
REG: F J Williams (1964)

burmanicum x dalhousiae
'Michael's Pride'

H: C Michael
REG: C Michael (1963)
N: J C Micheal (1963)

Rhododendron 'Michael's Pride'

xanthostephanum(s) x burmanicum
'Saffron Queen'
AM 1948

REG:  C Williams
N: J C Williams (1948)
R: J C Williams
I: J C Williams (1948)
INC: ICRA (1958)

arboreum(s) x thomsonii
Red Admiral Group

H: J C Williams (pre 1937)
G:  C Williams
N: J C Williams
R: J C Williams (pre 1937)
I: J C Williams
INC: ICRA (1958)

Rhododendron 'Saffron Queen'

pseudochrysanthum x
williamsianum
'Veryan Bay'

H: J C Williams (1929)
G:  C Williams
N: F J Williams (c.1964)
REG: F J Williams (1993)

sulfureum(s) x flavidum
Yellow Hammer Group

H: J C Williams (pre 1931)
N: J C Williams
R: J C Williams (pre 1931)
INC: ICRA (1958)

lavender form of impeditum(s) x
augustinii
Blue Tit Group

H: J C Williams
N: J C Williams
R: J C Williams
I: J C Williams (1933)
INC: ICRA (1958)

Rhododendron 'Veryan Bay'

haematodes(s) x williamsianum
Humming Bird Group

H: J C Williams
N: J C Williams
I: J C Williams (1933)
R: J C Williams
INC: ICRA (1958)

haematodes(s) x thomsonii
'Charles Michael'

N: C Williams (1948)
I: C Williams (1948)
INC: ICRA (1958)

cinnabarinum(s) x maddenii
Royal Flush Group

H:  J C Williams (pre 1926)
N: J C Williams
R: J C Williams (pre 1926)
INC: ICRA (1958)

Rhododendron 'Blue Tit'

burmanicum x edgeworthii
'Mella'

H: C Williams (pre 1952)
N: C Williams
R: C Williams (pre 1952)
INC: ICRA(1958)
DIED OUT AT CAERHAYS

Rhododendron 'Humming Bird'

calophytum(s) x sutchuenense
Robin Hood Group

H: J C Williams
N: J C Williams
R: J C Williams
I: J C Williams (1933)
INC: ICRA (1958)
DIED OUT AT CAERHAYS

fortunei subsp discolor Houlstonii
Group(s) x orbiculare
Robin Redbreast Group

H: J C Williams
N: J C Williams
R: J C Williams
I: J C Williams (1933)
INC; ICRA (1958)
DIED OUT AT CAERHAYS

haematodes(s) x griersonianum
'May Day'
AM 1932. AGM 2002

REG: A M Williams
N: A M Williams
I: A M Williams (1932)
R: A M Williams
INC: ICRA (1958)

Rhododendron 'May Day'

griffithianum hybrid
'Caerhays'

REG: J C Williams
N: J C Williams (pre 1958)
R: J C Williams
INC: ICRA (pre 1958)

cinnabarinum subsp. xanthocodon
Concatenans Group x cinnabarinum
subsp. Cinnabarinum
Blandfordiiflorum Group
'Caerhays John'

H: C Williams and C Michael
R: C Williams and C Michael (pre 1956)
REG: ICRA (1994)
DIED OUT AT CAERHAYS

cinnabarinum subsp. xanthocodon
Concatenans Group x cinnabarinum
subsp. Cinnabarinum
Blandfordiiflorum Group
'Caerhays Lawrence'

H: C Williams and C Michael
R: C Williams and C Michael (pre 1956)
REG: ICRA (1994)
DIED OUT AT CAERHAYS

cinnabarinum subsp. xanthocodon
Concatenans Group x cinnabarinum
subsp. Cinnabarinum
Blandfordiiflorum Group
'Caerhays Philip'
AM 1966

H : C Williams and C Micheal
I: F J Williams (1966)
REG: F J Williams (1966)
R: C Williams and C Michael
DIED OUT AT CAERHAYS

Rhododendron 'Caerhays Lavender'

'Caerhays Pink'
Rhod selection from davidsonianum

Flower pink with red spots, name
given by trade to best pink form
from Caerhays

Evergreen azalea parentage
unknown
'Caerhays Lavender'

Raised unknown grown at
Caerhays probably since 1930s

decorum x williamsianum
'Tinners Blush'

R: F J Williams (1960)
REG: C H Williams and J Parsons
(2006)
N: F J Williams
H: F J Williams (1960)
G: F J Williams (1968)

Rhododendron 'Tinners Blush'

decorum x williamsianum
'High Sheriff'

R: F J Williams (1960)
REG: C H Williams and J Parsons (2006)
N: F J Williams
H: F J Williams (1960)
G: F J Williams (1968)

tethropeplum x cinnabarinum
'Polgrain'

R: J C Williams
REG: C H Williams and J Parsons (2006)
H: J C Williams (1930s)
N: J C Williams
G: J C Williams (1940's)

tethropeplum x cinnabarinum
'Penvose'

R: J C Williams
REG: C H Williams and J Parsons (2006)
H: J C Williams (1930s)
N: J C Williams
G: J C Williams (1940's)

Rhododendron 'Polgrain'

moorii x euchates
'Penvergate'

R: F J Williams
REG: C H Williams and J Parsons (2006)
H: F J Williams (1954)
G: F J Williams (1960)

aureum x hanceanum
'Nancor'

R: Rt Hon C Williams (1950s)
REG: C H Williams and J Parsons (2006)
H: Rt Hon C Williams (1950s)
N: F J Williams
G: Rt Hon C Williams

Rhododendron 'Penvergate'

(pink) decorum x campylocarpum
'Rescassa'

R: P Tregunna (1967)
REG: C H Williams and J Parsons (2006)
H: P Tregunna (1967)
N: P Tregunna (2006)
G: P Tregunna (1972)

moupinense x chrysodoron
'Maisie'

R: J Parsons
REG: C H Williams and J Parsons (2006)
H: J Parsons (1999)
N: J Parsons
G: J Parsons (2002)

Rhododendron 'Nancor'

delavayi x unknown
'Winter Intruder'

S: F J Williams (1960)
REG: C H Williams and J Parsons (2006)
G: F J Williams (1967)

elliotii x eriogynum
'Caerhays Rebecca'

R: F J Williams (1960)
REG: C H Williams and J Parsons (2006)
H: F J Williams (1960)
S: F J Williams
G: F J Williams (1967)

Rhododendron 'Caerhays Rebecca'

'Moser's Maroon' x griersonianum
'Treberrick'

S: C H Williams
R: F J Williams
REG : C H Williams and J Parsons (2006)
H: F J Williams (1997)
N: C H Williams (2006)
G: F J Williams (2000)

yunnanense x Trewithen Orange Group
'Emma Williams'

REG: C H Williams and J Parsons (2006)
N: F J Williams (1970s)
G: P Tregunna (1970s)

impeditum
'J C Williams'

unknown

Rhododendron 'Emma Williams'

calophytum x sutchuenense
'Assaye'

R: J C Williams (1963)
N: F J Williams (1963)
REG: F J Williams (1963)

(Wilson 6771) brachyanthum
x (Wilson 1773) flavidum
'Brachydum Primum' AM 1924

I: J C Williams (1924)
INC: (1958)

callimorphum x neriiflorum
'Dimidatum'

G: J C Williams (1918)
N: Sir Issac Balfour (1919)
INC: (1958)

lutescens x edgeworthii
Kittiwake Group

R: J C Williams (1933)
N: J C Williams (1933)
INC: (1958)
DIED OUT AT CAERHAYS

Rhododendron 'J C Williams'

arboreum x sutchuenense
'Snow Bunting'

I: J C Williams
INC: (1958)

campanulatum x fortunei
'Susan'

R: J C Williams Pre (1933)
N: J C Williams
INC: (1958)
DIED OUT AT CAERHAYS

spinuliferum x lutescens
Spinlut Group

R: J C Williams Pre (1926)
N: J C Williams
INC: (1958)
DIED OUT AT CAERHAYS

Evergreen azalea
'Greenway'

I: F J Williams (1975)
REG: F J Williams (1975)

moupinense x sulfureum
Golden Oriole Group

R: C Williams (1947)
N: C Williams (1947)
I; C Williams (1947)

Lithocarpus pachyphyllus seeds

Lithocarpus variolosus

Quercus phellos

Quercus skinneri

Quercus myrsinifolia

# Appendix 6
## Rare & evergreen oaks at Caerhays
## (Lithocarpus & Quercus)

**Lithocarpus Collection**

**Planted 1920's**

X2 L. cleistocarpa

L. edulus

L. hancei

X2 L. pachyphyllus

L. uvarifolius

L. henryi

**Planted 1940's**

X2 L. pachyphyllus

**Planted 1960's**

L. cleistocarpa

**Planted 1980's**

X2 L. pachyphyllus

**Planted 2000**

L.variolosus NH 79

**Planted 2008**

L.corneus

**Planted 2009**

X4 L. lepidocarpus

**Quercus Collection**

**Planted 1920's**

x 5 Q. acuta

x2 Q. lamellosa

Q. oxyodon

Q. libani

Q. kelloggii

Q. phillyreoides

Q. glauca

Q. crassifolia

x6 Q. myrsinifolia

Q. phellos

Q. denudata

**Planted 1960's**

Q. ludoviciana

Q. lamellosa

**Planted 1980's**

Q. semecarpifolia

Q. variabilis

Q. x turneri 'Pseudoturneri'

Q. libani

x2 Q. phellos

**Planted 1990's**

Q. crassifolia

Q. x turneri 'Pseudoturneri'

**Planted 2000**

Q. leucotrichophora

**Planted 2001**

Q. oxyodon (NH)

**Planted 2003**

Q. x bushii

Q. dentata 'Carl Ferris Miller'

**Planted 2005**

Q. skinneri

Q. pontica

Q. dentata 'Carl Ferris Miller'

**Planted 2006**

Q. palustris

Q. aliena

**Planted 2007**

Q. cerris 'Argenteovariegata'

Q. x dentata

Q. x wislizeni

**Planted 2008**

Q. ellipsoidalis 'Hemelrijk'

Q. morii

**Planted 2009**

Q. gilva

Q. macdonaldii

x2 Q. nuttallii

Podocarpus lawrencii

Podocarpus 'Kilworth Cream'

Podocarpus nivalis 'Kaweka'

Podocarpus acutifolis 'Gold Lady'

# Appendix 7
## The Podocarpus Collection at Caerhays

| No. | Male/Female | Species | Date Planted | No. | Male/Female | Clonal names and varieties | Date Planted |
|---|---|---|---|---|---|---|---|
| 3 | M/F | acutifolius | 1999 | 1 | F | macrophyllus 'Aureus' | 1986 |
| 1 | | gracilior | 2003 | | | | |
| 1 | | henkelii | 2005 | 1 | F | nivalis 'Bronze' | 2006 |
| 2 | F | lawrencei | 2009 | 1 | F | nivalis 'Christmas Lights' | 2006 |
| 1 | | latifolius | 2005 | | | | |
| 1 | M | nivalis | 2008 | 1 | M | nivalis 'Clarence' | 2004 |
| 1 | | macrophyllus | 2005 | 1 | F | nivalis 'Green Queen' | 2006 |
| 3 | | nubigenus | 1997 | | | | |
| 15 | M/F | salignus | 1920's | 1 | M | nivalis 'Hikurangi' | 2006 |
| 4 | | totara | 1920's | | | | |
| 1 | | totara var hallii | 1920's | 1 | M | nivalis 'Kaweka' | 2005 |
| | | | | 3 | M | nivalis 'Kilworth Cream' | 2002 |

| No. | Male/Female | Clonal names and varieties | Date Planted | | | | |
|---|---|---|---|---|---|---|---|
| 1 | | acutifolius 'Gold Lady' | 1999 | 1 | F | nivalis 'Kralingen' | 2002 |
| | | | | 3 | F | nivalis 'Livingstone' | 2006 |
| 1 | F | cunninghamii 'Kiwi' | 2002 | | | | |
| 1 | M | cunninghamii 'Roro' | 2006 | 1 | M | nivalis 'Otari' | 2002 |
| 1 | | elongatus 'Blue Chip' | 2007 | 1 | M | nivalis 'Park Cover' | 2006 |
| 8 | F | lawrencei 'Blue Gem' | 2007 | 1 | | nivalis 'Rockery Gem' | 2002 |
| 1 | M | lawrencei 'Maori Prince' | 2002 | 1 | F | nivalis 'Red Embers' | 2006 |
| | | | | 4 | M | nivalis 'Ruapehu' | 2005 |

Podocarpus 'County Park Treasure'

Podocarpus 'Flame'

Podocarpus 'Spring Sunshine'

| No. | Male/ Female | Clonal names and varieties | Date Planted |
|-----|--------------|----------------------------|--------------|
| 3 | M | nivalis 'Soldier Boy' | 2005 |
| 1 | | nivalis 'Trompenberg' | 2002 |
| 1 | | nubigenus 'Pendula' | 1994 |
| 1 | | nubigenus 'Pendula' | 1994 |
| 2 | | totara 'Aureus' | 2007 |
| 1 | | totara 'Aureus' (hallii 'Aureus') | 1984 |

| No. | Male/ Female | Hybrids | Date Planted |
|-----|--------------|---------|--------------|
| 2 | F | 'Blaze' (lawrencei x nivalis) | 2008 |
| 1 | F | 'Chocolate Box' (lawrencei x nivalis) | 2002 |
| 5 | F | 'County Park Fire' (lawrencei x nivalis) | 2005 |
| 0 | F | 'County Park Treasure' | 1999 |
| 2 | M | 'Flame' (lawrencei x nivalis) | 2008 |
| 2 | F | 'Havering' (hallii x nivalis) | 1999 |
| 1 | F | 'Jill' | 2006 |
| 2 | M | 'Lucky Lad' | 2005 |
| 4 | | 'Orangeade' (lawrencei x nivalis) | 2004 |
| 1 | | 'Pine Lake' | 2006 |
| 1 | | 'Red Tip' | 2002 |
| 5 | F | 'Spring Sunshine' (lawrencei x nivalis) | 2008 |
| 2 | F | 'Young Rusty' (lawrencei x nivalis) | 2008 |

| No | Podocarpaceae Related | Date Planted |
|----|-----------------------|--------------|
| 1 | Dacrydium cupressinum | 2002 |
| 2 | Dacrycarpus dacrydioides | 2005 |
| 1 | Microstrobus fitzgeraldiana | 2006 |
| 1 | Dacrydium franklinii - Huon Pine | 1970's |
| 2 | Saxegothaea conspicua - Prince Alberts Yew | 2001 |
| 1 | Prumnopitys andina | 2008 |
| 1 | Prumnopitys taxifolia | 2005 |
| 1 | Halocarpus bidwillii | 2009 |
| 1 | Phyllocladus Trichomanoides | 2009 |
| 1 | Afrocarpus falcatus | 1999 |

Podocarpus 'Young Rusty'

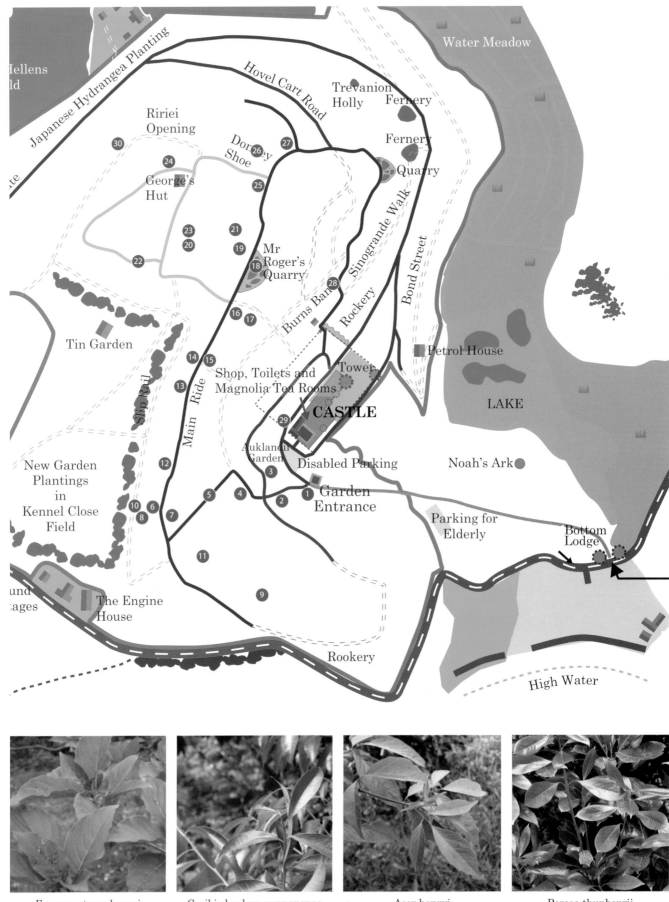

Emmenopterys henryi

Craibiodendron yunnanense

Acer henryi

Persea thunbergii

# Appendix 8
# A selection of Champion Trees at Caerhays

| No. | Genus | Species |
|---|---|---|
| 1 | Magnolia | x veitchii |
| 2 | Lithocarpus | pachyphyllus |
| 3 | Craibiodendron | yunnanense |
| 4 | Magnolia | campbellii |
| 5 | Ilex | perado subsp. perado |
| 6 | Camellia | reticulata 'Captain Rawes' |
| 7 | Stewartia | pteropetiolata |
| 8 | Emmenopterys | henryi |
| 9 | Magnolia | campbellii 'Kew's Surprise' |
| 10 | Meliosma | simplicifolia subsp. pungens |
| 11 | Persea | thunbergii |
| 12 | Magnolia | 'Star Wars' |
| 13 | Acer | henryi |
| 14 | Quercus | lamellosa |
| 15 | Magnolia | 'Philip Tregunna' |
| 16 | Acer | palmatum 'Sango-Kaku' |
| 17 | Magnolia | 'Delia Williams' |
| 18 | Magnolia | 'Lanarth' |
| 19 | Quercus | oxyodon |
| 20 | Aesculus | wilsonii |
| 21 | Quercus | acuta |
| 22 | Magnolia | delavayi |
| 23 | Camellia | taliensis |
| 24 | Lithocarpus | cleistocarpa |
| 25 | Magnolia | nitida |
| 26 | Michelia | doltsopa |
| 27 | Pieris | 'Charles Williams' |
| 28 | Styrax | japonicus |
| 29 | Magnolia | 'Caerhays Belle' |
| 30 | Magnolia | 'J.C. Williams' |

Aesculus wilsonii

| Manor | Tax | Ploughs | People | Wood | Pasture | Animals | Value |
|-------|-----|---------|--------|------|---------|---------|-------|
| **Brannel** | 1h/1.5h | 20 / 9 | 10 sl, 12 vill, 18 smallholders | 40a | 4 x 2 leagues | 20 unbroken mares, 2 cattle, 150 sheep | 12 silver marks / £12 18s 4d |
| **Trevilveth** | 1f / 2f | 3 / 1 | 1 sl, 2 vill, 2 smallholders | 20a | 5a | 2 cattle | 20s / 5s |
| **Tretheake** | 1v / 1h | 7 / 2 | 6 sl, 4 vill, 8 smallholders | | 40a | 30 sheep, 1 cow, 2 goats | 20s / 15s |
| **Elerky** | 1h / 4h | 20 / 5 | 10 slaves, 17 villagers, 18 smallholders | 30a | 100a | 2 cattle, 30 sheep | 100s / 50s |
| **Goviley** | 1/2h/ 1h | 6 / 5 | 8 sl, 5 vill, 13 smallholders | 5a | 100a | 9 cattle, 8 pigs, 232 sheep | 40s / 30s |
| **Tregony** | 1/2v/ 1h | 5 / 2 | 5 sl, 3 vill, 6 smallholders | 12a | 100a | 3 cattle, 40 sheep, 20 goats | 25s / 15s |
| **Tucoyse** | 1v / - | 5 / 3 | 5 sl, 4 vill, 8 smallholders | 8a | 40a | 2 cattle, 20 sheep, 20 goats | 30s / 20s |
| **Treworrick** | 1/2v/ 1h | 5 / 1 | 2sl, 2 vill, 8 smallholders | 20a | 60a | 1 cow, 30 sheep, 3 goats | 10s / 5s |
| **Lanhadron** | 1f / 1v | 3 / 1 | 2 sl, 4 smallholders | 5a | 60a | 20 sheep | 10s/ 5s |
| **Levalsa** | 1f / 1v | 3 / 1 | 3 sl, 2 vill, 1 smallholder | 3 x 1 f | 60a | 1 cow, 12 sheep, 1 pig | 20s / 10s |
| **Trevesson** | 2f / 2h | 4 / 2 | 3 sl, 3 vill, 4 smallholders | 20a | 20a | 3 cattle, 6 pigs, 15 sheep | 20s / 10s |
| **Galowras** | 1f / 1v | 2 / 1 | 2 sl, 2 smallholders | 4a | 10a | 2 pigs, 30 sheep | 7s / 7s |
| **Bodrugan** | 3v / 1h | 10 / 3 | 4 sl, 4 vill, 12 smallholders | 4a | 200a | 1 cob, 6 pigs, 40 sheep, 20 goats | 60s / 30s |

# Appendix 9
## Schedule of Domesday Manors

This schedule on the opposite page shows those manors which had holdings on or around the present Caerhays estate, and which were noted in the Domesday Book of 1086.

A clear idea of the relative wealth of each holding can be gained from the details of labour, woodland, pasture, ploughs, value and tax paid.

**Tax** — This column indicates the taxable land first at the time of Edward (the Confessor) in 1066 and then 'now' (i.e. 1086).
The letter F stands for a furlong. A hide amounted to roughly 120 acres. A virgate was a quarter of a hide.

**Ploughs** — The column headed 'Ploughs' records first the number of ploughs that the land (arable) could support and then how many ploughs were really there, which was always fewer than the capacity.

**People** — People probably indicate the number of heads of households in any one settlement. They are then divided according to social status. Three divisions are used:
slaves, villagers and smallholders.

**Woodland & Pasture** — Woodland and pasture are usually expressed as areas, using the term acres. At that time, acres varied in size around the country and it is not certain that these were much like present-day statutory acres. It has been suggested that an acre varied according to the type of soil, and was defined in any one locality as the area that could be ploughed in one day by one plough. Areas are occasionally given by the length and width of a block of land.

**Animals** — Animals are those recorded in the Exeter version of the Doomsday Book. The count of animals was restricted to those on the lord's own land, or demesne, and does not therefore reflect the entire animal population.

**Value** — Two values are given for the worth of a particular place. The first figure given is the value in 1066, and the second figure, the value in 1086. Values had declined between 1066 and 1086 due to the destruction of resources during the conquest and to the changes in administration arising from re-allocation of the land to new owners. The values are given largely in shillings.

**Money** — S stands for Shilling. A shilling was 1/20th of a pound.
d stands for the silver penny of the time. 12 pennies in a shilling
A silver mark was worth 13 shillings and 4 pennies, or 2/3 of a pound

| Name | Earliest surviving reference and etymology of name | Manorial history | Current form |
|---|---|---|---|
| **Veryan parish** | | | |
| Higher Polmenna | 1293 as Penmene. Cornish. Pen 'head, end, top', + meneth 'hill' | Tretheake (refs from 1465 to 1776) | Single farmstead. No longer operational. |
| Lower Polmenna | 1408 as Penmeneth Woles. Cornish. Pen 'head, end, top', + meneth 'hill' + goles 'lower' | Tretheake (refs from 1465 to 1776) | Single farmstead. No longer operational. |
| Lanhassick | 1354 as Nanslosek. Cornish. Nans 'valley, + ? | Tretheake (refs from 1573 to 1776) | Abandoned. |
| West Portholland | 1465 as Porthsalen. Cornish. Porth + ? | Tretheake (refs from 1465 to 1776) | Coastal hamlet with terraced cottages. |
| Pengelly | 1465 as Pengylle. Cornish. Pen 'head, end, top', + kelli, 'copse' | Tretheake (refs from 1465 to 1776), though a part was within Caerhays manor by 1545 | Single farmstead, still operational. |
| Ventonveth | 1332 as Fentennergh. Cornish. Fenten 'spring, well' + margh 'horse'? | Tretheake (refs from 1465 to 1776), though part within Caerhays manor by 1545 | Single farmstead. No longer operational. |
| Tretheake Mill | 1623 as Trethake mills and Behennowes Mylles | Tretheake (refs from 1623 to 1776) | Millhouse now a private dwelling. |
| Higher Penvose | 1302 as Penfos. Cornish. Pen 'head, end, top' + Fos 'dyke' | Tretheake (refs from 1400 to 1776) | Single farmstead, still operational. |
| Lower Penvose | 1775 (mapped). Name as for Higher Penvose | | Single farmstead. No longer operational. |
| Corwenna | 1314 as Kaerwenan. Cornish. *ker 'fort, a round' + ? | Tretheake (refs from 1465 to 1776) | Single farmstead. No longer operational. |
| **Cuby parish** | | | |
| Treluckey | 1298 as Trelouky. Cornish. Tre 'farming estate' + personal name | Possibly in Goviley in 1345 | Single farmstead, operational |
| Treluckey Mill | ?1345 as Goviley Mill | Possibly part of Goviley manor? | Mill disused; group of residential cottages. |
| Pendraze | | | See history notes |
| **St Ewe parish** | | | |
| Treberrick | 1249 as Treburec. Cornish. Tre 'farming estate' + ? | Part of Caerhays by 1545 | Single farmstead, operational. |

# Appendix 10
# Manorial History

This schedule lists places in and around Caerhays. It details the early references, the manorial history, and notes on their history. The map in chapter 1, Early Settlements, will help identify sites.

| Name | Earliest surviving reference and etymology of name | Manorial history | Current form |
|---|---|---|---|
| **St Michael Caerhays parish** | | | |
| Penheskin | 1314 as Penesken. Cornish. ?Pen 'head, top, end' + ?Heschen 'wet ground, bog'. | Part of Caerhays by 1545. Lanhydrock manor in 1695. | Abandoned; site known from 1695 map. |
| Tolcarne/Tubbs Mill | ?1262 as John de Talcarn. Cornish. Tal 'brow, front, end' + Carn 'tor, rockpile' | Tywardreath priory in 1545. | Mill disused. Cottage and converted barn occupied. |
| Hennery Cottage | 1841 as Hennery Cottage. Presumably from Henry Moon. | | Abandoned; slight earthworks survive. |
| 'Herras' | Late 12C as Herys | Part of Caerhays by 1545 | Abandoned; location uncertain. |
| Polgrain | 1300 as Polgrun. Cornish. Pol 'pit, pool, stream, cove, creek' + growen 'gravel' | Part of Caerhays by 1545 | Small hamlet, one farmstead operational. |
| 'Polbrague' | 1628 as Polbrage. Cornish. Pol 'pit, pool, stream, cove, creek' + ? | | Abandoned, though uncertain if this was ever a settlement. |
| St Michael Caerhays: Churchtown | | | Cottages, former school, poorhouse and institution. |
| Rectory | 15th century. Now known as The Vean. | | Recently restored. |
| 'Helland' | 1302 as Hellaunde. Cornish. Hen-lann 'old cemetery'. NB Portholland contains the name and was first recorded in 1287. | Part of Caerhays by 1545 | Abandoned; location uncertain. Possibly under the site of old rectory just downhill from The Vean. |
| Lavyhale | Cornish. Lann + Yvhal, 'churchyard' and St Michael | Part of Caerhays by 1545 | Abandoned; location uncertain. |

| Name | Earliest surviving reference and etymology of name | Manorial history | Current form |
|---|---|---|---|
| Barton | 1841, though the settlement was shown as early as 1748. A barton in Cornwall is the lord's home farm. | The home farm of Caerhays manor. | Still the core farm of Caerhays. Salers and Highland cattle and sheep. |
| Caerhays | 1259 as Karihaes. Cornish. See chapter 2 for origin of name | By late 13th century Carhays was a manor held under Brannel by payment of a chief rent of two shillings. | Castle still occupied. |
| Hovel | c1720 as Hovel | | Pair of cottages, occupied, and outbuildings. |
| Trevanion | 1302 as Trevanyon. Cornish. Tre 'farming estate' + ? | | Abandoned by early 18thC. See chapter 1,3,6 &10. |
| Caerhays Mill | 1646 as Carhays Mill | The manor mill of Caerhays. | Abandoned in mid 19th century. |
| Pound | 1891 | | |
| East Portholland | 1287 as Portalan. Cornish. Porth, 'cove, harbour') + hen-lann 'old cemetery' | | |

## Gorran parish

| Name | Earliest surviving reference and etymology of name | Manorial history | Current form |
|---|---|---|---|
| Trevennen | c 1300 as Trevanion. Cornish. Tre 'farming estate' + personal name | Tywardreath Priory until Dissolution; then Duchy. | The main house is currently derelict. Farmhouse and farm occupied and operational |
| Trevarrick | 1327 as Trevarek. Cornish. Tre 'farming estate' + ? | Parts held by Gregors of Trewathenick and Fortescues of Penwarne in 18th century. | Group of farmsteads of which at least two are still operational. |
| Goddaricks | 1327 as Coydarek. Cornish. Cos 'wood' + ? | Part of Trevennen by 1520. | Small barn survives. |
| Coosey | 1810 as Coosehais. Cornish. Cos 'wood' + ? | Presumably part of Trevennen. | Ruined cob barn beside green lane. |
| Trewolla | 1679 as Trewolla. Cornish. ?Tre 'farming estate' + ? | Trevennen manor | Single farmstead, operational. |
| Rescassa | 1269 as Roscada. *Ros 'promontory, hillspur, moor' + ? | Split ownership. Part in Lanhadron manor, owned by Arundels of Lanherne in 1459. Part in Caerhays by 1545. | Hamlet, with one farmstead operational; others residential. |
| Penvorgate | Penvergate 1748 | | Single farmstead, operational. |
| Tregavarras | 1269 as Tregavarred. Cornish. Tre 'farming estate' + ? | Fragmented ownership. Part was in Caerhays manor by 1545 | Several farmsteads, but none operational. |

# Further notes on site history

## Veryan parish

**Higher Polmenna** - Shown as a single homestead in 1748. Strip fields still open in 1840 in field to east of farmstead called Stitch Close in 1695.

**Lower Polmenna** - Shown as a hamlet in 1748. Still two farmsteads in 1851.

**Lanhassick** - Last referred to in 1884? Shown as a single homestead in 1748.

**West Portholland** - Shown as a hamlet in 1748. In 1841 occupiers included an innkeeper, a shoemaker, and numerous agricultural labourers; in 1851 a thatcher, a shopkeeper and a dress maker; in 1871 a mariner, a fisherman, a draper and a miller.

**Pengelly** - Usually referred to as one with Portholland.

**Ventonveth** - In 1545 a lease was held of Caerhays manor at the same time that Tretheake retained an interest in part of the land. In 1644 two free tenants of Tretheake each held half the 'village'. Shown as a hamlet in 1748.

**Tretheake Mill** - Sometimes called Corwenna Mill (1636, 1841).

**Higher Penvose** - In 1644 there were three separate tenants, two free and one customary. Shown as a hamlet in 1748. Five households in 1841.

**Lower Penvose** - Buildings shown here on 1775 map of Tretheake estate

**Corwenna** - The round may well be that which survives on the ridge top immediately east of Morvah. Shown as a hamlet in 1748.

## Cuby parish

**Treluckey** - The 'vill' of Treluckey mentioned in 1345. Shown as home of gentleman in 1748. Two households in 1861. Little Treluckey distinguished by 1698 and still there in 1851.

**Treluckey Mill** - Could be the Goviley Mill mentioned in 1345. Shown as hamlet in 1748. Mill and two cottages in 1841.

**Pendraze** - Field names at South end of Treluckey field system hint at the site of a former settlement.

## St Ewe parish

**Treberrick** - Part of Treberrick held by Caerhays and worth 66s 8d in 1545; there was a also a free tenant of Caerhays at Treberrick in 1545. Thomas Tonkin wrote in the early 18C that it had been sold by John Tanner to Charles Trevanion and was then occupied, as a country seat, by a younger brother of William Slade of Trevennen. By 1824, however, it was just a farmhouse, though still farmed by Slades until at least 1851.

## St Michael Caerhays parish

**Penheskin** - Free tenant of Caerhays manor in 1545. Mapped in detail in 1695; one house with four small enclosures, one an orchard, the others meadows. Last recorded in 1884? The bog mentioned in the name would be in the valley to the west.

**Tolcarne/Tubbs Mill** - Rents due to Tywardreath priory for Tolcarne Mill in

1545-6. Caerhays manor also had a corn mill at Tolcarne in 1545. In 1757 a fulling mill is mentioned. In 1829 two grist mills are operating; both Tolcarne and Tubbs Mills mentioned in 1841. Closed down and dismantled c 1920.

**Hennery Cottage** - Occupied 1841 by Henry Moon, basket-maker with a large family.

**'Herras'** - Tonkin in the early 18C suggested that 'Hurris, or Herys, was formerly the seat of a knightly family'; he cites Richard Carew's listing of Henricus de Herys as holding a knight's fee in the time of Richard I (i.e. late 12C). Field names suggest that any settlement lay on the slopes between Treluckey and Polgrain. Still occupied in 1545, when 'Harres ' had 42 acres and paid rent for 66s 8d, but not shown by Thomas Martyn in 1748, so gone by then.

**Polgrain** - Held by a free tenant of Caerhays manor in 1545. Shown as hamlet in 1748 (Martyn). Four households in 1841, one a farmer and one a smith. Second smaller farmstead established a short way to the north, beside road, in the early twentieth century; still operational. One of the surviving cottages may have 17th century origins.

**'Polbrague'** - Field names on the rounded hill SW of Caerhays churchtown. May suggest a former settlement, perhaps a predecessor of the Barton farmstead itself.

**St Michael Caerhays Churchtown** - See chapter on Church for details.

**Rectory** - In 1313 John de Trevayngnon, clerk, had licence to farm the glebe or 'sanctuarium' of the chapel of St Michael of Kerihayes for five years, paying rent to the Rector. After the 15th century Rectors of St Stephen in Brannel resided at Carhays. Glebe terriers provide detail on house, farm buildings and land, including the field called Lower Sentry, its name derived from Sanctuary. The rectory was shifted a short distance uphill to the NE in the early nineteenth century and was constructed as an imposing small country house overlooking the northern approach to Caerhays Castle. It seems likely that this was undertaken for Charles Trevanion Kempe who was instituted to the Rectory of Caerhays in 1806 and was incumbent for much of the next half century. This house was abandoned for much of the second half of the twentieth century, but has recently been carefully restored.

**'Helland'** - Helland may originally have been the estate's principal settlement, possibly dominant over both Caerhays and Trevanion around the turn of the second millennium. The place is perpetuated now by field names on the southern slope of the ridge on which the old Rectory stands and on the lower northern slopes of Caerhays hill.

This position, low on the side of a valley running down to what may have still been a tidal River Luney in the early medieval period when the 'old cemetery' was established, is more typical of early lann sites than the present church's hilltop perch a quarter of a mile to the north. Supporting the possibility that this Helland was perhaps the site of an aboriginal church, and possibly even an earlier form of the parish name, is the early reference (in 1287) to 'Portalan', Porth Helland, the harbour of Helland, at the far south-western corner of the parish, now East Portholland. Recall that the earliest surviving reference to Caerhays is roughly contemporary (1259) and that Caerhays is closer to Portholland than Helland: so why Porth Helland and not Porth Karihaes? More work needs to be done to establish whether anything survives of the medieval settlement of Helland, and then whether there is any trace of the lann and its early Christian structures. In 1543, when Helland was in the hands of a family called Arundell (perhaps a branch of that which had preceded the Trevanions at Caerhays), the place was still substantial – 60 acres of land (i.e. that subjected to ley husbandry), plus 20 acres of meadow and 6 of pasture, the sort of area that would support around three peasant households. In 1545 Helland was occupied by a free tenant of Caerhays manor (presumably Arundell).

**Lavyhale** - Still occupied in 1545 when Lavyhale had 70 acres worth £2 10s 4d, but not shown by Thomas Martyn in 1748, so gone by then. Presumably the churchtown farm.

**Barton** - Barton of 'Caryhays' was worth £10 pa in 1545. Uncertain when this settlement was established – in place and shown as home of gentleman by 1748 (Thomas Martyn). Farmer working 300 acres in 1851, 400 in 1861 and 334 in 1871. By 1891 head of main household was termed Farm Manager and one of the other two was headed by a herdsman from Scotland. Early nineteenth century farmhouse with well-preserved rear domestic yard in which hand pump survives.

**Caerhays** - See body of book for details.

**Hovel** - In 1841 two households with agricultural labourers and lime burner (presumably working the kiln at Porthluney). By 1851 four households including a gardener (note the large walled garden with glass houses in the sheltered valley immediately to the north) and a dress maker. By later Victorian period this was the home of the gamekeepers.

**Trevanion** - According to Thomas Tonkin (writing c 1730), Trevanion adjoined Caerhays to the north. The Trevanion family moved to Caerhays in 1390s, but others remained, or took over – the land was occupied by John Polmorva in 1409. Still occupied in 1545 when Trevanyon was worth £5, the second most substantial holding after the Barton itself.

**Caerhays Mill** - 1852 sale catalogue notes that it was then occupied by John Whiting. Had three pairs of stones for making flour and grist. The 1851 census returns records Whiting plus two young millers (each 15 years old). Apparently shifted to East Portholland by the Williams family when the park was improved.

**Pound** - Later nineteenth century settlement serving Caerhays. Named from proximity to a small pound next to the road. Occupied in 1891 by an engine driver (who was also a blacksmith) and his family who included two daughters working as dress makers. Another cottage was occupied by a gardener.

**East Portholland** - The name indicates that this was the harbour of the once important, but now lost settlement of Helland. Partly within Veryan parish, and this includes the likely site of the Portsalen Mill recorded in 1545, its leat probably reused in the 19C mill whose building still stands. The 1841 census returns recorded 16 households (and two unoccupied houses). Most heads of households were agricultural labourers – no less than 15 such labourers would have left East Portholland for the fields each morning; and an elderly publican William Nicholls welcomed them home in the evening. A fisherman was recorded in 1851, suggesting that the harbour was still in use then, and by 1861 a miller was recorded, presumably operating the then newly rebuilt Portholland Mill. By 1861 we learn the name of the pub, The Cutter Inn.

## Gorran parish

**Trevennen** - Trevennen manor contained Trevennen itself, plus neighbouring Trevascus, Goddaricks and Trewolla and also Pengelly in St Erme parish. Mill was at Tolcarne/Tubbs Mill, in St Michael Caerhays Parish. In 1447 the reeve was burdened with 5s carriage of a millstone to the mill. Moor or wetland to S and E of Trevennen mentioned in 1517 deed was enclosed as part of Trevanion deer park. A dovecote at Trevennen was mentioned in 1520. Manor belonged to Priory of Tywardreath and on Dissolution given by Henry VIII to the Duchy of Cornwall. When surveyed in 1651, the manor had eleven freehold and two leasehold tenants, and by then included some land in Trevarrick. Still owned by Duchy in 1847 (Cornwall Register). In 1846 recorded as the seat of Major Gully, eldest son of late William Slade Gully Esq, Sheriff of Cornwall 1797-8, who died in 1816. The Slade Gully estate was sold in 1919.

**Trevarrick** - Shown as hamlet by Thomas Martyn 1748. Twelve households recorded in 1841 census returns, including five farmers and seven agricultural labourers, plus four carpenters and an apprentice carpenter.

**Goddaricks** - Probably originally a farmstead cut out of Trevarrick land.

**Coosey** - On lane between Rescassa and Trevennen. Occupied by two households in 1841 headed by an agricultural labourer and a carpenter.

**Trewolla** - Hals suggests that this was the home of the Trewollas, a family whose arms had three owls. Sold in the time King Charles II to Charles Trevanion for £900.

**Rescassa** - Clear signs of former strips in surviving field shapes and as cropmarks. Reference in 1459 to 'town and fields'. Numerous other documentary suggestions that this was a hamlet in later medieval times. Some Lanhadron court rolls survive; include inquiry in 1471 whether a tenant had cut down 12 elms on his Rescassa tenement. Another in 1539 inquired whether another tenant had encroached upon the lord's land at Rescassa Moor and 'killed furze, heath and willows'. A 1733 lease of a fragmented property describes *'one-fourth part of Barrett's tenement in Rescassa, being two fields known as Trewolla ground and Pencarne, and the field called Dorevean and moor, and also the hall, entry and chambers over of a dwelling house at Rescassa, the herb garden, the quarry, the lower part of the barn, the pigs' house, the south end of the lower meadow and the east end of the mowhay.'* Shown as a hamlet by Thomas Martyn 1748. Sixteen households in 1841 (and five unoccupied dwellings): included four farmers and ten agricultural labourers as well as a tailor, a grocer and a gardener

**Penvorgate** - Martyn shows as a hamlet. Recorded as a farm in 19th century census returns. Surviving house is of 18th century form.

**Tregavarras** - Field pattern clearly derived from strip fields. Some survive as earthworks in western part that was taken in as a deer park by Williams family of Caerhays in 19th century. Lease of 1615 included moor at Porthluney. Shown as a hamlet by Thomas Martyn 1748. Still a hamlet in 1841 when there were nine households and one unoccupied dwelling; included three farmers and nine agricultural labourers.

# Appendix 11
# Principal Sources; Further Reading;
# Acknowledgements

## Principal sources and further reading.

Airs, Dr Malcolm    The Strange History of Paper Roofs
        Ancient Monuments Society: Transactions Volume 42 1998
Benney, DE.      An Introduction to Cornish Watermills, Bradford Barton, Truro.  1972
        Includes notes on Tubbs Mill
S.Baring-Gould MA       Cornish Characters and Strange Events    Two Volumes  1908
        Includes a chapter on the dream of Mr John Williams
Richard Carew of Antonie, esq    The Survey of Cornwall  1602
Cornwall County Council, 1996. Cornwall Landscape Assessment 1994,
        Countryside Commission and Cornwall County Council:
        Describes and interprets Cornwall's landscape and its historic character
Colson-Stone Partnership 1994. Caerhays Castle, Historic Landscape Survey and Restoration Plan
        A study of the ornamental part of the estate.
Colvin, Howard  A Biographical Dictionary of British Architects 1600-1840 (3rd edition) 1995 YaleUP
Davis, Terence    ed Sir John Summerson       The architecture of John Nash  Studio Books  1960
Folliott-Stokes, AG, 1912.    The Cornish Coast and Moors, Greening and Co, London.
        Portholland descriptions
Gascoyne, J., 1699.    A map of the County of Cornwall, newly surveyed by Joel Gascoyne,
        Reprinted by Devon and Cornwall Record Soc, 1991.   First medium scale map of Cornwall
The Gentleman's Magazine: Various editions 1740-1817
Gilbert, C.S.    An Historical Survey of Cornwall, Ackerman, London. 2 vols. 1817 & 1820
        Most observant of the early 19th century topographers
Gilbert, D, 1838. The Parochial History of Cornwall (4 volumes) Nicholls, London.
        Includes historical notes by Hals and Tonkin
Gregor, Sarah Loveday    Memoirs   c.1851   Cornwall Record Office  CRO DDG.1952
Henderson, Charles      Royal Institution of Cornwall: Henderson Papers
Henderson, C., 1935. Essays in Cornish History, Clarendon, Oxford.
        Includes a chapter on Caerhays derived from the first detailed research on the families and place
Henderson, C.    The 109 Ancient parishes of the Four Western Hundreds of Cornwall,   1955
        JRIC, II.3, 1-104.       Med church and chapel material; also chapel at house.
Herring, P.   Medieval Cornish deer parks,   The Lie of the Land 2003
        Proceedings of Exeter University & Devon Gardens Trust conference, ed by Robert Wilson-North,
        The Mint Press, Exeter
Hitchins, F and Drew, S.   The History of Cornwall (2 volumes), Penaluna, Helston.1824
Hunkin, Rt. Rev. JW, Bishop of Truro   A tribute to JC Williams 1861-1939; an obituary
Imperial Dictionary of Universal Biography   Edited John Francis Warner   Published c 1865
Isham, K.   Lime Kilns and Limeburners in Cornwall, Cornish Hillside Publications, St Austell. 2000
        Caerhays and Portholland kilns mentioned and described.

Lake's Parochial History of Cornwall written by Joseph Polsue   c 1865-1872  4 volumes
   *This includes:* William Hals (1655-1737)   Parochial Histories  unpublished 1737
      Thomas Tonkin, (1680-1742 )  unpublished 1742,
Loudon, John Claudius    An Account of the Paper Roofs used at Tew Lodge Oxon     1811
D & S Lyson's Parochial History (1814) Cornwall ( Volume 111 for Cornwall)
Martyn, T., 1748. A New and Accurate Map of the County of Cornwall from an Actual Survey,
   Copy at Royal Cornwall Museum, Truro.1st comprehensive map of settlements and roads
McCabe, Helen        Houses and Gardens of Cornwall      Tabb House 1988
McClean, Brenda     George Forrest, Plant Hunter
   Antique Collector's Club, *in association with The Royal Botanic Garden, Edinburgh*    2004
Moule, Thomas     The English Counties Delineated: or, A Topographical Description of England, 1838
Padel, O.J.    Cornish Place-Name Elements, English Place-Name Society, Vol 56/57, Nottingham 1985
   The definitive source for the meaning and history of Cornwall's place-names
Penhallurick, R.      Tin in Antiquity, The Institute of Metals, London     1986
   Material on the Roman coins from Caerhays and thoughts on the Porthluney creek
Pett, Douglas Ellory.   The Parks and Gardens of Cornwall, Alison Hodge, Penzance  1998
Pilcher Donald         The Regency Style            Batsford 1947
Potts, R.    A Calendar of Cornish Glebe Terriers, 1673-1735, DCRS, NS 19   1974
   Terriers for 1680 and 1727, details of buildings, fields, trees, land use, etc
Pounds, NJG.   The Parliamentary Survey of the Duchy of Cornwall, Part 2,   1984
   Devon and Cornwall Record Society NS 27  Trevennen described
Edmund Prideaux (1693-1745)         Topographical Drawings:
   Reproduced by permission of Mr & Mrs P Prideaux-Brune
Rowse, A.L  Tudor Cornwall   Jonathan Cape 1941
Rowse, A.L.   The Byrons and Trevanions, Weidenfeld and Nicolson, London    1978
   A reworking of Henderson's material on the Trevanions.
Royal Cornwall Gazette March 24 1848
Stoate, TL, Hearth Tax Returns for Cornwall
Stoate, TL, 1987. The Cornwall Military Survey 1522 with the Loan Books and a Tinners Muster Roll
   c1535, Stoate, Bristol.  In 1522-6 Hugh Trevanion of St Michael Carhays was assessed at 60
   pounds, number 43 in the order of wealth in Cornwall.
Summerson  John      Georgian London        Pleiades Books  1945
Thorn, C and Thorn, F.    Domesday Book, Cornwall, Phillimore, London and Chichester     1979
Tyack, Geoffrey. For his generous help and for 'Nash the Incomparable', Country Life, June 23 2005.
Walker, Violet W & Margaret J Howell   The House of Byron Quiller Press, London1988
Williams, Colonel G.T.G   Extensive family research and compiled reports.
Williams, F.J. 'J.C.Williams- An Enthusiast'.  Lecture, November 1998
Handwritten notes possibly by Borlase, copied by Tonkin, transcribed by Gregor at the end of the
   18thC.  The notes are found on page 159  (or 146, deleted) of the microfilm known as Borlase
   parochial notes in the Royal Institution of Cornwall
SCSTyrrell   Personal papers, records and photographs

Books on the history and domestic architecture of Cornwall are not included.

# General:

  With the exception of some later 19thC legal documents deposited by Coode solictors with the Cornwall Record Office,  the Trevanion family papers have vanished.  So far, therefore, little material has been found for the main period of Caerhays' development, aggrandisement, and house, garden and deer park creation. We have to rely on often oblique or fleeting references to the family and to Caerhays in other archives and public records, as well as the material remains themselves.

  The Cornwall and Scilly Historic Environment Record (HER, held and maintained by Cornwall Council) and Listed Building records (held by English Heritage) were consulted to obtain a baseline for the archaeological remains and buildings. Further field work has been undertaken by Peter Herring and Stephen Tyrrell.

  The Cornwall Record Office (Cornwall Council) and the Courtney Library of the Royal Institution of Cornwall (Truro) and other archives were visited to study historic maps and documents, and to research early sites, boundaries, settlements and field names.

## Maps

Maps consulted included early small-scale county and hundred maps such as those by Christopher Saxton (1579), John Norden (c1597), Joel Gascoyne (1699) and Thomas Martyn (1748) and then the larger-scale 19th and 20th-century published maps (Ordnance Survey 1813, 1876 and 1906) and the 1841 parish Tithe Apportionment Map (with their accompanying schedules giving details of land use, ownership, occupancy and land value). The Caerhays Estate has its own archive of documents and maps. These include:

The "Book of Maps, .. the property of Michael Williams esq M.P."
Surveyed and mapped by W.Smith , Manaccan 1853
"Plan of Carhaise Manor....the property of John T P Bettesworth Trevanion esq".
Surveyed 1802 by Thomas Corfield.

Charlie Johns and Sean Taylor of Cornwall County Historic Environment service assisted in preparation of the map of early settlements in chapter one.

## Illustration credits:

We have tried to trace the origin and owners of all photographs used, crediting the owner where possible. We apologise for omissions or inaccuracies in this list. Certain illustrations have been provided by photographic libraries of pictures stated to be within the public domain, and therefore available for reproduction. Where requested, the origin of a particular picture has been noted alongside the illustration.

The Williams Family and the Burncoose and Caerhays Estates have provided many of the photographs and illustrations and these are used with their permission.
Other photographs were taken and supplied by

| | |
|---|---|
| Twinkle Carter | Stephen Dance |
| David Green | Mike Greenslade |
| Peter Herring | Michael Levett |
| Jaimie Parsons | Karol Pawlak |
| Courtenay Smale | Richard Stone |
| S.C.S.Tyrrell | |

and are used with permission

Particular thanks are given to the staff at both Caerhays and Burncoose.

The lakes and Porthluney beach at sunset

# Appendix 12
# Activities at Caerhays

Web addresses and telephone numbers

## Caerhays Estate

The Estate Office, Gorran, St Austell, Cornwall, PL26 6LY
Telephone: 01872 500025  Fax: 01872 501870
Email: estateoffice@caerhays.co.uk
Website: www.caerhays.co.uk

## Burncoose Nurseries

Gwennap, Redruth, Cornwall TR16 6BJ
Telephone: 01209 860316  Fax: 01209 860011
Email: info@burncoose.co.uk
Website: www.burncoose.co.uk

## The Vean

Telephone: 01872 500025  Fax: 01872 501870
Email: estateoffice@caerhays.co.uk
Website: www.thevean.co.uk

## Holiday Lets

These can be arranged through the Estate Office,
who also have details of other holiday houses available.
Telephone: 01872 500025  Fax: 01872 501870
Email: estateoffice@caerhays.co.uk

## KPK Builders and Developers Ltd

Burncoose, Gwennap, Redruth, Cornwall TR16 6BJ
Telephone: 01209 860472  Fax: 01209 860213
Email: kpk.builders@virgin.net

## Tourism
Garden Tours
Guided Walks
Caerhays Castle House Tours
Castle Gift Shop
Magnolia Tea Rooms in the Castle Courtyard
Plant sales at Caerhays
Holiday Cottages
Beaches
Beach Café
Car Parks

## Education
Annual Royal Horticultural Society lecture series
Botanic and Garden Lectures
Agricultural & Educational Visits

## Accommodation
The Vean
The Old Village Hall
Holiday Cottages
Self Catering Accommodation
Serviced Accommodation
Spring Garden Breaks

## Property Management
Estate Cottages
Building Maintenance
New Building Work
KPK Builders and Developers Ltd

## Landed Estate
Land Management
Home Farm
Pedigree and Rare Breed Conservation
Forestry
Woodland and Timber
Heritage Estate Management

## Retail Operations
Caerhays Garden Shop
Burncoose Nurseries
Porthluney Beach Café
Internet Shopping
Mail Order Shopping

## Corporate Events and Hospitality
Country Sports and Shooting
Weddings
Product Launches
Corporate and Business Meetings
Parties & Celebrations
Film and Photographic Locations

## Horticulture and Gardens
Caerhays Castle Gardens
Burncoose Nurseries and Gardens
Nurseries and Mail Order Plants
Landscaping and Garden Design

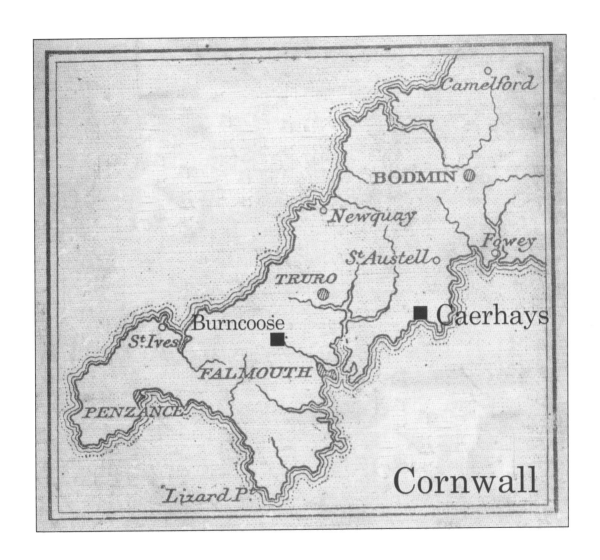

Camelford

BODMIN

Newquay

Fowey

St Austell

TRURO

Burncoose

Caerhays

St Ives

FALMOUTH

PENZANCE

Lizard P.

Cornwall

Magnolia 'Caerhays surprise'

Rhododendron 'Penvergate'

Caerhays Castle from the east.

An aerial photograph of Caerhays Castle and the coast from the north west